THINK *LIKE AN*
IMMIGRANT

A blueprint for turning challenges into
opportunities in a new land

UDOH ELIJAH UDOM

Think Like An Immigrant: A blueprint for turning challenges into opportunities in a new land Copyright © 2025 by Udoh Elijah Udom

Cover Design | Print Layout: Kingdom Branding

The opinions expressed in this book are those of the author. They are not meant to be political, offensive, or harmful. They also do not necessarily express the viewpoints of anyone or any organization connected to the author. This book reflects the author's present recollections of personal experiences over time. Some names have been changed, some events have been compressed, and some dialogue has been recreated.

ISBN 979-8-9901550-4-6 (Paperback)

Library of Congress Control Number 2025948560

1st Printing
Printed in the United States of America

The opinions expressed in this book are those of the author. They are not meant to be political, offensive, or harmful. They also do not necessarily express the viewpoints of anyone or any organization connected to the author. This book reflects the author's present recollections of personal experiences over time. Some names have been changed, some events have been compressed, and some dialogue has been recreated.

TABLE OF CONTENTS

FOREWORD

In this seminal work, *Think Like an Immigrant*, Udoh Elijah Udom advocates a vital set of strategies and behavior patterns that would ensure progress and success for immigrants in their new countries of residence. His emphasis is on migration patterns from the global-South to the global-North, which is the larger direction in which relocation is currently taking place. An immigrant himself who has resided in many global-South and global-North countries, the author does not only speak from experience but also makes inferences and offers critical advice based on his interactions and dialogues with immigrants from various countries and cultures.

Think Like an Immigrant breaks new ground by advocating essential survival strategies that go far beyond the standard guidance typically offered to immigrants, such as finding employment, improving legal status, or enrolling children in school. While such formal advice is important, immigrants frequently underestimate the cultural, social, and behavioral adjustments required to truly flourish beyond simply fulfilling expected standards.

The author presents a comprehensive blueprint for navigating the challenges of adaptation, emphasizing the importance of preserving one's cultural identity while embracing the host country's culture, living with integrity and accountability, respecting the law, steering clear of harmful influences and self-destructive habits, and building meaningful connections with inspiring individuals and communities. Others include never giving up even in the face of seeming failure, taking advantage of skills enhancement opportunities, volunteering and giving back to the community, and consolidating healthy family relationships - within the new country and the home country.

Think Like an Immigrant is, therefore, an appropriate symbolic title for Udom's book. While immigrants are often stereotyped as aimless, desperate, poor, unskilled, and backward, the author underscores the point that when they subscribe to his "twenty-five principles of highly successful immigrants," they and their progeny become invaluable innovators and contributors to the advancement of their receiving countries in practically every sector: education, healthcare, business, industry, technology, and science. To "think like an immigrant" one must essentially think like and embody the vision, ideology, and ingenuity of a *successful* immigrant.

The book in your hand is a must read, not just for immigrants but for citizens of host countries who inadvertently have to live and interact with immigrants.

Philip Effiong
Professor
Michigan State University

PREFACE

In the shadow and light of migration

Immigration has long been one of the defining features of modernity, a recurring chapter in the story of global interdependence. Yet for all the economic, cultural, and intellectual vitality that immigrants bring to their new homelands, they continue to be cast as ambiguous figures in the public and academic imagination - neither fully welcome nor entirely rejected. In scholarly and policy circles, immigrants are often spoken of in terms that oscillate between utility and threat. The literature is saturated with an uneasy ambivalence. While immigrants are frequently portrayed as contributors to national growth and development - filling labor shortages, sustaining aging populations, and diversifying the cultural landscape - they are also depicted as burdens on welfare systems, disruptors of national identity, or, more abstractly, as "*shadow citizen*s" who exist within but not fully as part of the nation-state.

Shadow citizens

Shadow Citizens are people who, by chance or design, live on the margins of society. They are both in and out, but mostly out.

Because they are not viewed as legal citizens with full rights and privileges, they are ultimately thrust outside of the mainstream. Unnoticed and marginalized, they still find creative ways to survive and, more importantly, to be impactful on so many levels. These *Shadow Citizens* wear different immigrant statuses: they are undocumented, legal, and somewhere between legal and undocumented. They are periodically recognized, real or imagined, through language, manner of speaking, religious practices, behavior, dress style, and physical appearance. These social group identifiers have evolved into a basis for categorizing immigrants as threats and for subjecting them to acts of discrimination and denigration based on their particularities. Because religion, for instance, is a yardstick by which a *Shadow Citizen* is sometimes determined, non-Christians are often stereotyped as pro-terrorist and therefore castigated or deprived a sense of belonging in major immigrant receiving countries.

Regardless of status, most *Shadow Citizens* typically come from countries that are described as "developing", including, but not limited to, Asian, African, Central American, South American, and Arab countries. These are people who usually fall within the category of "black", "brown", "person of color" or "aliens."

Many *Shadow Citizens*, even after attaining legal residential status, citizenship, and positions of significant success, simply give up on struggling for acceptance. But they never give up on survival or attaining their dreams of success and, over the years, have emerged as some of the most resilient, educated, and productive members of society, regardless of their vulnerability to various forms of victimization. This is evident in their accomplishments and the prestigious positions they hold in various sectors of society: healthcare, technology, education, sports, business, and science, among others.

In sum, the term *shadow citizens*, used by legal scholars and sociologists, is especially poignant. It encapsulates the in-between status of millions of people who, though they may work, pay taxes, raise families, and participate in civic life, remain outside the boundaries of full belonging. They are not invisible, yet not fully seen; not excluded outright, yet not embraced. This book seeks to illuminate these tensions, to examine the personal, political, and philosophical dilemmas of immigration as experienced by those who live in its margins and at its center.

What is striking about the discourse surrounding immigration is the extent to which it remains mired in contradiction. Stakeholders in the immigration debate - governments, employers, civil society organizations, media, and academia - rarely agree on the value or role of immigrants. For employers in some developed countries with limited supply of labor, immigrants are often indispensable workers. For policymakers, they may represent votes, tax revenue, or a national security challenge. For humanitarian organizations, they are lives in need of dignity and protection. Meanwhile, for the average citizen of a receiving country, immigrants are often filtered through a lens of fear, competition, or cultural anxiety. This ambivalence functions not merely at the level of individual attitudes but becomes embedded in institutional policies and national ideologies.

The countries that receive immigrants - particularly those in the Global North - often exhibit what might be termed a politics of selective hospitality. These countries want immigrants to work in agriculture, construction, health care, and domestic service. They want innovation from immigrant entrepreneurs and scholars, and they benefit from the cultural pluralism that enriches art, cuisine, and intellectual life. Yet the same societies that welcome immigrants for their labor and creativity may recoil from the presence of their foreignness when it touches upon national identity, social cohesion, or resource distribution. Immigration policies, therefore, are frequently designed not to integrate but to extract - prioritizing economic gain while offering limited pathways to citizenship, political voice, or social equality.

Within this context, immigrants themselves often live in a state of dual consciousness - balancing hope and alienation, belonging and exclusion, gratitude and resentment. They are deeply invested in their new societies yet continually reminded of their outsider status. They are portrayed as aspirational figures in public success stories while simultaneously being subjected to suspicion, surveillance, and sometimes violence. This paradoxical existence breeds a form of resilience that is both admirable and exhausting. The dream of a better life coexists with the reality of systemic discrimination, economic precarity, and psychological displacement.

Compounding this condition is the fact that many immigrants cannot return home. For refugees and asylum seekers, their countries of origin are often war zones, failed states, or sites of political persecution. Even for economic migrants, return is not always a viable option - either because the cost is too high or because their departure has created new dependencies among the families and communities they left behind. Thus, the immigrant condition is not just about movement, but about stasis - about being caught between a past that cannot be reclaimed and a future that remains uncertain.

This emotional and existential limbo is rarely captured in the economic models or political debates that dominate the discourse. Much of the academic literature on immigration, especially in disciplines like economics and political science, tends to frame the issue in terms of costs and benefits, integration of metrics, or demographic trends. While such approaches are valuable, they often miss the lived experience of migration - the trauma of displacement, the daily acts of adaptation, the quiet dignity of persistence.

In reducing immigrants to data points or policy problems, much of the scholarship inadvertently replicates the logic of exclusion it seeks to analyze.

Even sociological and anthropological studies, which often aim to center the voices of immigrants, can fall into the trap of othering - treating immigrants as subjects to be observed rather than as co-creators of the societies in which they live. This book takes a different approach. It is rooted in the belief that an immigrant is not merely a figure of study but a full human being, whose story is not ancillary to the receiving country's story but central to it. By focusing on personal narratives, cultural reflections, and theoretical interrogations that foreground immigrant voices, this book aims to shift the conversation from what immigrants do for society to what immigration reveals about society itself.

One of the key insights of this book is that immigration is not an event but a condition. It is not something that ends at the border or after a certain number of years in a new country. For many, the psychological and social impacts of immigration endure across generations. Children of immigrants often inherit their parents' traumas and dreams, living with a hyphenated identity, e.g., Nigerian-American, that can be both enriching and alienating. The concept of home becomes complicated, more of an idea than a place. Citizenship may be granted on paper, but the feeling of belonging is harder to come by.

This dynamic raises fundamental questions about the meaning of citizenship, the boundaries of community, and the responsibilities of the state. If full inclusion remains elusive for many immigrants despite their contributions and commitments, then perhaps it is not the immigrants who are failing to integrate but the societies that are failing to accommodate.

In this light, immigration becomes a mirror in which nations see the contradictions of their own ideals - equality versus exclusion, openness versus control, diversity versus assimilation.

It is also important to remember that the global context of migration is shaped by deep structural inequalities. Immigration does not occur in a vacuum. It is the result of centuries of colonialism, uneven development, environmental degradation, and geopolitical conflict. The borders that some people cross with ease are the same ones others die trying to traverse. The countries that receive immigrants often played a role in creating the conditions that forced those immigrants to leave in the first place - through war, trade policies, or climate emissions. Thus, to speak of immigration without addressing global justice is to tell an incomplete story.

Nevertheless, the immigrant experience is not only one of suffering or marginalization. It is also a story of creativity, resistance, and reinvention. Immigrants are not merely victims of systems but active agents who build new lives, forge new identities, and transform the societies they join. Their contributions are not only economic but cultural, intellectual, and emotional. They teach us about adaptability, empathy, and the meaning of community in a world defined by movement and change.

The optimism that many immigrants carry is not naïve but radical. It is an optimism forged in adversity, grounded in the belief that a better life is possible even in the face of exclusion. This hope is not a denial of the difficulties they face, but a refusal to be defined by them. It is this spirit that animates the stories in this book - the spirit of those who dream, not in spite of the odds, but because of them.

Why I wrote this book

In the book in your hand, the goal is not to romanticize immigration or to ignore the real challenges it presents. Rather, the aim is to offer a more nuanced, humane, and intellectually honest account of what it means to move, to stay, to belong, and to be excluded. It is to challenge the reductive narratives that dominate public discourse and to open space for deeper reflection - on who we are, how we live together, and what kind of world we want to build.

This book was born out of the urgent and often precarious realities faced by immigrants around the world. It is both a call to action and a guide for understanding. On one hand, it urges receiving countries to listen more carefully, think more critically, and act more compassionately toward immigrants. In an era marked by rising nationalism, tightening borders, and increasing inequality, the way we treat immigrants is not merely about them - it is a reflection of us. It tests our values, institutions, and shared humanity. Let us hope we rise to the challenge.

At the same time, this book serves as a resource for immigrants themselves. It is designed to help them navigate life in two worlds: their homeland, now distant or unreachable, and their new country of residence. Drawing from years of research and interviews with immigrants, this book explores both what drives them forward and what holds them back.

Unlike critics who fault immigrants for seeking new opportunities or for aspiring to the rights and privileges of citizenship, this book takes a different approach. It is an educational discourse - one that encourages adaptation over blame, understanding over judgment.

It speaks especially to newcomers, offering them practical insights on how to adjust and thrive without alienating their new communities.

STRUCTURE OF THE BOOK

This book is divided into three key sections:

1. *Section I: Challenges faced by immigrants - The Journey and the Challenges*: This section explores the immigrant experience from the initial decision to leave one's homeland through the struggles and adjustments that follow arrival in a new country. It examines the emotional, legal, cultural, and social hurdles that define the immigrant journey.

2. *Section II: Thinking like an immigrant - The Mindset Shift* Success in a new environment requires more than hard work - it demands a new way of thinking. This section invites immigrants to rethink inherited mindsets and adopt new perspectives suited to their current reality. Growth begins when we recognize that the rules and expectations of one world do not always apply to another.

3. *Section III: Principles of highly Successful immigrants*: Learning from those who have already succeeded can light the path forward. This concluding section presents twenty-five principles - habits, strategies, and values - drawn from the lives of highly successful immigrants. These insights serve as a guide or beacon for others who are just beginning their journey or struggling to find their footing.

CONCLUSION

This book aims at building bridges - between immigrants and their new communities, between old identities and new realities, and between fear and understanding. Whether you are an immigrant yourself, a policymaker, or simply someone seeking to understand this vital global issue, this book invites you to think, reflect, and act with greater empathy and intention. Finally, this book, not only underscores the latter fact, but also highlights the numerous challenges immigrants face. Subsequently, it outlines essential tools and resources available to help them survive and thrive in their new countries of residence.

Acknowledgement

I would like to express my heartfelt gratitude to the immigrants who generously shared their personal stories and experiences with me. Your openness and courage have deeply enriched this work. I am also sincerely thankful to Professor Philip Effiong, my dear friend Mr. Shiv Varma and Mr. Tokunbo Kehinde for their insightful editing and invaluable guidance throughout the manuscript process. Your keen eye and thoughtful feedback helped shape this project into its final form. Finally, to my dear wife, Boi-Betty Udom, thank you for always being there, especially when I faced technical challenges. Your unwavering support and patience mean more than words can say. I am truly grateful to you all.

Terminologies

Immigration: Usually associated with international relocation to a new country or region with the intention of staying and living there, whether temporarily or permanently.

Migrant: A person who moves away from his or her place of birth or usual residence, whether within a country or across an international border, temporarily or permanently, and for a variety of reasons.';

Emigrate: The act of leaving one's residence or country of origin to live in another.

Immigrate: When a person immigrates, he or she comes to another country to live permanently.

Migrate: Moving from one place to another, sometimes within and across borders. This may be part of a back-and-forth pattern while at other times it may be influenced by factors like environment, weather and security.

Forced Migration: Human migration flows in a way the movers have no choice but to relocate.

Voluntary Migration: Human migration flows in a way that the movers respond to perceived opportunity, not force.

Sending country: The country of origin of immigrants.

Receiving country: The country that opens its borders to receive people from other countries or the country to which immigrants choose to relocate to.

Global North: Refers to a group of countries with a high degree of power, wealth, and economic influence, many of which are situated in North America, Europe, and Australia. Other such countries include Israel, Japan, and South Korea.

Global South: Consists of the world's developing and least developed regions, often located in the tropics or Southern Hemisphere. Most Global South countries can be found in Africa, Latin America, the Caribbean, Asia (excluding Israel, Japan, and South Korea), and Oceania (excluding Australia and New Zealand).

INTRODUCTION

SOME IMPORTANT CONSIDERATIONS

*"I will not allow my mistakes of the past compromise
my hope for the future."*
- Charles F. Glassman (medical coach)

All over the world, immigration patterns and their cost-benefits continue to evoke controversy and remain an enduring issue of interest and concern to world leaders and their citizens. Like wars, diseases, climate change, terrorism, poverty, politics, and hard drugs, immigration will continue to be a topic for private and public conversation, whether at governmental institutions, across agencies of the United Nations, in boardrooms, in workplaces, at street corners, in houses of worship, in restaurants and bars, and at family dining tables. Governments and citizens of countries that attract large immigrant populations often look askance at the newcomers and relate to them with intentional and sometimes veiled feelings of caution and uncertainty. Essentially, therefore, suspicions about immigrants may or may not be in full display, which periodically makes it difficult for immigrants to decide on how to relate to citizens of their host countries.

Negative attitudes towards immigrants are not a recent phenomenon or peculiar to a few countries. It is estimated that about sixty-five countries around the world have built or are building walls along their borders to keep out legal and undocumented immigrants. Historically, the Chinese and the Roman Empires were among the first monarchies to build walls along their borders. In the last few decades, escalating security concerns, racism, and ethnocentrism (partly due to fears provoked by World War II) have fueled a new spate of wall-building to keep away immigrants. A prime example is the Berlin wall built by the Communist East German government in 1961 because of longstanding distrust between the Soviet Union and its satellite states on one side and Western Europe and the United States on the other. That same year, the Turkey-Syria border wall was built to prevent people crossing from Syria into Turkey.

The trend continued in the 1970s when the United States and South Korea constructed the Korean wall between 1977 and 1979 along the length of the demilitarized zone (DMZ) to deter infiltration attempts from North Korea into South Korea. 1986 witnessed the construction of India's 2,500-mile border wall, estimated at the cost $1.2 billion, to prevent migration from Bangladesh. In 2002, Israel commenced the building of a West Bank barrier designed to separate Palestinian territories from Israel. About 708 kilometers long, the wall is also described as Israel's "apartheid wall". To stem the flow of refugees from Syria, Afghanistan, and Iraq, in 2015 Hungary's right-wing government constructed a four-meter-high fence along its border with Serbia. With construction beginning in 1909, the walls along the US-Mexican borders are still being built in 2025 to keep immigrants from Central and Southern American countries from crossing Mexican borders into the United Stares.

Many receiving countries feel that they do immigrants a favor by opening their borders and giving them the opportunity to escape social, cultural, and political difficulties in their countries of origin.

These countries also pride themselves on providing immigrants access to widespread economic opportunities, security, and high standards of living. In return, they expect and demand that immigrants express gratitude by being submissive and unconditionally loyal to the receiving countries for the kindness shown to them.

A strong case can indeed be made for the compassion that receiving countries show immigrants, especially those whose lives were in danger in their countries of origin. It is, therefore, reasonable that gratitude should be expected of immigrants. However, it is also important for receiving countries to remember and/or acknowledge the complex realities of migration and the sacrifices and challenges that immigrants often face during the immigration process. Not least is their vulnerability to xenophobic confrontations and assaults, all of which could deter genuine expressions of appreciation. Giving an entry visa to someone is one thing, but providing an enabling environment and opportunities for the individual to maximize their potential in a new setting is quite another.

NON-ZERO-SUM RELATIONSHIP

It is important to understand that immigration benefits all the stakeholders - the receiving and the sending countries, and immigrants alike. Many receiving countries attest to the role of immigrants as engines of development in various sectors. Commenting on the role of immigrants in the United States, President John F. Kennedy said, *"Everywhere, immigrants have enriched and strengthened the fabric of American life"*.[1] This statement is significant, coming from a President tasked with the responsibility of overseeing the affairs of his country.

---

1 "JFK and a Nation of Immigrants: Transcript," John F. Kennedy Presidential Library and Museum, accessed February 10, 2025, https://www.jfklibrary.org/about-us/social-media-podcasts-and-apps/jfk35-podcast/season-1/jfk-and-a-nation-of-immigrants/transcript.

As an immigrant and having studied the life of immigrants for many years, I have concluded that immigrants are the new *international currency*. Many countries peg their currency to the US dollar, which provides long-term predictability of exchange rates for business planning, subsequently helping to consolidate economic stability. Similarly, many countries peg or plan their development projects in hopes of a constant inflow of immigrants to supply a much-needed labor force. Immigration has not only served as a fountain of labor force; immigrants have also contributed to the development and sustenance of the infrastructure of receiving countries. Such contributions by immigrants are much more beneficial to receiving countries than verbal expressions of gratitude.

Receiving countries

To fully understand how immigrants contribute to the development of their new countries of residence, one should embark on a visit to some of the countries in the Middle East, including Saudi Arabia, the United Arab Emirates (UAE), Qatar, Kuwait, and Oman. These countries, despite having unfavorable climatic conditions, have become "a must visit" for tourists because the leaders have been wise to open their borders to immigrants. These immigrants have become a key part of the economic growth of these countries, contributing to the construction of their cities, running businesses, and working in the petroleum and manufacturing sectors. The hard work, diligence, and dedication of these immigrants is the most effective way that they demonstrate their thankfulness. This is certainly more practical than, say, mounting billboards on major streets around the world thanking the receiving countries for their magnanimity in granting visas to foreigners.

Besides Middle Eastern countries, the developed countries of North America and Europe have benefitted and continue to benefit enormously from immigration.

Historical records and writings of the Founding Fathers, for instance, acknowledge how vital immigrants have been to the development and progress of the United States. Thomas Jefferson was steadfast in his belief that immigrants were instrumental in America's self-governing success, providing much needed perseverance and diligence. He, therefore, asked a fundamental rhetorical question, *"Shall oppressed humanity find no asylum on this globe?"*[2]

According to a recent study by the Migration Policy Institute (2024), immigrants boost America's overall economic growth by expanding the labor force and increasing consumer spending. Immigrants also start new businesses at higher rates than US-born citizens. They have been involved in the development of 30 percent of patents in strategic industries in recent years, and more than 40 percent of Fortune 500 companies were founded by immigrants or children of immigrants (Gelatt, (2024).

In 2020, the United States, under President Donald Trump, restricted the issuance of H-1B visas that would bring in much needed foreign engineers and other skilled workers from other countries, arguing that this entry permit results in the establishment of foreign businesses that replace Americans with lower-paid foreign workers from India and China. A few days before his inauguration as the 47th President, Donald Trump yielded to the advice of his principal non-elected advisers in engineering and business innovations, Elon Musk and Vivek Ramaswamy (both immigrants) and some tech companies on the need to grant more H-1B visas to attract highly skilled workers to the United States. Regardless of why Trump changed his decision, the move is in the best interest of the United States and would only help the country maintain its economic hegemony in the world.

---

2   "The Question of Immigration," Thomas Jefferson's Monticello, accessed February 12, 2025, https://www.monticello.org/the-art-of-citizenship/the-question-of-immigration.

The same positive effect of immigration has been the story in other high-income countries of Europe that attract immigrants. These countries benefit from migration through entrepreneurship, innovation and the increased supply of labor and skills. Immigrants also pay taxes and contribute to social security systems. One study shows that 83 percent of the native-born population in the twenty-two richest countries of the Organization for Economic Cooperation and Development (OECD) has experienced a significant welfare gain because of immigration from non-OECD countries (Aubry, et. al. 2016).

The Sending countries

Many sending countries, though classified as underdeveloped, are saturated with an untapped and highly skilled labor force. The citizens of these countries are often not provided with efficient channels through which to develop and utilize their skills, which is why they move to other countries. The sending countries do benefit from immigration, even though a significant percentage of their populations often complain and accuse developed countries of keeping them underdeveloped by encouraging human capital flight. While these countries may lose some of their highly skilled labor force, they benefit from remittances their migrant citizens send back to loved ones, family members, friends and acquaintances, a substantial portion of which goes into welfare support as well as educational and entrepreneurial projects that benefit the economy of recipient countries.

In 2024 alone, according to stakeholder reports, remittance flows from high-income to low- and middle-income countries remittance was estimated at $685 billion (Ratha, et. al. 2024). This is a massive amount of money that flowed into the treasury of developing countries.

Countries that benefit from remittances continue to experience an increase in household disposable incomes, which helps to reduce poverty. Such migrant-initiated remittances also help poor households to pay for social services like education, housing, and healthcare. They are a major source of capital for small businesses and other entrepreneurial activities and thus facilitate a rise in aggregate demand and economic growth.

Though immigration has led to a decrease in the labor pool of the sending countries, these countries benefit from the apparent economic loss. Where hiring opportunities are scarce in the sending countries, the exodus of highly skilled workers helps to alleviate unemployment, thereby increasing earnings for those workers who do not emigrate.

It is sad to report that authoritarian leaders in some countries overtly or covertly encourage emigration by their citizens as this reduces the number of political activists who are likely to challenge them and pose a threat to their control of power. How does this benefit the sending countries? The departure of potential agitators tends to reduce the likelihood of conflict, especially where such conflict can engender bloodshed and death. If that is a benefit to the sending countries, it is a temporary benefit. Just because activists leave or are forced out of a country does not automatically lead to political stability in the sending countries.

BENEFITS ENJOYED BY IMMIGRANTS

Most immigrants audaciously move to a foreign country in search of what they could not have in their countries of origin. In moving to a developed country with a strong economy, immigrants are given access to more job opportunities, higher wages, improved educational facilities and greater potential for career advancement, resulting in the overall improved quality of life for themselves and their families. Besides being given the opportunity to escape political persecution and experience improved standards of living, emigration also reunites individuals with family members already living abroad.

OVERVIEW

Just as Egypt would be nonexistent without the River Nile; developed countries would also not be sustainable without immigrants. Without the River Nile, Egypt's environmental stability, agricultural potential and trading opportunities would be adversely altered. Similarly, no matter how economically developed a country is, it will eventually have to rely to a significant extent on a skilled workforce sourced from overseas to help maintain the efficiency of its industrial complex.

In the same vein and contrary to the opinion of some native-born citizens of the receiving countries, immigration is a non-zero-sum game. All participants and stakeholders are beneficiaries to various degrees. Immigration should be viewed as a bridge to the future. In every global-North country that I have been to, there is abundant evidence that immigrants have enriched and strengthened the fabric of their economies and the quality of life of their citizens.

Immigration has helped alleviate labor deficits in many developed countries with a high number of retired and out of work elderly people. Because immigrants are typically younger and more likely to be of working age, they are used by industrialized countries to replenish the shrinking labor pool resulting from an aging population, particularly in sectors like healthcare and construction where there is a high demand for an energetic labor force.

The significance of immigrants is even more apparent when assessing the agricultural industry in global-North countries.

In the United States, according to data from the Bureau of Economic Analysis, agriculture, food and related industries that depend heavily on immigrant workers, contributed roughly $1.537 trillion to the Gross Domestic Product (GDP) in 2023. The output of America's farms contributed $222.3 billion of this sum - about 0.8 percent of the country's GDP (USDA 2024). One can only imagine the impact on this sector if there were no immigrants to plant and harvest crops. Harvesting, packaging, and shipping of these crops to different parts of the country and the world at large would be severely impeded. Large numbers of immigrants also perform jobs that Americans prefer to avoid, like picking up trash, mowing the lawn, trimming, and cutting trees and cleaning the streets. This fact should be taken into consideration by leaders and citizens who are quick to denigrate immigrants.

Immigrants usually travel long distances to their destinations. The journey can be hazardous, tiring, and expensive. On arrival in the receiving country, they are confronted with nostalgia and other sociocultural challenges. They are often vulnerable to acts of discrimination and xenophobia by citizens based on factors like national origin, race, and language. Regardless of these challenges, many immigrants are resilient and would not be deterred from pursuing their goals.

Although it is not certain to whom the following statement is attributed, it is important within the context of the immigrant experience, "Success is not final, failure is not fatal. It is the courage to continue that counts."[3] No matter how toxic the living condition is, immigrants typically respond by putting on their armor of success and working hard to meet the goals that they set for themselves.

---

3   Pixelstorm, "Quotes Falsely Attributed to Winston Churchill," International Churchill Society, July 25, 2023, https://winstonchurchill.org/resources/quotes/quotes-falsely-attributed.

This book highlights and examines the challenges immigrants face or are likely to face and offers practical solutions to overcoming the obstacles that they will inevitably encounter. To achieve this objective, twenty-five standard principles adopted by highly successful immigrants are illustrated and explained. It is my hope that this information will serve as a beacon for immigrants as they embark on a journey of success and fulfillment in their host countries.

CHAPTER I

SINS OF ASSUMPTION

Many immigrants make the false assumption that once they set foot on their new country of residence their life woes will either come to an end or be considerably reduced. Life does not come with guarantees. The problems immigrants face, irrespective of nationality, are determined by several factors, including cultural, economic, and political structures in the receiving country. On arrival in a foreign country, immigrants may not experience the same problems they encountered in their countries of origin, which triggered their decision to emigrate in the first place. But they should be ready to face unanticipated and unfamiliar problems in their new country of residence.

Immigrants should always remember that no country, no matter how advanced, is devoid of problems and their green pastures may hold some withered areas.

Notwithstanding, according to Charles Swindoll, *"Life is 10 percent what happens to us and 90 percent how we react to what happened."*[4] This maxim means that our habits and how we respond to our problems will determine our success or failure. It is particularly relevant to contemporary immigrants given constant changes in immigration policies in the receiving countries and the resulting obstacles they pose. The attitudes, behavior patterns and actions of immigrants have a much larger impact on how they handle challenges than the challenges themselves. Their ability to adapt to new situations is essential for success.

NEWCOMERS

Before embarking on their transnational journeys, many immigrants do not know or do not care to find out if their preferred destinations are as "green" as they imagine them to be based on information gathered from private conversations with friends, books, articles or the Internet. Grand claims about freedom and economic opportunities may be little more than public relations baiting orchestrated by receiving countries.

---

4   Title of book by Pastor Charles R. Swindoll, founder of Stonebriar Community Church in Frisco, Texas, 2023.

Some of the advanced countries that attract immigrants can be likened to a cage filled with insects; peering into the cages are immigrants like gullible hungry birds. While the latter are desperate to get into the cage, some already on the inside are equally desperate to get out as they discover that the insects are not that tasty and, in some instances, may actually be lethal.

When many immigrants realize that their new dwellings are not as "green" as they imagined them to be, they become exasperated and consider or embark on relocation to new countries or back to their home countries. Only relatively few immigrants choose the option of returning to their countries of origin. Most immigrants, regardless of the difficulties they encounter, see their situation as a *fait accompli* and decide to stay and fight for survival. The result is that many immigrants live in two worlds (see my book: *Living in Two Worlds*, forthcoming 2026); they physically take up residence in foreign countries but remain emotionally attached to their homelands.

Another false assumption often made by immigrants is tied to this statement by internationally renowned anti-apartheid activist, Nelson Mandela: *"Education is the most powerful weapon which you can use to change the world."*[5] Because immigrants are part of a highly educated demographic, when they move to a new country they generally feel confident that their skills would be appreciated and that they would be able to maximize their potential. This is a reasonable and understandable expectation. In some countries, the United States, for instance, studies show that immigrants are statistically more educated than native-born citizens (Olsen & Batalova, 2020). However, in recent years, many receiving countries have tightened their immigration policies and show growing skepticism towards immigrants.

---

5 "Nelson Mandela," Oxford Reference, accessed February 17, 2025, https://www.oxfordreference. com/display/10.1093/acref/9780191843730.001.0001/q-oro-ed5-00007046.

Consequently, though immigrants are among the most educated individuals in host countries, many still fall short of achieving their goals in these countries, even in countries like the United States where opportunities abound for the expression of talent. This is why "thinking like an immigrant" is critical.

Because many immigrants are educationally empowered, yet struggling to make ends meet, it goes without saying that education or technical skills alone cannot guarantee them success in their new country of residence. For some immigrants, a "terminal degree" from a highly ranked institution does not guarantee a "better life" even if it leaves them with a psychological sense of success. Education is certainly important, but even more important is how the knowledge is utilized or the purpose it serves. The latter depends on several factors, including how enabling the environment is, the demand for the field of study and the prejudices that immigrants face. Are immigrants able to find their niche and practice their trade without fear or favor? In many countries, immigrants are treated as "shadow citizens," discussed above, and are not accorded access to opportunities that would guarantee their success and growth, despite their education and talents.

When highly qualified immigrants complain about the lack of opportunities for growth in their new country of residence, I usually ask them a set of questions, e.g.,

Is it really the lack of opportunities or your attitude to life that has blinded you to opportunities that are readily available to you?
Is it because of existing immigration policies?
Is it your perspective about life and the world?
Could it be your habits or life principles?
Is it your health situation?
Is it the people you surround yourself with?
Who are your friends?
Do you have a development plan for yourself?

The above questions address factors which, singularly or collectively, can hinder one's progress irrespective of a high level of education.

Many immigrants do not know the value of the skills they have. This lack of self-awareness is tantamount to ignorance and, according to Myles Munroe, a renowned Evangelist, *"The greatest enemy of man is ignorance of self. Nothing is more frustrating than not knowing who you are or what to do with what you have"* (Munroe 1995). Some immigrants know their professional capabilities but lack the ability to "sell" themselves. Others think because they are technically qualified and residing in a developed country, they need not work as hard as they once worked in their countries of origin to be successful. There is also the widespread misconception by immigrants that they only need to put in minimal effort to achieve their goals in receiving countries since these countries are very wealthy. This *El Dorado* image of their new country of residency creates the false impression of streets lined with gold. Minimal effort is simply a dead end on the road to progress.

While education is a powerful tool with which to jumpstart life in a foreign country, I have to disagree with the great Nelson Mandela who argued that *"Education is the most powerful weapon which you can use to change the world."*[6] To be successful as an immigrant, you have to think critically and come to terms with your beliefs and behavior patterns, which may be shaped by your ancestral culture or your immediate environment, all of which can impact your progress positively or negatively. These may include but are not limited to being clear as to why you emigrated, deciding what you want in life, believing in yourself, taking responsibility for your actions, living a life of thankfulness, cultivating the habit of giving, self-control, setting clear goals, having integrity, remaining enthusiastic,

---

6   "Nelson Mandela," Oxford Reference, accessed February 17, 2025, https://www.oxfordreference. com/display/10.1093/acref/9780191843730.001.0001/q-oro-ed5-00007046.

embracing change, and most importantly, clearly defining your goals and taking action to achieve them.

TURNING CHALLENGES INTO OPPORTUNITIES: A GUIDE FOR IMMIGRANTS

The primary objective of this book is to prepare immigrants to face unanticipated challenges and to transform obstacles into opportunities. Immigrants often encounter unique burdens in their new countries of residence, many of which are hidden, misunderstood, or underestimated. This book seeks to illuminate these challenges and provide strategies for overcoming them with resilience, adaptability, and purpose.

Rather than criticizing immigrants or the policies of sending and receiving countries, the book offers a constructive guide. It is not about blame - it is about empowerment. Immigration policies, regardless of their perceived benefits or drawbacks, are legitimate tools used by nations to preserve their territorial integrity and national security. However, it is hoped that leaders of both sending and receiving nations will recognize the immense value immigrants bring and work toward building respectful and mutually beneficial relationships.

To thrive in a new environment, immigrants must be prepared to think differently. As Alvin Toffler famously stated in *Future Shock* (1984), *"The illiterate of the twenty-first century will not be those who cannot read and write, but those who cannot learn, unlearn, and relearn."* Learning, unlearning, and relearning are habits, and they are essential to transformation. Successful people develop credible life principles and surround themselves with inspiration drawn from those who have navigated similar paths with perseverance and wisdom.

This book was not written as a theoretical lecture or academic treatise. Rather, it is a practical, real-world guide grounded in the lived experiences of hundreds of highly successful immigrants. Through in-depth interviews, I uncovered the principles, habits, and mindsets that helped them rise above adversity and thrive. These findings have been distilled into twenty-five core principles that form the backbone of this book.

The purpose of highlighting these success stories is not to romanticize the immigrant journey, but to provide a blueprint for others to follow. The growth potential for immigrants is truly limitless if they are willing to embrace change, adopt a growth mindset, learn from failure, seek out new opportunities, develop resilience, and have the courage to replace self-defeating habits with productive ones. Reframing challenges as opportunities can lead to improved mental and physical health, a more optimistic outlook, and ultimately, greater chances of success and longevity.

One of the major impediments to immigrant progress is the continued adherence to the same ideals, behaviors, and mindsets that hindered productivity in their country of origin. Immigrants must be willing to critically examine their habits and take decisive action to align their lives with new realities. For life to change in a meaningful way, habits must also evolve.

Thinking like an immigrant means acknowledging that your frame of reference is no longer the same. A farmer does not think like a pilot, and likewise, an immigrant must not think like someone who never had to leave their homeland. This mental shift is explored in depth in Challenge # 1 below.

It is difficult to adequately capture the bravery, tenacity, audacity, and intellectual capacity of immigrants. However, immigrants need to understand that, despite their skillsets, well-thought-out life principles and decisions are the *sine qua non* for success in a foreign country. They can have all the education from the best institutions in the world, but if their thoughts and attitudes towards life do not align with the cultures and laws of their new countries of residence, their effort to achieve their goals will end in failure.

Ultimately, this book serves as both a warning and a roadmap meant to protect today's immigrants from repeating the mistakes of their predecessors, whether caused by ignorance, misinformation, or information overload. By learning from those who have succeeded before them, contemporary immigrants can avoid unnecessary hardship, accelerate their growth, and step boldly into their potential.

SECTION I

CHALLENGES FACED BY IMMIGRANTS

INTRODUCTION TO SECTION I

"But today our very survival depends on our ability to stay awake, to adjust to new ideas, to remain vigilant and to face the challenge of change."[7]

Martin Luther King Jr.

It is unlikely that anyone simply wakes up one morning and decides to abandon or hate their homeland. As the popular Nigerian saying goes, *"na condition make crayfish bend"*. Translated, "difficult circumstances often force people into situations they would otherwise avoid." In her poem Home, a Somali-British writer and poet, Warsan Shire, reflects on this reality, writing, *"No one leaves home unless home is the mouth of a shark."* Just as sharks deploy various techniques to hunt and devour their prey, so too do the leaders of some countries use oppressive tactics to persecute, kill, or deny their citizens basic human rights. In such environments, people often feel trapped inside the jaws of a predator. When the situation deteriorates so drastically that citizens feel endangered by the very nations meant to protect them, emigration becomes a necessity for survival and the hope of a safer future for themselves and their families.

Relocating to another country regardless of how advanced or stable it may be, inevitably presents new and unfamiliar challenges. Life's struggles, like disease, know no borders. People in both wealthy and impoverished nations face hardships, though the severity and nature of these challenges may vary. There is no utopia on Earth, no green pasture without patches of dryness. At times, fleeing one's homeland may feel like leaping from the proverbial frying pan into the fire.

---

7   "Martin Luther King Jr.," Goodreads, accessed February 23, 2025, https://www.goodreads.com/quotes/197767-but-today-our-very-survival-depends-on-our-ability-to.

The challenges immigrants face are multifaceted and often begin even before departure, stemming from uncertainties about what awaits them in their new country. These challenges are amplified for those who remain deeply attached to their cultural roots and struggle to let go of traditional customs, which may hinder their ability, or willingness, to assimilate into a new way of life. Immigrants may be disappointed to discover that the high-paying job opportunities they had hoped for are scarce or inaccessible. Access to education, healthcare, and professional networks can be limited. They may also lack trusted mentors or supportive communities to lean on during times of hardship.

Some of the challenges immigrants face in their new countries may mirror those they tried to escape. For instance, people who flee tribalism or ethnic conflict might find themselves subjected to racism or religious discrimination in their unfamiliar environment. As the saying goes, "No matter what you call a dog, it's still an animal". In other words, changing the label does not change the underlying reality. Whether you call negative treatment of immigrants discrimination or tribalism, the effect is the same on the wellbeing of the people affected. Similarly, while many host countries publicly hail immigrants as "engines of development", underlying attitudes often remain hostile, with xenophobia and prejudice undermining these proclaimed ideals.

Immigrants must navigate a landscape filled with both expected and unforeseen obstacles - some tangible, others psychological, but all potentially capable of stalling progress or crushing hope. One persistent challenge is the cultural clash between the traditions of their homeland and the values and social norms of their new country. These tensions are particularly pronounced in areas such as marriage, family dynamics, and economic expectations, leaving many immigrants feeling conflicted and overwhelmed by the new realities they face.

To fulfill its objective, the author delves deeper into the social and cultural challenges that are common to the immigrant experience, regardless of their destination.

CHALLENGE #1

DISMANTLING COLONIAL MENTALITY

Colonization did not just redraw political boundaries or reshape economies; it also left behind a lasting psychological impact known as *colonial mentality* in the people of the colonies. This deeply rooted mindset causes people in formerly colonized countries to view the values, cultures, and traditions of their colonizers as superior to their own.

While often subtle, the effects of this mindset are far-reaching, influencing personal choices, societal expectations, and national development. Among the most affected are immigrants from previously colonized countries, many of whom carry this mentality across borders. They often arrive in Western nations with high expectations, believing life will be unequivocally better. However, when the realities of immigration do not meet their ideals, the dissonance between perception and experience breeds frustration and disillusionment. This essay explores the roots of colonial mentality, how it shapes immigrant expectations, and the unique challenges it poses for those trying to build new lives abroad.

UNDERSTANDING COLONIAL MENTALITY

Colonial mentality, also known as a colonial mindset, refers to the internalized belief that one's native culture, identity, language, and values are inferior to those of the colonizer. This psychological condition manifests as admiration for and imitation of Western or colonial ways, often at the expense of one's own traditions and self-worth.

The concept is particularly relevant in post-colonial societies in Asia, Africa, Latin America, and the Caribbean, where colonial powers ruled for extended periods and systematically undermined local institutions and belief systems.

The term is rooted in postcolonial theory, which analyzes the cultural, political, and psychological legacy of colonialism. Colonizers often imposed their language, religion, educational systems, and governance structures on indigenous populations. Over time, this led to a systemic devaluation of native identity and pride. Schools taught Eurocentric histories, churches promoted Western religious superiority, and media portrayed Western beauty standards and lifestyles as ideal. As a result, generations grew up believing that success, civility, and progress were synonymous with being "more Western."

COLONIAL MENTALITY AND THE EMIGRATION URGE

One of the most pervasive effects of colonial mentality is the idealization of the West, particularly Europe and North America, as the ultimate destinations for a better life. This belief is deeply embedded in the psyches of many people from formerly colonized nations. Education systems that glorify colonial powers, media that highlight Western prosperity, and even family narratives passed down through generations reinforce the notion that true opportunity lies abroad.

Thus, emigrating becomes not just a personal ambition but a social and cultural goal, sometimes even a *rite de passage*. Success is often defined by one's ability to leave the "developing" world and integrate into the "developed" West. This mindset frequently downplays or outright ignores the potential for advancement within one's own country, leading to a neglect of local opportunities and innovation.

While economic disparity is a valid and significant driver of migration, colonial mentality adds a psychological dimension that can make emigration feel like an imperative rather than a choice. People begin to see migration not merely as a path to better wages or education but as a necessary step to attain dignity, respect, and social mobility.

THE ILLUSION VS. REALITY: IMMIGRANT DISILLUSIONMENT

Upon arriving in their new country of residence, whether in North America or Western Europe, immigrants often face a stark contrast between their expectations and reality. Colonial mentality, having painted an idealized image of life in the West, does not prepare individuals for the social, economic, and emotional complexities of immigration. The disillusionment arises when immigrants realize that:

1. **Employment is not guaranteed** – Even with educational qualifications, immigrants often face underemployment or unemployment due to lack of local experience, language barriers, or systemic discrimination.
2. **Social integration is challenging** – Language, cultural differences, and social isolation can impede the development of meaningful relationships and a sense of community.
3. **Racism and xenophobia are prevalent** – Many immigrants encounter overt or covert racism that contradicts the egalitarian ideals they associated with the West.
4. **Financial burdens are high** – The cost of living, coupled with low-paying jobs, means many struggles to achieve the financial security they anticipated.

This gap between imagined prosperity and lived experience leads to a feeling of disappointment or disenchantment when one's hopes or expectations are not met, often arising from a lack of fulfillment or reality. For some, disappointment becomes a deep source of frustration. They may become resentful, grumpy, disengaged, or disoriented by the realization that the West is not a utopia. Others internalize their struggle as personal failure, further feeding feelings of inferiority and self-doubt.

COLONIAL MENTALITY AS A BARRIER TO ADAPTATION

Colonial mentality not only shapes immigrants' expectations but also hinders their adaptation and resilience in their new environments. Some of the key challenges or barriers to adaptation include:

1. *Identity crisis*: Immigrants grappling with colonial mentality often experience an identity crisis. They may feel caught between a devalued heritage and an unattainable ideal. In trying to assimilate, they might suppress their cultural identity - changing their names, accents, or appearance to "fit in." Yet, full acceptance is often elusive, leaving them feeling rootless.

2. *Reluctance to Build Local Networks*: Believing that proximity to "Western" individuals or institutions is a marker of success, some immigrants avoid communities from their own ethnic backgrounds. This limits their access to support networks that could ease their transition and reduce isolation.

3. *Underestimation of Local Knowledge and Skills*: Colonial mentality can cause immigrants to devalue the skills and experiences they bring with them. A teacher, engineer, or entrepreneur from a developing country

may see their expertise as inferior, leading them to accept roles far below their capability.

4. *Struggles with Self-Worth and Motivation*: When immigrants perceive themselves as inherently "less than," it can lead to a lack of motivation to advocate for their rights, pursue higher education, or seek leadership roles. This perpetuates cycles of low achievement and poor mental health.

Being told their background and values are inferior to the West deepens immigrants' disillusionment.

THE CULTURAL DISCONNECT
AND FAMILY DYNAMICS

Immigrants with colonial mindsets often impose the same beliefs on their children, creating intergenerational conflicts. Children born or raised in the new country may embrace aspects of both cultures, leading to identity tensions within families. Parents may struggle to maintain authority if their cultural values are seen as outdated or irrelevant.

Additionally, the pressure to succeed in the West, often viewed as redemption for past colonial inferiority, can place immense stress on immigrant families. Children may be pushed to achieve unrealistic goals in academics, career, or social mobility. When these goals are not met, blame, guilt, and family discord can arise.

RECLAIMING IDENTITY:
BREAKING THE COLONIAL MINDSET

Overcoming colonial mentality is both an individual and collective process.

For immigrants, healing from this psychological inheritance is crucial not only for their personal well-being but also for building a meaningful life in a new country.

1. *Cultural Reclamation*: Reconnecting with one's roots - language, history, traditions - can foster pride and resilience. Celebrating one's heritage, rather than viewing it as a barrier to success, helps immigrants build a strong and confident identity.

2. *Community Empowerment*: Ethnic communities that promote cultural pride and mutual support serve as critical resources for new immigrants. Organizations that offer language classes, cultural events, and professional mentoring can help counter feelings of isolation and inferiority.

3. *Redefining Success*: Moving beyond Western definitions of success to create individualized, culturally grounded aspirations helps immigrants find satisfaction and motivation. Whether through entrepreneurship, community leadership, or art, redefining success opens new paths to fulfillment.

4. *Mental Health Support*: Therapy and counseling that address the psychological effects of colonial mentality, particularly identity conflict and low self-worth, are essential. Culturally sensitive mental health professionals can guide individuals through the complexities of postcolonial trauma and adjustment.

CONCLUSION

The colonial mentality, deeply embedded in the psyche of individuals from formerly colonized nations, continues to shape the migration experience in profound ways.

By idealizing the West and devaluing their own cultural identities, immigrants often arrive in new countries with unrealistic expectations and fragile self-worth. When confronted with the realities of racism, economic struggle, and social alienation, many experience deep frustration and disillusionment. However, by recognizing the roots of colonial mentality and actively working to reclaim cultural pride and redefine success, immigrants can begin to overcome these challenges. Building inclusive communities and investing in culturally sensitive support systems is essential to breaking the cycle of inherited inferiority and empowering immigrants to thrive, both as individuals and as contributors to the global society.

CHALLENGE #2

FAMILY SEPARATION

Family separation is an increasingly common reality in today's world, driven by personal, economic, and safety concerns. People no longer simply migrate from one country to another, they also move within countries, from one city or region to another, in pursuit of better opportunities. This constant movement often comes at a steep cost, particularly the risk of weakened family bonds and the disruption of marital and parental relationships. It is a classic "damned if you do, damned if you don't" dilemma, where the options available to immigrants are often limited, difficult, and imperfect.

In the desperate search for a better life, many immigrants, often at the risk of harsh criticism, end up leaving their spouses and children behind when relocating to a new city or country. While these decisions are frequently made with the family's long-term well-being in mind, the immediate consequences of such separations can be emotionally and psychologically damaging.

No matter how stable a marriage may be, prolonged physical separation can lead to feelings of isolation or even abandonment in the partner left behind. In some cases, this emotional strain may result in *Separation Anxiety Disorder*, a condition marked by intense fear and worry over the absence or potential loss of a loved one. I experienced this firsthand during my frequent relocations while working with the World Health Organization (WHO) and the United Nations (UN).

The recurring separations from my family eroded the emotional and psychological connections that tie family members together. The pain and disconnection were so profound that I was compelled to author a book titled *Restless Citizens* (2010), which explores the hidden emotional burdens associated with working in transnational roles such as those at the WHO and the UN.

The book resonated with many within the UN community. It was a pleasant surprise being contacted by Phil Scarr, the 2nd Vice President of the UN Field Staff Union in Brindisi, Italy, to discuss the impact of family separation on the welfare of UN personnel. His letter is reproduced below:

> *Dear Dr. Udoh Elijah Udom. My name is Phil Scarr, and I am Currently assigned as the 2nd Vice President of the United Nations Field Staff Union - the staff representative body for international personnel assigned to UN peace-keeping and special political missions. We are currently looking into the subject of Family vs. Non-Family Duty Stations and I have been given to understand that you researched this very subject during your time with the World Health Organization and have also referred to some of the challenges arising from it in your book "Restless Citizens". I was therefore wondering if you would be willing to make some time to talk to me by telephone and perhaps share your views on the matter at some point during the weeks ahead.*
>
> *My apologies for writing to you "out of the blue" like this but I confess to having found the idea of trying to contact somebody who has apparently looked into this subject in some depth to be extremely appealing.*
> *Best Regards.*
>
>
>
> *Phil Scarr*
> *2nd Vice President, UN Field Staff Union,*
> *UNGSC/UNLB, Brindisi*
>
>

The family is a vital source of emotional security, happiness, and success. Its strength, much like that of an army, depends on the loyalty and closeness of its members. When significant members of a family are separated, particularly spouses, this loyalty can be strained or even fractured. Prolonged physical separation often results in loneliness, miscommunication, and emotional detachment. As the saying goes, *"an idle or confused mind can become the devil's workshop."* Both the spouse who relocates and the one who remains behind are vulnerable in different but equally damaging ways.

The psychological impact of long-term separation can be severe, often eroding emotional closeness and weakening the relationship. For many, family is the main reason for emigrating - to build a better life for their loved ones. But when separation leads to the loss of family bonds, the very purpose of migration is undermined. Immigrants must be mindful not to let the pursuit of a better life (which varies from person to person) come at the cost of their most valuable relationships. Wherever possible, steps should be taken to keep families together - for the wellbeing of individuals and the strength of the family.

CHALLENGE #3

NATIVISM

Nativism is one of the most powerful sentiments that poses a serious challenge to immigrants. At its core, it is a political philosophy that places the interests of native-born citizens above those of foreigners. It implies that government policies should prioritize citizens over non-citizens. This view is echoed by Clifton Fadiman, who once stated, *"When you travel, remember that a foreign country is not designed to make you comfortable. It is designed to make its own people comfortable"*. While many immigrants might find this perspective discriminatory, the truth is that even the least developed countries often adopt policies aimed primarily at protecting the interests of their own citizens - defending their sovereignty, securing their borders, and deciding who is allowed to enter or stay.

Nativism is not unique to any one region or political system; it is a global phenomenon, present in both rich and poor nations, and under both authoritarian and democratic governments. While protecting national interests is not inherently wrong, nativism often gives rise to xenophobia - fear and hostility toward foreigners. These anti-immigrant sentiments are among the first challenges many immigrants encounter in their new country of residence. Even in countries that enshrine equal rights and protections for all residents, including immigrants, laws alone cannot prevent discrimination by individuals or institutions.

In many countries, public opinion on immigration oscillates between hope and fear. For some political leaders and citizens, immigration is seen as a threat rather than an asset. Across history and continents, immigration has remained a divisive and emotionally charged topic. In response, some governments have tightened border controls and even constructed physical barriers to stem the flow of migrants. These anti-immigrant sentiments are fueled by perceived competition over jobs, housing, and public services - often intensified by differences in language, religion, culture, and political ideology.

While immigrants must be aware of such sentiments, they are also encouraged to adopt a mindset that fosters resilience and adaptability. As discussed further in Section III, successful immigrants often share core principles: perseverance, respect for local laws and customs, and the willingness to engage meaningfully with their new society.

A word of advice to immigrants: before criticizing the policies or people of your new country, take a moment to reflect on the reasons you left your homeland. Consider whether your current situation, despite its imperfections, is still an improvement in your situation. Remember that you had a choice in where to go, and by choosing to emigrate to your current abode, you implicitly agreed to abide by the laws and norms of your new country.

I am often struck by how quickly some immigrants forget the discriminatory systems, such as, tribalism or caste hierarchies, in their own countries that denied people opportunities based on ethnicity, class, or region. Complaints about racism, employment discrimination, or lack of opportunity in their host countries, while sometimes valid, must be viewed in the context of where they came from and why they left.

This is not to excuse racism or tribalism - both should be condemned in any society. The Universal Declaration of Human Rights, adopted in 1948 by 193 UN member states, was the first international legal instrument to outline the fundamental rights of all people, regardless of nationality. Unfortunately, many countries fail to uphold the very laws they helped draft and ratify. Despite these lofty commitments, national interests often take precedence. Immigrants, even in countries that promise equal rights, are rarely guaranteed full protection or freedom from discrimination. No nation offers unconditional rights to immigrants - often not even to its own citizens.

It is essential that immigrants remain aware of their status and approach challenges with a balanced perspective, avoiding a victim mindset or the tendency to blame others for unmet expectations. The reality is that most countries, to varying degrees, display nativist tendencies, especially when facing concerns about cultural preservation, economic pressure, and national identity in the face of growing diversity.

I have lived outside my country of birth for over three-quarters of my life, across more than five nations. I have studied the experiences of immigrants in over twenty countries across the Global South and Global North. The conclusion is clear: no country has clean hands when it comes to the treatment of immigrants. While many governments use inclusive rhetoric and humane terminology, when it comes to national sovereignty and protecting their own citizens, immigrants are almost always viewed as *shadow citizens* - outsiders, or worse, as threats. Immigrants are rarely a national priority. They should think as immigrants and accept the status gracefully, with whatever rights and privileges attached to it.

This is the truth immigrants must never forget no matter their contribution to the development of their new country or how prosperous they become in a foreign land.

If you left your homeland in pursuit of freedom, safety, or a better life, remember this: freedom is never truly free. The journey often comes with a price - facing discrimination rooted in your origin, your accent, your customs, or your faith. In your new country, you may be pressured to assimilate, to fit in, to leave parts of yourself behind. But whether you choose to fully adopt your host nation's culture, blend it with your own, or proudly preserve your heritage, never forget your story. Remember where you came from, what you endured to get here, and why you made that choice. In the face of nativism, your identity is both your armor and your legacy. Hold it close.

CHALLENGE #4

ASSIMILATION

Assimilation is the process through which individuals or groups of differing ethnic, racial, or cultural backgrounds are absorbed into the dominant culture of a society. In today's globalized world, true cultural homogeneity is rare. Migration has ensured that few, if any, countries remain culturally uniform. Nations that attract immigrants are increasingly becoming multinational and multicultural. In these societies - especially those with large immigrant population, residents often form a tapestry of "disparate people", differentiated by national origin, ethnicity, culture, race, and a host of other social, behavioral, emotional, and spiritual traits. Efforts to transform these diverse populations into a single, homogeneous national identity through assimilation have often met with limited success. For many countries, the attempt has proven to be a complex and, at times, frustrating endeavor.

When immigrants leave their homeland, it is often said that only their feet leave with them - their hearts, ancestral values, and cultural identities remain rooted in the place they call home. One of the first and most pressing challenges they face in their new environment is the pressure to assimilate. Most receiving countries expect immigrants to adapt quickly and fully to prevailing cultural norms. As the old saying goes, "*What is good for the goose is good for the gander*". If a country opens its doors to immigrants, it is seen as reasonable for those immigrants to reciprocate by embracing its dominant culture. Assimilation can foster harmony and good neighborliness, enabling meaningful inter-ethnic and inter-racial relationships and contributing to national unity and stability. By embracing assimilation, immigrants may better integrate into society and pave the way for future generations to thrive.

BARRIERS TO ASSIMILATION

Despite its perceived benefits, assimilation is not a straightforward process. Immigrants face a range of barriers - social, cultural, legal, and political—that make assimilation difficult. Among the most significant obstacles are prejudice, discrimination, stereotyping, and restrictive immigration laws and policies.

Prejudice - defined as preconceived opinions not grounded in reason or experience —is a major challenge. Immigrants often encounter biased attitudes from both native-born citizens and even other immigrant groups. Imagine the discouragement of arriving in a new country with hope of maximizing potential, only to be met with suspicion or hostility before being given a chance to prove oneself.

In many economically advanced nations, prejudice against immigrants from less developed countries is particularly common. Ironically, this prejudice sometimes stems not only from perceived differences in language or culture, but also from the high levels of education, professionalism, and innovation immigrants often bring. Female immigrants and native-born women alike also face other form of prejudice: sexism. Some of these attitudes stem from entrenched ideologies, such as the ultra-nationalist belief in cultural or racial superiority. As Klitzke (2001) noted, some view immigrants as members of "lower races"- a dangerous and unfounded notion that still shapes public opinion and policy in some places.

Regardless of how accomplished immigrants may have been in their home countries, they are too often treated as inferior in their new homes.

Stereotyping is another major barrier to assimilation. It is rooted in broad, inaccurate generalizations and assumptions. A common stereotype, for example, is the notion that immigrants are a "public charge" - individuals who rely on social benefits without making meaningful contributions to their communities. While some immigrants may require temporary support from public and private entities during difficult times - often due to circumstances beyond their control - labeling all immigrants as burdens is both unfair and demoralizing.

This attitude echoes Abraham Maslow's well-known remark: "*If the only tool you have is a hammer, you tend to see every problem as a nail*". In other words, when a society fixates on a single narrative or scapegoat, it oversimplifies complex issues and applies solutions that do more harm than good. Blaming immigrants for a nation's socioeconomic challenges is a prime example of this misguided thinking.

The reality is that immigrants are often major contributors to the development of their new societies. In many countries, they are entrepreneurs, educators, inventors, caregivers, and members of the armed forces. For example, in the United States in 2019, there were 3.2 million immigrant entrepreneurs employing over eight million people - both native-born and immigrant (New American Economy, 2022). Major technological and commercial innovations - from the iPhone to Uber to Amazon - have been fueled by immigrant talent. Across industries and borders, immigrants are vital to global progress and development.

Assimilation remains a complex and deeply personal journey. While host countries may expect it, and immigrants may strive toward it, the process is fraught with barriers that must be understood and addressed. True integration involves mutual respect: immigrants adapting to a new culture, and host societies recognizing and valuing the contributions immigrants make. Only then can assimilation become not a tool of erasure, but a bridge toward shared identity and inclusive progress.

CHALLENGE #5

KNOWLEDGE GAP

Living in a foreign country as an immigrant can be overwhelming, particularly for those who are illiterate or semi-literate. Some immigrants, such as those who relocate after winning a visa lottery, may arrive in developed countries without the education, language proficiency, or vocational skills typically required to thrive in a competitive labor market. Winning a visa does not necessarily equate to having a specialized talent or the tools needed to navigate a new society successfully.

For many in this situation, the lack of formal education or relevant job skills presents immediate obstacles. Unemployment or underemployment in low-paying, labor-intensive jobs become a common reality. In addition, the inability to read, write, or use technology often prevents access to essential services and information. Everyday tasks, such as, understanding public transportation, reading signs, filling out forms, or accessing healthcare, can become daunting challenges. The communication barrier compounds social isolation and makes integration into the broader community more difficult. Moreover, limited literacy and unfamiliarity with local laws and systems increase vulnerability to exploitation, scams, and misinformation.

A particularly critical challenge immigrants face is the knowledge gap surrounding immigration policies and procedures. This gap often leads to confusion and unintentional non-compliance.

Many arrive in their new countries with little to no understanding of what is expected of them, what rights they possess, or how to navigate bureaucratic systems. They also frequently lack insight into the cultural norms and social expectations of the host society. This lack of preparedness can hinder their ability to adapt and succeed.

In some cases, the absence of accurate information, or the presence of misinformation, is even more harmful than direct discrimination. As the biblical saying goes, "*My people perish for lack of knowledge*" (Hosea 4:6). Without a clear understanding of their environment, immigrants may find it difficult to make informed decisions about their future, which in turn limits their aspirations and stifles their creative potential. The uncertainty born from this knowledge gap can fuel anxiety, fear, and a diminished sense of agency.

In this book, immigrants are encouraged to actively seek out information about their destination countries before and after arrival. By striving to understand the local culture, laws, and immigration policies, they can better assess whether a particular country aligns with their goals and values. Such preparation is vital - not just for legal compliance, but for building a fulfilling life in a new home.

CHALLENGE #6

SUDDEN WEALTH: A HIDDEN DANGER
FOR IMMIGRANTS

Many immigrants arrive in new countries driven by the hope of a better life - one that promises economic opportunity, stability, and upward mobility. Through perseverance, long hours of work, and strategic thinking, many have achieved remarkable success. Some, however, find themselves catapulted into wealth overnight, whether through high-paying jobs, successful businesses, inheritances, legal settlements, or even lottery winnings.

While sudden wealth may seem like a dream come true, it can quickly turn into a nightmare if not handled wisely. Immigrants who come into unexpected riches must recognize that along with financial prosperity comes a new set of challenges - some of which can be deeply personal and even destructive.

This phenomenon has a name: *Sudden Wealth Syndrome*. It is a psychological condition marked by anxiety, confusion, guilt, and an identity crisis. Those affected often struggle with decisions about spending, saving, and giving, and may feel overwhelmed by new social expectations and financial responsibilities. If left unaddressed, this syndrome can spiral into what experts refer to as *financial dysmorphia*, a distorted and unhealthy obsession with money, material possessions, and status.

There is nothing inherently wrong with becoming wealthy. The danger lies in not being prepared for it. Many immigrants, particularly those who have experienced poverty or financial instability in their home countries, are often unequipped to manage sudden wealth responsibly. For some, it feels like an endless stream of abundance - manna from heaven that will never stop flowing. But this illusion is dangerous. All wealth, no matter how large, is finite. Without careful planning and self-discipline, it can vanish just as quickly as it appeared.

The pursuit of prosperity is natural, and for many, it is the very reason they left their homelands. But wealth, when mismanaged, has led immigrants into avoidable crises—strained marriages, troubled children, broken friendships, and even legal troubles. These outcomes are often rooted in emotional impulsiveness, the absence of financial literacy, and the misguided belief that success means showing off. Sudden wealth can seduce people into a destructive cycle of overspending, promiscuity, egotism, and financial recklessness.

Let this be a clear warning: wealth without wisdom is a trap. Success must be matched with humility, education, and a long-term vision. Immigrants who work hard and earn their wealth deserve to enjoy it, but they must do so with discernment. Financial security is not just about making money; it is about keeping it, growing it, and using it to build a legacy—not just for oneself, but for future generations.

In conclusion, sudden wealth can be both a blessing and a burden. Immigrants who find themselves in fortunate financial positions must take the time to educate themselves, seek professional advice, and stay grounded in their values. Only then can wealth become a true instrument of empowerment rather than a path to regret.

CHALLENGE #7

CULTURAL DIFFERENCES

Cultural differences refer to the variations in values, beliefs, customs, and behaviors that exist between people from different cultural backgrounds. These differences can profoundly influence how individuals communicate, relate, and adapt in a new society. For immigrants, cultural adjustment is often one of the most complex challenges of resettlement. While many successfully navigate unfamiliar customs and overcome xenophobic attitudes, others struggle with the clash between their native traditions and the cultural norms of their host country.

This cultural dissonance can affect various aspects of life - language use, gender roles, parenting styles, religious expression, and even basic social interactions. Some immigrant practices may be misunderstood or frowned upon in the host country, while aspects of the new culture may feel foreign, uncomfortable, or morally conflicting to the newcomer.

Understanding these differences and identifying potentially problematic areas, whether in legal expectations, social etiquette, or workplace behavior, is crucial for smooth integration. Without this awareness, immigrants risk misunderstandings, isolation, or unintentional conflict. Cultural differences, if not managed wisely, can lead to a "conflict of cultures", straining gender and parent-child relationships, and obstructing successful integration. Immigrants must, therefore, approach cultural adaptation with openness, sensitivity, and a willingness to learn - while still preserving the core values of their identity.

CULTURAL INTEGRATION:
A BALANCING ACT FOR IMMIGRANTS

One of the most profound challenges immigrants face in a new country is not just finding work or learning the language, it is deciding how to navigate the cultural divide between their ancestral traditions and the norms of their host society. This tension between holding on and letting go is a quiet battle that plays out daily in homes, workplaces, schools, and places of worship.

RESISTANCE TO ADAPTATION

While discrimination and xenophobia are unfortunate realities immigrants may encounter, a more subtle and sometimes more damaging issue is the refusal to adapt. Some immigrants cling so tightly to their cultural roots that they resist the social norms, legal expectations, and values of their new country. This can create a kind of cultural paralysis - like trying to climb a coconut tree while holding heavy objects in both hands. Holding on to an old mindset in a new context can lead to frustration, confusion, and missed opportunities.

Attempting to maintain two distinct cultural identities without integration can also trigger culture shock. Immigrants may find themselves torn between which practices to uphold and which to discard - unsure of how to honor their heritage while also fitting into their new environment. This confusion can manifest in family life, especially in areas such as work ethics, gender roles, parenting, and spousal relationships.

The dilemma deepens when immigrants attempt to blend religions, values, or social customs without a clear framework.

Even after taking the oath of citizenship, many remain emotionally tied to their countries of origin. Their hearts remain at home, even though their bodies have moved on. This emotional split can create a form of divided loyalty, making full integration difficult.

However, integration does not have to mean total assimilation or cultural erasure. Many immigrants successfully strike a balance - preserving meaningful aspects of their heritage while adapting to the key social, legal, and cultural expectations of their host country. For example, it is common to see Chinese, Russian, Kenyan, Yemeni, or Korean immigrants who celebrate their traditional festivals, speak their native languages at home, and still respect local laws and social norms.

The goal, therefore, is intentional cultural integration - an honest effort to adapt where necessary while maintaining a healthy respect for one's cultural roots. Immigrants should ask themselves:

- Which parts of my culture can I preserve without isolating myself?
- What new practices must I adopt to succeed and thrive here?
- Am I resisting change out of fear, pride, or lack of understanding?

Striking this balance takes time, humility, and reflection. But the reward is a stable, respectful identity that honors both the old and the new - a key ingredient for successful settlement and lasting peace of mind in a new homeland.

PARENTING ACROSS CULTURES: GUIDANCE FOR IMMIGRANT FAMILIES

A growing trend among immigrants is to leave their children behind - sometimes temporarily, sometimes for extended periods - while they move abroad to pursue education, employment, or better opportunities. These parents often intend to reunite with their children later, hoping to expose them to improved educational and economic prospects. In the meantime, the children are raised by either one parent or extended family members, who serve as surrogate caregivers. However, long-distance parenting presents serious emotional and practical challenges. Despite their best intentions, many immigrant parents find it difficult to instill values, monitor behavior, or provide consistent guidance from afar.

Parenting becomes even more complex once children reunite with their parents in a foreign country. Immigrant families typically fall into three categories:

1. Native-born children raised in the home country who later move abroad;
2. Foreign-born children, born and raised in the new country; and
3. Bi-racial or bi-national children, often referred to as *Third Culture Kids* (TCKs) - those growing up between multiple cultural identities.

Each group has distinct needs and faces unique challenges, particularly around identity, sense of belonging, and cultural adaptation. TCKs often struggle with language barriers, rootlessness, emotional isolation, and confusion over where they truly belong.

This is where cultural sensitivity in parenting becomes critical. One of the most important lessons for immigrant parents is this: do not rigidly apply parenting styles from your country of origin in your new environment. While ancestral values may be deeply held and well-intentioned, they can clash with the norms, laws, and expectations of the host society. For example, physical punishment or authoritarian parenting styles that may be socially accepted - or even encouraged - in one's home country could be considered abusive or unlawful in the new country. Ignoring these differences can lead to legal consequences and serious damage to the parent-child relationship.

At the same time, parents must avoid the opposite extreme - adopting a hands-off approach and allowing children to grow up without structure or guidance. This is a common pitfall when parents, overwhelmed or unsure, retreat from active parenting to avoid "cultural conflict." The result is often children who feel emotionally neglected, lack discipline, and are left to be shaped entirely by outside influences.

Immigrant parents must find a balanced approach:

- Adapt their parenting methods to respect the rights of the child as understood in the host country.
- Stay involved emotionally and physically, maintaining open communication and trust.
- Instill values like respect, responsibility, and community-mindedness that are universally appreciated across cultures.
- Educate themselves about local parenting norms, child protection laws, and school expectations.

- Model flexibility and cultural intelligence, teaching children how to embrace both their heritage and their present reality.

By blending the best of their ancestral values with the practical expectations of their new society, immigrant parents can raise well-adjusted, respectful, and culturally competent children. Effective parenting in a new country requires humility, learning, and constant engagement - but it is worth every effort for the future of the family.

Good parents understand that discipline and presence are essential to raising well-rounded children, which is why they neither spare the rod nor substitute their presence with presents. "Sparing the rod" is not about endorsing physical punishment but rather refusing to set firm boundaries and enforce consequences, which leads to a lack of structure and accountability in a child's life. Equally harmful is the tendency to compensate for emotional absence with material gifts - presents can never replace presence. Children crave connection, guidance, and consistent love far more than toys or gadgets. By being present and firm, parents cultivate respect, emotional security, and responsibility, laying a solid foundation for their child's future.

Challenge #8

Female Empowerment and the Changing Dynamics of Immigrant Families

Female empowerment refers to the process by which women gain the ability and freedom to make decisions, access opportunities, and shape the course of their lives - both in the private and public spheres. The United Nations outlines five key components of women's empowerment:

1. A woman's sense of self-worth;
2. Her right to make her own choices;
3. Her power to control her life within and outside the home;
4. Her access to resources and opportunities;
5. Her capacity to influence social and economic systems for justice and equality.

While these principles are universal, their impact is especially profound, and at times disruptive, within immigrant families who relocate from traditional societies to more progressive, developed countries.

In many parts of the Global South, patriarchal norms are deeply entrenched. Women are often raised to be deferential, to manage domestic affairs, and to prioritize family above personal ambition. Speaking up, questioning a husband's decision, or asserting independence is often culturally frowned upon. Men, in turn, are socialized to expect obedience, service, and emotional dependence from their wives.

However, when families immigrate to Western societies where women's rights are legally protected, culturally normalized, and institutionally supported, the old order begins to crumble - often abruptly. Women gain access to formal education, professional development, legal support systems, and social networks that encourage self-expression and ambition. The result is frequently a transformed worldview, particularly for those who had previously been denied a voice.

EMPOWERED RICH WOMEN SAYING TO HER HUSBAND, I AM PAYING THE BILLS: DO WHAT I TELL YOU TO DO, WHILE CHILDREN WATCH THE DRAMA IN DISMAY.

As Eleanor Roosevelt aptly noted, *"A woman is like a tea bag - you can't tell how strong she is until you put her in hot water"*. This quote captures the essence of the indomitable spirit that resides within every woman, waiting to be tested and unleashed when faced with challenges and adversity. If women are inherently powerful, imagine how they will be when empowered - putting gasoline in fire?

For many immigrant men, the "hot water" is the unanticipated independence and assertiveness their wives begin to express in their new country due to empowerment in education and high paying jobs. A wife who once deferred to her husband's every decision may now demand joint decision-making, challenge outdated norms, or pursue a career that redefines her role within the household.

This shift has led to significant marital strain. Many male immigrants - particularly those who financed their wives' education or vocational training express disillusionment when those investments lead not just to family advancement, but to their wives seeking autonomy, reducing their domestic availability, or in some cases, questioning the marriage itself.

Importantly, empowerment does not equate to rebellion or disrespect. But without adequate preparation for these cultural and gender-role transformations, what should be a shared journey toward mutual growth can become a source of resentment, fear, or emotional distance. Men who once held unilateral authority may feel displaced, emasculated, or unsure of their role in the family, especially in societies that no longer validate patriarchal dominance. This cultural dissonance plays out in various forms:

- *Conflict over domestic roles*: Empowered women may refuse to be the sole caretaker or housekeeper, expecting their spouses to share responsibilities.
- *Financial independence*: Women who earn their own income may insist on joint financial decisions or maintain personal savings, which some men interpret as distrust or rebellion.
- *Parenting approaches*: Empowered women may advocate for gender-equitable parenting, resisting traditional expectations that sons are prioritized over daughters.

- ***Religious and cultural practices***: Women may question or reinterpret faith and cultural rituals once deemed unquestionable, leading to spiritual or philosophical rifts.

In many immigrant communities, this evolving gender dynamic has contributed to a rise in marital dissatisfaction, separation, and divorce. Some men, unprepared for these shifts, react with control, withdrawal, or even violence - behaviors that are legally actionable in their new societies.

However, the narrative need not be adversarial. Female empowerment, when embraced as a shared value rather than a threat, can lead to more balanced, respectful, and fulfilling relationships. Immigrant men must also be empowered - emotionally and intellectually - to adapt to new norms, recognize the evolving role of women, and redefine masculinity in terms of partnership rather than power.

A PATH FORWARD

While often labeled a Western ideology, women's empowerment is increasingly relevant across cultures. Interestingly, during interviews with various European and American men, many expressed – privately - a discomfort with true gender equality, even as they publicly support women's advancement. One man confided, "God created women to be men's helpers - not the other way around. So, all this noise about men not being helpful is ridiculous." Such views highlight a lingering resistance to shifting gender dynamics. Yet, we live in a new era - one where male dominance is increasingly seen as outdated. For peace and harmony in conjugal relationships, especially within immigrant families navigating new cultural landscapes, several foundational principles are essential:

- *Communication is key*: Open dialogue about evolving roles, expectations, and fears fosters mutual understanding. Avoiding hard conversations only widens the emotional gap.
- *Cultural education*: Both partners should actively learn how their host country's norms around gender, family law, and marital roles differ from their own traditions.
- *Mutual respect*: Empowerment is not about competition. It is about cooperation and mutual growth.
- *Counseling and community support*: Many organizations offer culturally sensitive counseling to help immigrant couples and families navigate the pressures of change and adaptation.

When handled with emotional intelligence and mutual respect, women's empowerment can strengthen the fabric of immigrant families - helping them adapt and flourish without discarding the beauty of their cultural roots.

CHALLENGE #9

DIVORCE: UNDERSTANDING CULTURAL
SHIFTS IN MARRIAGE AND SEPARATION

In today's globalized world, women - like men - are increasingly accessing higher education, employment, and mobility. Industrialization, urbanization, and modern transportation have made it easier for women to emigrate in pursuit of better opportunities. Many young women now live independently, earn their own income, and feel empowered to make life decisions on their own terms - including the decision to marry, or not to marry, and, when necessary, to leave a marriage that has become toxic or unfulfilling.

This shift is especially visible when women from traditionally patriarchal societies immigrate to developed countries in the Global North. Here, laws, cultural norms, and strong advocacy for gender equality protect women's rights in ways that can be unfamiliar or even shocking to many immigrants from the Global South. In these societies, women are not expected to submit to their husbands without question, and marriage is seen as a partnership, not a hierarchy.

Practices that may be culturally accepted in some Global South communities—such as controlling a woman's finances, limiting her freedom, denying her education, or demanding exclusive domestic service - are often viewed in the Global North as signs of emotional abuse or gender-based oppression. Immigrant women who were once silent about these issues now find strength through education, legal awareness, and community support.

Many begin to speak up, seek help, and, when necessary, choose divorce as a legitimate and healthy path to reclaiming their dignity and well-being.

The idea that divorce is a *taboo* is still deeply ingrained in many immigrant cultures. In such environments, women who leave their marriages are often seen as failures or rebels. However, in most developed countries, divorce is not viewed as a personal failure but as a legal and social mechanism to protect individuals from harmful relationships. This shift in cultural perception must be understood and respected by immigrants, particularly men, who may feel threatened or confused by these changing dynamics.

RISING DIVORCE RATE AMONG IMMIGRANT FAMILIES

From New York to Paris, London to Toronto, rising divorce rates among immigrant families reflect not just social instability, but a broader cultural evolution. Women are no longer willing to suffer silently under the weight of oppressive traditions. As I spoke to immigrant families across various destinations, I was surprised by the number of separations and divorces - not because women were "rebellious," but because many had found the courage and legal support to walk away from loveless, abusive, or controlling relationships.

Some men struggle to adjust. The traditional sense of male authority - the expectation that they alone control family decisions - is increasingly challenged. For some, this perceived erosion of power leads to emotional withdrawal, domestic conflict, or even abandonment of the marriage altogether. In these cases, what is really at stake is not the marriage, but the male ego and its unwillingness to adapt to new realities.

ADVICE TO IMMIGRANTS:
NAVIGATING MARRIAGE IN A NEW CULTURE

Marriage can often feel like a gamble. Many couples enter it with high hopes and vows of "for better or worse," only to find themselves at odds before long. Romantic moments give way to blame and resentment. Even in ancient texts, we see this dynamic - Adam, for instance, blamed God for giving him Eve, calling his helper a source of trouble rather than support. This pattern of miscommunication and unmet expectations is hardly new. As Socrates once said, *"By all means, marry; if you get a good wife, you'll become happy; if you get a bad one, you'll become a philosopher."* What he meant by becoming a philosopher is up for debate, but the challenges of marriage - especially for immigrants - remain real.

Starting life in a new country brings immense cultural shifts, and marriage is often the first space where those tensions show. To thrive in this new environment, immigrants should consider the following:

1. *Understand the Laws of Your New Country*: Marital laws in most developed nations prioritize individual rights and protect both spouses from abuse, coercion, or neglect. Ignorance of these laws is not an excuse for harmful behavior. Learn your rights—and your partner's.

2. *See Marriage as a Partnership, not a Power Structure*: Successful marriages are built on mutual respect, open communication, and shared responsibilities. Control, silence, or fear should never replace love and understanding.

85

3. *Accept That Divorce Is Not a Disgrace*: While often stigmatized in traditional cultures, divorce can be a healthy and necessary step toward healing when a marriage becomes harmful. Staying in a toxic relationship for the sake of appearances only deepens emotional wounds.

4. *Embrace Change, Do not Resist It*: Cultural expectations may shift in a new country. Men, especially, must be willing to grow alongside their empowered wives. Equality in marriage does not weaken the family - it strengthens it.

5. *Seek Help Early*: Do not wait until your relationship reaches a crisis point. Counseling, mediation, and community support groups are widely available and often culturally sensitive. Seeking help is a sign of strength, not weakness.

CONCLUSION

Immigrants must approach marriage in a new cultural landscape with humility, adaptability, and a commitment to growth. Empowered women are not threats - they are partners. And while divorce can be painful, it can also be a path to peace, healing, and renewal when marriage no longer serves the well-being of those involved. By embracing change and seeking understanding, immigrant families can build strong, respectful, and enduring relationships in their new homes.

CHALLENGE #10

HABITS: THE HIDDEN FORCES
BEHIND IMMIGRANT SUCCESS

One of the most powerful yet overlooked factors shaping success - especially for immigrants - is habit. While motivation can spark the desire to move forward, only habits create the consistency and discipline necessary for lasting achievement. Former Olympian Jim Ryun once said, *"Motivation is what gets us started. Habit is what keeps us going."* This insight holds true for many immigrants who relocate in search of a better life but struggle to sustain that progress once the initial excitement fades.

Leaving one's country of origin is a courageous first step, but settling successfully in a new environment requires more than courage - it demands the cultivation of productive, adaptable, and winning habits. Immigrants who maintain the same habits they had in their home countries, without adjusting to the expectations and culture of their new society, may find themselves at odds with local norms and unable to thrive.

HOW HABITS SHAPE THE IMMIGRANT EXPERIENCE

Habits govern daily decisions, among which are: how we use time, how we handle money, how we interact with others, and how we respond to challenges. For immigrants, habits such as punctuality, effective communication, goal setting, financial discipline, and time management, are not just optional, they are essential.

In many developed countries, lateness, disorganization, or unreliability can quickly damage one's professional reputation or cost a job opportunity.

WINNING HABITS FOR IMMIGRANTS

Aristotle is often quoted as saying, *"95% of everything you do is the result of habit"*. Whether or not the exact figure is accurate, the message is clear: our habits shape our lives. For immigrants building a future in a new country, developing winning habits is not just beneficial, it is essential. Here are a few key habits that can make a meaningful difference:

- *Learn from failure instead of blaming others*: Mistakes are part of growth. Owning them builds resilience and earns respect.
- *Stay self-motivated, even without external praise*: Progress often depends on inner drive, especially in unfamiliar environments.
- *Set clear, measurable goals and work toward them consistently*: Success is built on small, intentional steps, not wishful thinking.
- *Be adaptable when conditions change*: Flexibility opens doors that rigidity will close.
- *Maintain integrity and honesty, even when shortcuts are tempting*: Trust is hard to earn and easy to lose - honest conduct builds a strong foundation.

Most receiving countries expect immigrants to be law-abiding, hardworking, and respectful of local norms. These are not discriminatory expectations - they are standards applied to all residents. Immigrants who fail to develop constructive habits risk falling behind, facing legal issues, or becoming socially and economically isolated. But with the right habits, immigrants can not only integrate - but they can also thrive.

THE DOUBLE-EDGED SWORD OF HABIT

An old Chinese proverb states, *"Habits are first cobwebs, then cables."* In other words, habits begin subtly but gain strength over time, eventually becoming powerful enough to control us. Many habits seem harmless at first - like occasional lateness, minor overspending, or indulging in gossip - but when repeated, they form behavior patterns that are hard to break and potentially harmful.

The danger is not only in bad habits, but in being unaware of them. Immigrants may carry cultural habits that were normal in their home country but are frowned upon - or even penalized - in their host country. For example:

- In some cultures, negotiating deadlines is common; in others, deadlines are non-negotiable.
- In some regions, gender roles in marriage are rigid; in others, equality and mutual respect are legal and cultural imperatives.
- In some societies, personal connections open doors; in others, formal procedures and merit are emphasized.

Failing to adapt habits in these areas can lead to frustration, isolation, or even legal challenges.

THE SLIPPERY SLOPE OF HARMFUL HABITS

Like addiction, habits often start with seemingly innocent behaviors. For instance, a non-drinker may try alcohol at a friend's party just to fit in. Over time, occasional drinking can become a social habit, then a dependency. This progression illustrates how habits can take control when not carefully monitored.

The Apostle Paul observed in 1 Corinthians 6:12, *"All things are lawful for me, but not all things are profitable. All things are lawful for me, but I will not be mastered by anything."* The goal is not to avoid all pleasures, but to ensure that we remain in control of our choices and not the other way around.

Habits do not just shape behavior - they shape character. Over time, we become the sum of the habits we cultivate. Albert Gray once noted, *"The common denominator of success... lies in forming the habit of doing things that failures don't like to do"*. In other words, successful people train themselves to consistently do what needs to be done, regardless of how they feel.

HABIT FORMATION

The good news is that habits can be unlearned and replaced. Therefore, build habits that serve you. Immigrants must become intentional about forming habits that support their new goals and responsibilities. Some practical recommendations include:

- *Practice punctuality*: Being consistently on time is a sign of respect and professionalism.
- *Prioritize communication*: Clear, respectful communication builds trust in both personal and professional relationships.
- *Pay your bills on time*: This builds credit, trust, and financial stability.

- *Be content and avoid unnecessary comparisons*: Gratitude and realistic expectations help maintain emotional balance.
- *Cultivate emotional intelligence*: Avoid constant complaining, overthinking, or blaming others for setbacks.

Bad habits such as procrastination, pessimism, gossiping, or financial recklessness can quietly sabotage even the most promising new beginnings. Good habits, on the other hand, empower immigrants to integrate successfully, advance in their careers, raise healthy families, and fulfill the dreams that inspired their migration in the first place.

In conclusion, while the journey of immigration begins with motivation, it is sustained by the daily disciplines and habits we choose. Habits are the invisible architecture of success. By building strong foundations in the form of good habits, immigrants can, not only survive in a new land, but thrive.

Challenge #11

Language:
The gateway to belonging and success

Language is one of the most powerful tools for social inclusion, and one of the greatest barriers immigrants face when settling in a new country. Whether a nation is officially monolingual or multilingual, language proficiency profoundly affects an immigrant's ability to adapt, find their niche, and succeed.

Some countries - such as Switzerland, India, South Africa, Nigeria, and the United States - are officially multilingual, yet many of their citizens may speak only one of the national languages. For example, although Switzerland recognizes German, French, Italian, and Romansh as official languages, most Swiss citizens are fluent in only one or two, depending on their region. As someone who lived in Switzerland for seven years, I observed firsthand how language could either build bridges or create silent walls, even among Swiss nationals themselves.

In other countries - such as Japan (Japanese), Bangladesh (Bengali), and Bahrain (Arabic) - a monolingual identity dominates, meaning most citizens speak a single official language, with limited use of other languages. For immigrants arriving in these nations without fluency in the national language, daily life can quickly become a struggle.

WHY LANGUAGE PROFICIENCY
MATTERS FOR IMMIGRANTS

Language affects virtually every area of immigrant's life including, but not limited to:

- *Employment*: Without the ability to communicate effectively, immigrants are often confined to low-wage, labor-intensive jobs, regardless of their qualifications.
- *Education*: Immigrant children who lack fluency in the host country's language often face significant disadvantages in school, including being misclassified into remedial classes or placed in underperforming institutions.
- *Healthcare*: Misunderstandings due to language barriers can lead to inadequate treatment or misdiagnoses.
- *Housing*: Securing accommodation becomes difficult when one cannot read listings, negotiate leases, or understand rental contracts.
- *Social integration*: Making friends, participating in community events, or even engaging in casual conversations can become nearly impossible without basic language skills.

The lack of language proficiency does not just hinder progress, it can erode confidence, foster shame, and increase vulnerability to discrimination, exploitation, and xenophobia. It can also lead many immigrants to feel isolated, helpless, or even invisible.

Sadly, children of immigrants often inherit the consequences of language illiteracy. For example, in situations where parents cannot advocate effectively for their children's education or well-being due to language limitations, opportunities for upward mobility shrink.

THE PSYCHOLOGICAL AND SOCIAL TOLL

When people cannot communicate, they struggle to form relationships, understand their rights, or express their needs. This disconnection often causes:

- Loneliness and social anxiety
- Depression and emotional withdrawal
- Loss of self-worth and identity confusion

Moreover, many immigrants report being treated as unintelligent or inferior simply because of a heavy accent or lack of fluency. Over time, this can chip away at their dignity, especially when their value is measured solely by their ability to speak the dominant language.

LANGUAGE AS AN INSTRUMENT OF EMPOWERMENT

Fortunately, language is a skill that can be learned - and investing in it pays enormous dividends. Immigrants who commit to learning the local language often experience:

- Greater self-confidence
- Improved job prospects
- Increased civic participation
- Better mental health
- Stronger family advocacy, especially in navigating schools, healthcare, and legal systems

Children benefit especially when their parents are fluent enough to support their education, communicate with teachers, and help with homework. In fact, language acquisition can be one of the strongest indicators of long-term integration and success for immigrant families.

What immigrants need to do

The most important philosophy immigrants should engrave in their mind is that if you "master the language, you master your destiny." When you master the language of your new country of residence, you can influence, direct, and control your own environment. The other pertinent advice for immigrants are:

1. Make language learning a top priority. Do not wait for fluency - start with basic communication skills and build from there.
2. Join language classes in community centers, religious institutions, or online platforms.
3. Immerse yourself in the new language: watch TV, listen to local radio, read newspapers, and practice speaking in everyday interactions.
4. Encourage your children to help you learn. Many children adapt more quickly and can be valuable learning partners.
5. Accept mistakes as part of the journey. Every conversation is an opportunity to learn.

Language is more than grammar and vocabulary, it is access, it is confidence, and it is belonging. For immigrants, overcoming the language barrier is not just about fitting in; it is about surviving, thriving, and creating a meaningful life in a new land. It opens doors to employment, education, healthcare, and human connection.

Without it, the promise of a better future remains out of reach. Make learning the language of your host country not just a goal, but a *mission*. It is the bridge between who you were and who you are becoming.

FINAL THOUGHT

A common and often overlooked challenge for many immigrants is their accent. In my experience as a college instructor, I have had immigrant students who demonstrated outstanding proficiency in English - often writing at a higher level than many native-born American students. Yet, when they spoke, their strong foreign accents sometimes overshadowed their intellectual ability, creating an unfair disconnect between how they were perceived and what they were truly capable of.

It is important to recognize that accents are a natural part of speaking a second language and do not reflect poor language skills. In fact, they are a sign of bilingual or multilingual strength.

However, if you understand the official language of the host country well but feel your accent is holding you back in communication or connection, here are some practical and encouraging steps you can take to boost clarity, confidence, and integration.

1. *Embrace Your Accent - It Tells a Story*
    *   Your accent is part of your identity and reflects your multilingual journey.
    *   Many successful people have strong accents. An accent is not a barrier to respect or success if communication is clear.

2. Focus on Clarity, Not Perfection
- You do not need to lose your accent - you need to be understood.
- Work on pronunciation, intonation, and rhythm to improve clarity.

3. Practice Regularly with Native Speakers
- Join community groups, language exchange meetups, or conversation clubs.
- If possible, engage in environments where the language is spoken naturally - churches, volunteer centers, co-working spaces, etc.

4. Listen & Mimic
- Watch local news, TV shows, or podcasts in the official language.
- Try to repeat phrases aloud, mimicking the speaker's tone and cadence (shadowing technique).

5. Consider Accent Coaching
- If the accent affects job opportunities or confidence, consider working with a speech coach or English as a second language (ESL) pronunciation specialist.
- There are also apps like ELSA Speak or Speechling--a digital language-learning platform designed to help users improve their speaking and pronunciation skills in a variety of languages.

6. Build Relationships Despite the Accent
- Relationships thrive on authenticity, trust, and kindness - not perfect pronunciation.
- Be patient with yourself and others; communication is a two-way street.

Your goal is to connect, not to sound exactly like a native speaker. Fluency, not flawlessness, is the path to integration and meaningful relationships. Many people will appreciate your effort and courage to speak their language.

Challenge #12

Other Challenges:
Internal Obstacles to Success

While many of the challenges immigrants face are external - language barriers, cultural clashes, legal hurdles, and economic constraints - others are internal and psychological. These internal struggles often manifest as negative thinking patterns, limiting beliefs, emotional immaturity, or the inability to regulate ambition, and can have just as much impact on one's ability to succeed and thrive. Immigrants may find themselves dealing with:

- Negative thoughts rooted in past trauma or fear of failure.
- Procrastination and inaction, especially when overwhelmed by the demands of adapting to a new environment.
- Pride or a lack of humility, particularly after attaining financial or professional success.
- Chronic dissatisfaction, which can stem from deep-seated poverty mindsets or a fear of slipping backward.

While external challenges often take the spotlight in the immigrant experience, internal psychological barriers can be equally powerful and limiting. Recognizing and addressing these inner struggles, such as fear, pride, procrastination, and negative thinking, is essential for achieving lasting success and personal growth in a new environment.

THE PITFALLS OF PRIDE AND ARROGANCE

One significant internal challenge is the erosion of humility, particularly when immigrants rise quickly from economic hardship to positions of comfort or affluence. Some immigrants who transition from minimum-wage jobs to six-figure incomes or prestigious careers begin to lose touch with the very qualities - resilience, humility, gratitude - that fueled their success in the first place. A lack of humility and gratitude can be dangerous. It:

- Discourages feedback from significant others, making it harder to grow emotionally and professionally.
- Damages relationships, especially with friends and community members who may feel alienated or disrespected.
- Obstructs self-awareness, causing individuals to overestimate their abilities or become blind to their flaws.

True humility invites openness, reflection, and continuous learning - qualities that are essential for sustained success and integration in a new society.

THE TRAP OF DISCONTENTMENT

Another recurring challenge is a lack of contentment. Many immigrants come from environments marked by scarcity and struggle. Upon achieving a measure of success, they may fall into the trap of material comparison and competitive living - feeling the need to prove their worth by showcasing wealth, status, or luxury. This often leads to:

- Excessive materialism;
- Chronic dissatisfaction with one's income, possessions, or even family;
- Envy and resentment toward others who seem more accomplished.

This state of mind can be corrosive. Egotistical immigrants may never feel their income is high enough, their home big enough, or their children successful enough. This constant striving not only leads to stress and anxiety but may also poison relationships through jealousy, competition, and emotional burnout.

On the contrary, cultivating contentment helps immigrants:

- Appreciate the progress they have made!
- Reduce anxiety and mental fatigue
- Focus on meaningful goals rather than shallow appearances
- Build stronger, more authentic relationships.

Contentment is not about settling for less; it is about recognizing that self-worth and fulfillment come from within, not from external validation.

A BROADER LANDSCAPE OF CHALLENGES

In addition to these emotional and psychological barriers, immigrants also grapple with:

- Unrealistic expectations
- Pressure to support family back home
- Social isolation

- Identity confusion or dual citizenship loyalty syndrome
- Discrimination and micro-aggressions
- Parental stress and generational conflict

Each of these challenges deserves attention. For lack of space to discuss all these challenges, it suffices to single out "Discrimination and micro-aggressions" for discussion here. This is what immigrants deal with every day.

"Discrimination and micro-aggressions" refer to different forms of unfair or harmful treatment that people can experience, often based on their identity (such as race, gender, religion, sexual orientation, disability, etc.). For clarity, here is a breakdown:

Discrimination

This is unfair or unequal treatment of individuals or groups based on certain characteristics. It can be:

- *Direct:* Obvious and intentional (e.g., not hiring someone because of their ethnicity).
- *Indirect*: Subtle but still harmful, often built into systems or policies (e.g., workplace policies that disadvantage certain groups without explicitly targeting them).

Examples:

- Refusing to rent an apartment to someone because of their religion.
- Paying women less than men for the same job.

Microaggressions

These are subtle, often unintentional comments or actions that express prejudice or stereotypes toward marginalized groups. They may seem small but can have a big emotional impact over time.

Examples:

- Saying, "You speak English so well" to someone born in the country, implying they do not belong.
- Interrupting or ignoring someone repeatedly in meetings based on their gender or race.

In sum, discrimination is often overt and institutional, while micro-aggression is every day less obvious slights. Both contribute to an environment of inequality and exclusion. The key takeaway here is that not all obstacles are visible, and the most dangerous ones are often internal.

KEY TAKEAWAY

Despite these hurdles, the immigrant journey is one of hope, resilience, and transformation. Immigrants are among the most adaptable, hard-working, and visionary people in any society. The very act of leaving one's homeland and starting over in a foreign land is an act of courage and bravery.

To succeed, however, immigrants must do more than adjust externally - they must also undergo an inner transformation: overcoming pride, letting go of toxic competitiveness, embracing humility, and cultivating contentment. These traits do not make a person passive; rather, they anchor the mind and heart in wisdom, emotional intelligence, and lasting fulfillment.

The conditions that shape a person's quality of life differ significantly from country to country and often serve as powerful motivators for immigration. While the pursuit of a better life drives many to relocate, the journey is rarely without obstacles. As discussed in the preceding sections, immigrants face a range of challenges - cultural, psychological, legal, social, and personal - that can influence their decisions and disrupt their long-term goals.

Amid these challenges, it is vital for immigrants to remember one foundational truth: they are living in a foreign country with customs, laws, and social expectations that may be very different from those of their home country.

Success in a new environment requires more than hard work; it demands cultural intelligence, flexibility, and a willingness to learn and grow.

Immigrants must think and act like immigrants, meaning they should remain aware, adaptive, and respectful of the norms and systems in their host countries. This includes:

- Learning the local language(s) to improve communication and integration,
- Understanding and obeying local laws and regulations,
- Adapting to workplace expectations and social customs,
- Respecting cultural differences while maintaining the core values that define their identity.

By being proactive and open-minded, immigrants can not only overcome the initial hurdles but also thrive - building meaningful lives for themselves and contributing positively to the societies they now call home.

SECTION II

UNDERSTANDING HOW SUCCESSFUL IMMIGRANTS THINK

INTRODUCTION TO SECTION II

*"You are today where your thoughts have brought you;
you will be tomorrow where your thoughts take you."*[8]

James Allen

For many immigrants, moving from one's homeland to a foreign country is far more than just a change of address - it is a pilgrimage of self-actualization, a courageous leap into the unknown in search of a better life, freedom, and opportunities for personal and collective growth. It is a profound decision rooted in hope, resilience, and the desire to maximize one's potential. But while the destination promises greater possibilities, the journey is often fraught with cultural, social, emotional, and systemic obstacles - as explored in the preceding chapter.

To navigate these challenges and thrive in unfamiliar territory, it is not enough to carry our belongings; we must also reshape our mindset. This is the essence of thinking like an immigrant - embracing change, cultivating adaptability, and becoming intentionally strategic about how we perceive and respond to our new environment.

One cannot arrive in a new country and expect a better quality of life while clinging to old patterns of thinking shaped by a different social, political, or cultural context. The world we knew is not the world we now inhabit. To succeed, we must be willing to question our assumptions, relearn social norms, and redefine what success and belonging look like in a new land.

---

8   James Allen Quotes, accessed March 22, 2025, https://www.brainyquote.com/quotes/james_allen_133802.

This transformative mindset begins with self-awareness, is sustained by diligence, and is directed by intentionality. It means taking ownership of our inner life - our thoughts, beliefs, and attitudes - because these are the forces that shape our external reality. Our thoughts influence how we interpret challenges, how we respond to setbacks, and how we engage with others. If we internalize a sense of defeat, we will carry ourselves accordingly. But if we cultivate thoughts of possibility and growth, we will act with purpose and resilience. It is this timeless truth that moved the ancient Chinese philosopher Lao Tzu to admonish us:

> *"Watch your thoughts, they become your words;*
> *watch your words, they become your actions;*
> *watch your actions, they become your habits;*
> *watch your habits, they become your character;*
> *watch your character, it becomes your destiny."*

In the immigrant journey, this insight is not philosophical poetry - it is practical survival. The mind of the immigrant must be both alert and open. Every new interaction, every unfamiliar system, every cultural difference becomes an opportunity to grow and adapt. Thinking like an immigrant means letting go of rigid thinking and embracing flexibility, resilience, and a long-term vision for success.

In essence, a better life is not merely the product of better circumstances, thinking right is the bedrock of our success. The quality of our thoughts determines the quality of our choices, and those choices chart the course of our lives. When we manage our thoughts wisely, we lay the foundation for a future that not only meets our expectations but often exceeds them.

Thinking like an immigrant 101:

A new mind for a new world

Immigrants often approach the world in profoundly different ways, shaped by unique histories, cultural values, and personal experiences. These thought patterns, especially how they perceive themselves in relation to their new countries, often determine their success or failure in adapting to a new life.

In my book, *The Future of My Past* (2022), I explore how certain cognitive tendencies, such as, *retrospection* (looking back on past events) and *contraction bias* (how past experiences shape current perceptions), can influence our decisions and behaviors. While the past may contain pain, struggle, or trauma that led to emigration, it is still an essential part of who we are. As Pan-Africanist, Marcus Garvey, famously said: *"A people without the knowledge of their past history, origin and culture is like a tree without roots."*

No matter what opportunities your new country offers, your identity is rooted in where you were born, raised, and educated. Ignoring or rejecting past experiences does not elevate you, rather it disconnects you from the foundation that shaped your values, resilience, and perspective.

Upon arrival in a new country, many immigrants are overwhelmed by excitement and the desire to assimilate quickly. Some begin to criticize or even resent their countries of origin, developing a form of self-hatred rooted in shame or denial. But successful immigrants take a different path. They reflect on their past - not to dwell in it, but to learn from it. They carry forward the strengths and lessons of their upbringing to build a stronger, more meaningful future.

In contrast, those who fail to adapt often cling too tightly to the old ways, resisting the new environment without discernment. Yet "thinking like an immigrant" means doing more than blindly adopting everything new or clinging to everything old. It requires comparing, evaluating, and choosing wisely preserving constructive values and habits from both worlds while discarding what no longer serves personal or communal growth. Cultivating such discernment leads to a more sustainable well-being and a deeper sense of belonging.

For immigrants living in countries of the Global North, holding a blue, red, or brown passport may offer a sense of legitimacy or accomplishment. But do not be lulled into a false sense of belonging. A passport is, in many ways, just a symbol, a kind of international PR badge. It does not erase your origins. You remain a "hyphenated" citizen, a person whose identity straddles two worlds (see my book, *Living in two worlds*, forthcoming 2026). Your connection to your country of origin is inalienable, no matter how underdeveloped it may be.

If you have found success abroad, never forget those who helped raise, nurture, or support you before you left. Stay connected. Extend kindness and respect to those you left behind, regardless of their current situation. Life has a way of shifting, and you may one day need the very people you once overlooked. As Wilson Mizner is quoted to have said, *"Be nice to people on your way up because you'll meet them on your way down"*. To express this maxim differently, never be in a hurry to disown your country of origin because as the Bible teaching goes, *"The stone that the builders rejected could become the cornerstone*" (Psalm 118:22). The message from Mizner and the Bible is that the day may come when your new country is no longer safe or welcoming, and the very country you disowned may become your refuge again.

In the same vein, don't curse your past - use it to build your future because that is where you are going to spend the rest of your life. Your roots are not a burden but a resource.

THINKING LIKE AN IMMIGRANT 102:

ONCE AN IMMIGRANT, ALWAYS AN IMMIGRANT

"Thinking Like an Immigrant 102" builds on a foundational reality: once you become an immigrant, you are marked by that identity for life - socially, politically, and psychologically. Regardless of how many years you have lived in a host country, or whether you have gained permanent residency or even naturalized citizenship, your immigrant status remains a lens through which you are seen, and through which you may need to continue seeing yourself.

Many immigrants in Global North countries come to believe that citizenship automatically places them on equal footing with native-born citizens. Legally, this may be true. But socially and politically, the story is more complicated. Naturalization may offer legal recognition, but it does not erase the subtle and overt ways in which immigrant identity continues to shape perception, experience, and opportunity. In many cases, you are not seen as a full member of "We the People," particularly in societies where nativism - whether explicit or systemic - remains strong.

THE REALITY OF DIFFERENTIAL TREATMENT

This differential treatment should not automatically be interpreted as personal animosity or hatred. Governments have an obligation to prioritize the interests and welfare of their native-born citizens.

Immigration policy, public services allocation, employment preferences, and cultural expectations often reflect this priority. While such policies may be frustrating - especially if they impede your goals - they are rarely designed with the specific intent of harming you. Rather, they are expressions of a social contract built around national identity.

In this light, immigrants must recalibrate expectations. Discomfort in the face of exclusionary policies or attitudes does not justify adopting a victim mindset or engaging in a blame game. Instead, the challenge is to adapt - both psychologically and strategically. Remember: the journey to becoming an immigrant likely stemmed from challenges or limitations in your country of origin. Ask yourself honestly - despite the unequal treatment - are you better off now?

ATTITUDE IS EVERYTHING

The worst reaction to immigrant marginalization is to internalize it in ways that lead to bitterness, cynicism, or withdrawal. As the Stoic philosopher Epictetus wisely noted, "*It's not what happens to you, but how you react to it that matters*". Similarly, psychologist William James observed that "*The greatest discovery of my generation is that a human being can alter his life by altering his attitudes*". These are not just motivational quotes - they are practical frameworks for survival and success as an immigrant.

A negative mindset leads to distrust, miscommunication, and fractured relationships with native-born citizens. It narrows your outlook and stunts your ability to integrate meaningfully. It is not easy - but cultivating a mindset of resilience, openness, and humility is crucial.

YOU ARE A GUEST IN SOMEONE ELSE'S HOUSE

Clifton Fadiman once wrote, *"When you travel, remember that a foreign country is not designed to make you comfortable. It is designed to make its own people comfortable"*. This is a sobering truth, and one that immigrants must internalize. You did not build the house you have moved into. You are a guest - perhaps a long-term one, perhaps one who contributes more than many of the natives - but a guest nonetheless.

This is not a call for self-deprecation. Rather, it is a reality check. Do not expect full equality in treatment, because nations, like families, prioritize their own. Just as you would not give a stranger more food than your child, governments instinctively protect their native-born populations first. This is not always fair - but it is consistent with human behavior across cultures and histories.

Even in your own homeland, people from neighboring villages or regions cannot claim rights to land or resources that belong to your community without friction. Why, then, expect to be granted full equity in a land that is not your birthplace?

THE IMMIGRANT IDENTITY: BURDEN OR ADVANTAGE?

Yes, immigrants are often relegated to the margins when it comes to access to power, public benefits, and cultural acceptance. They are "shadow citizens, recognized but not fully embraced. And yet, being an immigrant can also be a position of power. You carry the strength of dual perspective, cultural adaptability, and a survival instinct honed by challenge.

Success is possible. Immigrants often outperform native-born citizens in business, academics, athletics, and innovation. But social capital - belonging, trust, entitlement - remains elusive. This is the paradox of the immigrant experience: high achievement but partial acceptance.

FINAL THOUGHT

Rather than resist this reality, learn to navigate it with wisdom. Understand the rules, adapt your expectations, and focus your energy on building a life within the constraints that exist - while working slowly, steadily, and respectfully to broaden the space you are allowed to occupy.

"Once an immigrant, always an immigrant" is not a sentence of limitation - it is a framework for awareness, growth, and adaptation.

THINKING LIKE AN
IMMIGRANT 103:

YOUR PERSPECTIVES

The third principle in the "Thinking Like an Immigrant" series centers around a fundamental but often overlooked idea: changing your perspective. For immigrants, this is not just an abstract philosophical concept - it is a survival skill, a success strategy, and a psychological tool for growth.

To change your perspective means to alter the way you view a situation, idea, or issue. It is about stepping outside of your own assumptions and examining life through different cultural, emotional, or experiential lenses. This mental shift is crucial for immigrants, who are often uprooted from one cultural universe and replanted into another. Navigating this new reality requires more than just language proficiency or legal documentation, demands mental flexibility, emotional intelligence, and cultural adaptability.

THE RISK OF A RIGID MINDSET

Many immigrants struggle not because of external circumstances, but because of internal resistance to change. A rigid mindset - often shaped by deep-rooted cultural traditions - can become a major obstacle to integration and fulfillment in a new country. Take, for instance, a real-life example: A friend of mine, also an immigrant in the United States, filed for divorce from his wife.

When I asked him why, he responded:

"Though I am in the United States, I cannot compromise my ancestral values. In our home country, household chores are strictly a woman's duty. But here, my wife expected me to assist with tasks like laundry or taking out soup to thaw for dinner. I saw these demands as cultural violations. These irreconcilable differences led me to file for divorce."

His reasoning might seem outdated or even offensive in some cultural settings, yet it underscores a broader issue: the unwillingness to shift perspective. Instead of adapting to the realities of a new social environment, he clung to the framework from his country of origin - one that no longer fits the context of his new life.

Was his decision justifiable? The answer would vary depending on the cultural lens through which it is viewed. But it is evident that failure to adapt contributed directly to personal and relational breakdown.

PERSPECTIVE SHIFT:
THE GATEWAY TO TRANSFORMATION

Changing perspectives is not about discarding your culture or erasing your identity. Rather, it is about expanding your worldview, learning how to hold your cultural heritage in one hand while embracing the new reality with the other. When immigrants embrace this dual perspective, several transformative things happen:

- *Empathy increases*: You begin to understand others' experiences, even if they differ greatly from your own.

- *Biases weaken*: Long-held prejudices or assumptions begin to dissolve.
- *Growth accelerates*: You become more flexible in your thinking, more creative in problem-solving, and more adaptable in relationships.

By viewing situations through a broader lens, you position yourself not just to survive, but to thrive.

PRACTICAL WAYS TO CHANGE YOUR PERSPECTIVE

Stephen Covey states emphatically that, "To change ourselves effectively, we first had to change our perceptions". Perspective refers to the way individuals understand and interpret social situations, emphasizing the importance of social interactions, relationships, and structures. It involves considering different viewpoints and how social factors influence thoughts, feelings, and behaviors. This perspective helps in analyzing various societal issues, including rights and responsibilities. Humans are cultural animals. Much of our present behavioral patterns which affect the way we think, and act were ingrained in us early in life. If you do not like your thinking pattern or your attitude towards issues of popular concern, change your mindset by:

1. *Challenging your assumptions*: Ask yourself why you believe what you believe. Is this belief helping or hindering your success?
2. *Embracing discomfort*: Growth often comes from the unfamiliar. Instead of resisting discomfort, explore what it is trying to teach you.
3. *Thinking across boundaries*: Be willing to adopt models from other cultures, genders, and belief systems. Learn from everyone.

4. *Reframing challenges*: Instead of labeling a situation as a "problem", ask how it might be an opportunity to grow.

5. *Pause and reflect*: When you encounter resistance, internally or externally, take a step back. Examine your emotional responses and assess them rationally.

Mindset shifts do not happen automatically. They require conscious, intentional effort.

But every step toward a renewed mindset is a step toward freedom, empowerment, and greater success in your immigrant journey.

THE POWER OF A RENEWED MIND

The concept of renewing the mind is echoed in countless philosophies and religions. In a modern immigrant context, it means discarding harmful mental habits and replacing them with constructive attitudes and thought patterns. With a renewed mind, you will be able to:

- See yourself not as a victim, but as a builder.
- See challenges not as threats, but as lessons.
- See others not as competitors, but as collaborators.

Ultimately, a changed perspective creates a changed reality. As your thinking evolves, so does your life.

CONCLUSION

Moving to a new country is not just a change in geography, it is a change in identity. If your mindset remains locked in the past, your present will suffer, and your future will be limited.

In other words, if you change how you think, you will change how you live.

Changing your perspective does not mean losing yourself; it means growing into a better version of yourself - one who is strong enough to hold the tension between past and present, tradition and change, comfort and growth.

To live victoriously in a foreign land, immigrants must train their minds to think flexibly, creatively, and compassionately. Because as Anais Nin argues, *"We don't see things as they are, we see them as we are"*. The quote emphasizes the subjective nature of perception. It suggests that our understanding of the world is shaped by our personal experiences, beliefs, and emotions, rather than an objective reality. Therefore, we must be careful not to allow our internal narratives to distort our perceptions, leading to different interpretations of the same situation. Even more important is the fact that our reality is not just external but is also a reflection of our internal state. In sum, how we see determines how we act, and we live.

THINKING LIKE AN IMMIGRANT 104:

SHUNNING BAD INFLUENCES

Thinking like an immigrant 104 means intentionally purging negative influences that prevent your personal growth. Let us return to the attitude of my friend in "Thinking like an immigrant 103" relating to what was or was not a woman's job.

Migrating to a new country is more than just crossing borders; it is a journey of transformation. One of the biggest challenges immigrants face is not just adapting to a new culture but letting go of the internal beliefs and influences that no longer promote their growth. In my journey of life as an immigrant, I have come to learn that "thinking like an immigrant" means intentionally identifying and purging negative influences that hold me back. But how to recognize a negative influence remains a serious dilemma for most immigrants. Here are signs of negative influences:

One major sign is cultural rigidity - the refusal or reluctance to adapt to changing cultures in a new environment. For example, in my friend's home country, household chores were considered the exclusive responsibility of women. That mindset was deeply ingrained in him. But that is not the culture in the United States. There lies the conflict of culture which sparked inter-marital conflict. He could not tolerate a simple request from his wife for him to help with simple household tasks like laundry or pulling soup from the freezer and microwave it before she came home to prepare dinner for the family.

He viewed such a request as a threat to tradition rather than an opportunity for partnership. It created tension and, ultimately, led to the breakdown of their marriage.

Another negative influence that affected my friend was unrealistic expectations of gender roles. In a new environment, such as the United States, where both partners often work and share responsibilities, clinging to outdated roles can strain a relationship. Expecting one person to carry all the domestic responsibilities because of cultural norms ignores the shared reality of life in many developed countries. It limits mutual respect and growth.

Another negative influence is resistance to change. Even in the smallest things, resistance to change can have the biggest consequences. My friend's refusal to help with minor household tasks was not about the tasks themselves - it was about holding on to a version of manhood that did not fit the new reality. Growth often begins with small acts of humility, compromise, and understanding.

Finally, there are people who are bad influences on us. They may include some of our family members, peer group members, church members, people we hang around with in the bar and even professional colleagues. No matter who or what these influences are, if your relationship is harming your mental health or emotional stability, your best decision is to end the relationship. Hanging around toxic people can create a negative and debilitating outlook on yourself and eventually isolate you from people who could actually be beneficial to you.

One of the greatest obstacles to progress is allowing yourself to be blinded by the people around you. Many immigrants, on arrival in their new countries of residence, choose isolationism. They seek out and get connected mainly to people of the same ethnic group or nationality. While there is nothing wrong with bonding with people who are culturally similar to you who have been in the country long before your arrival, the danger is that you will start thinking and acting like them if you do not diversify your source of interaction. The mere fact that you look like them or speak the same language does not mean you have the same goals in life.

The onus is on you to carefully assess these people to find out whether they will lift you up or drag you down. If you surround yourself with pessimistic and unmotivated people just because they look like you, you can easily be corrupted by misleading desires that can taint and adversely affect your life goals. Negative attitudes strip people of their well-being and a sense of peace. Even your worldview can become skewed by the incessant lack of enthusiasm among the people you interact with. Life becomes more manageable, and aspirations are more readily pursued when you delete negative people from your personal space.

To truly thrive as an immigrant, we must unlearn some of what we thought was unchangeable. Letting go of harmful beliefs does not mean losing our identity, it means reshaping it for a better, more inclusive future. The freedom to grow is one of the greatest gifts of migration. The question is: are we willing to take it?

LETTING GO TO GROW: A REFLECTION ON CULTURAL RIGIDITY AND PERSONAL CHANGE

Moving to a new country exposes us to new cultures and gives us an opportunity to learn and grow. Unfortunately, personal growth in a new environment does not happen automatically.

It requires a willingness to examine and sometimes let go of beliefs and habits that are no longer practical. As an immigrant, I have come to understand that true adaptation is not just about learning a new language or finding a job. It is about challenging internal patterns that quietly hold us back. In his book, *Future Shock* (1970), Alvin Toffler argues that "The illiterate of the 21st century will not be those who can't read and write, but those who cannot learn, unlearn, and relearn." This statement highlights the importance of lifelong learning and adaptability in the face of a rapidly changing world. My friend who considered helping his wife with house chores demeaning falls under the category of people who cannot learn, unlearn, and relearn.

One of the most powerful barriers to personal growth is cultural rigidity - the belief that traditions from home must remain unchanged, even in a new cultural setting. Some immigrants, especially those from traditional African and Asian countries still try to get involved in the choice of spouse for their children. Youths will not accept that mindset they brought to any of the global-North countries where children have the right and freedom to choose who they want to marry. Clinging to such practice in North America or Europe will lead to conflict and disconnection in family relationships. When you move to a new country, it is important to think and act in line with its language and culture. Holding on too strongly to your original language and culture can make it harder to grow and succeed.

Reflecting on my daily behaviors, I have come to realize that real growth requires more than survival in a new country. It requires intentional reflection, a flexible mindset, and the courage to evolve. Letting go of outdated beliefs and practices does not erase who we are - it refines who we can become.

THINKING LIKE AN IMMIGRANT 105:

CONTROLLING YOUR THOUGHTS

"You are today where your thoughts have brought you; you will be tomorrow where your thoughts take you." These words by James Allen, author of *As a Man Thinketh* (1902), ring especially true for immigrants - those brave enough to uproot their lives and plant themselves in unfamiliar soil. The immigrant experience is as much a mental journey as it is a physical one. Among the many challenges that come with resettlement - language barriers, cultural differences, legal uncertainties - the most silent and persistent battles are fought in the mind.

Controlling one's thoughts, or more precisely, developing *thought discipline*, is not simply a matter of maintaining a positive attitude. For immigrants, it can mean the difference between resilience and collapse, between strategic navigation and mental paralysis. In "Thinking Like an Immigrant 105: Controlling Your Thoughts", we learn that immigrants must actively manage their mental state not by suppressing their fears, insecurities, or anxieties, but by engaging them with analytical awareness.

Living in a foreign country exposes immigrants to a wide range of feelings and thoughts, both uplifting and distressing. Homesickness, uncertainty about the future, exclusion, and even subtle forms of discrimination can dominate one's mental space. Suppressing these thoughts may seem like a coping mechanism, but psychologists have found that suppression often has the opposite effect - it intensifies unwanted emotions. In fact, chronic suppression can lead to mental health issues like anxiety and depression. This is why thought control is not about avoidance; it is about intelligent engagement.

As the old proverb goes, "*You can't stop the birds from flying over your head, but you can stop them from building a nest in your hair*". Similarly, immigrants cannot always control the intrusive or unsettling thoughts that arise in difficult situations, but they can choose not to dwell on them or allow them to shape their identity and behavior. This skill - of not being ruled by every passing thought - is vital for immigrants, who often exist in uncertain legal, social, or professional territories.

In many ways, immigrants are "shadow citizens." They contribute to the economies, cultures, and communities of their host countries, yet are often reminded, subtly or explicitly, that they do not fully belong. Their successes, however significant, remain vulnerable to shifting immigration laws or rising nationalist sentiments. This is not unique to any one country; it is a global reality, a kind of geopolitical game that even immigrants' countries of origin play. Thus, maintaining control over one's internal narrative becomes essential.

This is where mental discipline acts as a form of quiet resistance. By mastering their thoughts, immigrants can maintain focus, reject internalized inferiority, and keep their long-term goals intact even amid societal exclusion.

The stoic philosopher, Marcus Aurelius, once said, "*You have power over your mind - not outside events. Realize this, and you will find strength*". For immigrants who must often contend with forces beyond their control, such strength is indispensable.

Moreover, thought control enhances adaptability. In an unfamiliar system, where expectations are different and social cues may be alien, clear and calm thinking allows immigrants to observe, learn, and respond strategically rather than react emotionally. This is not about hiding one's identity or emotions, but about choosing responses that serve one's long-term well-being.

The threat of *nativism* - an ideology that prioritizes the interests of native-born citizens over immigrants - is another external pressure that can destabilize an immigrant's mental peace. As societies face economic stress or cultural shifts, fearmongering often takes the form of blaming immigrants for job loss, increased crime, or cultural decline. This can fuel feelings of guilt or defensiveness in immigrants. But again, mental clarity helps to contextualize such hostility not as personal rejection, but as political behavior rooted in fear and misinformation.

In times like these, the maxim *"Know thyself"* becomes especially relevant. By knowing their values, goals, and emotional patterns, immigrants can build a resilient internal world that cannot be easily shaken by public opinion or political shifts. This self-awareness becomes a compass, especially when the external map is uncertain.

In conclusion, controlling one's thoughts is not a luxury for immigrants, it is a necessity. It is the foundation upon which everything else is built - confidence, adaptability, emotional balance, and long-term success. The external journey may be unpredictable, but the internal journey can be mastered. As the habits that govern our minds ultimately shape our lives, immigrants must learn to lead their thoughts with purpose, precision, and power.

We have been warned hy Lao Tzu, a Chinese philosopher to:

"Watch your thoughts, they become your words;
watch your words, they become your actions;
watch your actions, they become your habits;
watch your habits, they become your character;
watch your character, it becomes your destiny."

For the immigrant, this chain begins with one quiet, powerful choice: to control the mind before the world attempts to control it for them.

Thinking like an Immigrant 106:

Giving Back

The journey of immigration often begins long before a visa is stamped or a plane is boarded. It starts in the quiet, anxious moments - those long, sleepless nights where an individual weighs whether to leave behind familiarity, family, and home in pursuit of a better life. That decision is never simple. It requires deep thought, self-reflection, and courage. And for many, the factors guiding that decision include the economic strength, political stability, educational opportunities, and freedoms offered by the receiving country.

But while it is natural for an immigrant to evaluate what a country can offer, *Thinking Like an Immigrant 106* challenges that mindset. This stage of the immigrant's intellectual and moral evolution asks a deeper question: "What can I give back? Not only to the country that welcomed you, but also to the one that raised you."

The power of a renewed mind

In the early stages of emigration, the focus is understandably inward. Many immigrants flee hardship - poor governance, insecurity, unemployment, or lack of opportunity. These experiences often leave emotional scars and foster resentment toward their countries of origin. It becomes easy to place the blame squarely on failed leadership or broken systems. While these criticisms may be valid, they are incomplete.

We must ask: *Before leaving, did I contribute in any meaningful way to improve my country of origin?* Did I vote? Volunteer? Innovate? Educate others? Pay taxes? If not, then some of the responsibility belongs to us too. Blame without reflection is a missed opportunity for growth.

As an immigrant, you now live in a society that, by comparison, may offer better infrastructure, a stronger economy, or more inclusive systems. But remember: this system was not built overnight, nor did it emerge from thin air. It was built, maintained, and improved by ordinary people - citizens and immigrants alike - who made the decision to give back. As John F. Kennedy famously stated, *"Ask not what your country can do for you - ask what you can do for your country."* This call to civic responsibility transcends borders.

GIVING BACK TO THE RECEIVING COUNTRY

You may have chosen your new country because of its safety, opportunity, and prosperity - but now you are a part of it. You are no longer a mere beneficiary of its progress; you are a *participant in its future*. This realization should guide your actions.

Giving back does not always mean grand gestures or wealthy donations. It begins with simple but powerful commitments, such as:

- Being law-abiding and respectful of the culture and values of your host society.
- Contributing economically through hard work, entrepreneurship, or paying taxes.
- Volunteering in local schools, hospitals, or community projects.

- Mentoring newer immigrants, helping them navigate the complex systems that once challenged you.
- Educating your children to become responsible citizens who understand both their rights and their obligations.

When immigrants contribute actively and ethically, they do not just improve their own lives, they enrich the cultural and civic fabric of the nation. They show the world that immigration is not a burden, but a mutually beneficial exchange of values, skills, and humanity.

As Coretta Scott King wisely said, *"The greatness of a community is most accurately measured by the compassionate actions of its members."* Immigrants must be among those compassionate actors, proving through action that they are not just guests, but guardians of the shared future.

GIVING BACK TO THE SENDING COUNTRY

SENDING MONEY TO FAMILY AT HOME

It is easy for immigrants to forget their homeland, especially when it symbolizes hardship or trauma. But no matter how far one travels, the country of origin remains part of one's story - etched in language, family ties, food, memories, and values.

Giving back to your country of origin is not about romanticizing the past or ignoring its failures. It is about leveraging your new position to effect positive change, however modest. Immigrants send billions of dollars in remittances globally every year, helping to feed families, fund education, and support small businesses. But giving back can go far beyond financial aid to include intangible elements, such as:

- Sharing knowledge and skills by training others remotely or returning to teach.
- Investing in community projects, such as building schools, clinics, or tech hubs.
- Supporting reform movements, whether through journalism, advocacy, or policy input.
- Establishing scholarships for young people who lack the resources you once lacked.
- Promoting civic responsibility, encouraging fellow citizens to demand better governance and transparency.

You may have left your country because it failed to serve you, but if everyone with talent and drive departs and never looks back, the cycle of underdevelopment continues. To break it, immigrants must become not just success stories abroad, but agents of progress at home.

As African proverb says, *"If you want to go fast, go alone. If you want to go far, go together."* Giving back ensures that others can walk a path of dignity, not desperation.

THE LEGACY YOU LEAVE

Eventually, your immigration story will become part of your family history. Your children or grandchildren may ask why you left and what you did afterward. Let the answers inspire them. Let your legacy not just be defined by what you gained, but by what you gave in return to show gratitude to those who led you by hand.

History remembers immigrants not only for their sacrifices but for their *contributions*. Think of figures like Andrew Carnegie, who came to the U.S. as a poor Scottish boy and went on to fund thousands of public libraries. Or Ilhan Omar, who went from a Somali refugee camp to the U.S. Congress. Or even the countless unnamed immigrant nurses, scientists, farmers, teachers, and taxi drivers who help keep societies running every day.

Whether your impact is global or local, public or private, the principle remains: To whom much is given, much is expected.

CONCLUSION: THE IMMIGRANT AS A
BRIDGE-BUILDER

Immigrants occupy a unique space in today's interconnected world. You stand between two lands, two identities, and often two cultures. This duality is not a burden; it is a privilege. You are a bridge, capable of carrying ideas, values, and innovations between your country of origin and your country of residence.

Giving back is not only a moral duty but also a practical necessity. It reinforces your humanity, builds stronger communities, and reshapes narratives. It shows that immigration is not just an escape, it is a choice to build, uplift, and connect.

In the end, the immigrant who gives back writes a story not just of survival or success, but of significance. And that is the kind of legacy that transcends borders.

THINKING LIKE AN IMMIGRANT 107:

LEGACY

Immigration is more than just the pursuit of a better life. It is the chance to redefine not only your personal future but the future of those around you. *Thinking like an immigrant 107* challenges us to ask a profound question: *For what will I be remembered?* What lasting value will I leave behind, not only for my children, but for the communities that shaped me and those that accepted me?

Many immigrants are admired for their financial success. They send generous remittances to family members, fund projects back home, buy big houses, and drive expensive cars. These actions are often rooted in love and duty, and some of them are indeed commendable. But let us be clear: conspicuous consumption is not a legacy. Wealth that is spent on image and lifestyle does not outlive its owner. Legacy, by contrast, endures. It leaves footprints in time.

LEGACY: MORE THAN MONEY

Legacy is often misunderstood as simply wealth left behind. But real legacy transcends material inheritance. It is the *transformative* impact you have on people, institutions, and ideas. It is the values you live by, the principles you pass down, the lives you elevate, and the systems you build to continue your work even after you are gone.

According to Christian doctrine enshrined in Proverbs 13:22,

"A good man leaves an inheritance to his children's children". But inheritance is not just about bank accounts and real estate; it is about giving the next generation a better platform than the one you started with. For immigrants who often come from families that failed them; this is both a responsibility and an opportunity for them to stop the cycle of scarcity, not only within their families, but within their larger community.

WHAT SHOULD AN IMMIGRANT LEGACY LOOK LIKE?

An immigrant's legacy can take many meaningful forms - some tangible, others intangible. Below are few powerful examples:

1. ***Educational Impact***: Create scholarships for underprivileged students - especially those from your home country or immigrant communities in your adopted country. Support institutions that shaped your early life. Even mentorship is a form of legacy: teaching others what you have learned ensures knowledge is passed forward.

2. ***Community Development***: Build or support local infrastructure back home - libraries, clinics, clean water initiatives, vocational training centers. Even small investments in community well-being can multiply their impact for generations.

3. ***Business and Job Creation***: Instead of only sending remittances, think about creating sustainable businesses that provide jobs for others. A flourishing family business or social enterprise can uplift entire communities and serve as a long-term economic engine.

4. ***Civic and Cultural Engagement***: Establish or support organizations that preserve your cultural heritage, fight for immigrant rights, or engage in community development. This ensures your values are institutionalized and protected.

5. ***Raising Responsible Children***: One of the most enduring legacies is the kind of children you raise. Will they be responsible, compassionate, and purpose-driven? Will they be proud of the legacy you left and inspired to continue it?

I cannot end this discussion without citing "reputation" as a valuable legacy. Reputation is a legacy, though intangible, because it reflects the values, actions, and impact a person leaves in the minds and lives of others. A strong and positive reputation can inspire others to emulate the person, striving to live with similar integrity, values, and impact. Parents, be mindful; your children may not say anything, but they are always watching and will likely imitate your actions when opportunity presents itself.

FROM SURVIVAL TO SIGNIFICANCE

Many immigrants start out hustling - working long hours in factories, warehouses, restaurants, or ride-shares to provide for their families. This phase is one of survival. But once stability is achieved, immigrants must shift from *survival to significance*.

The goal should not just be personal comfort. It should be transformational impact. If you once experienced poverty or lack of access to education, you are in a unique position to ensure that others do not suffer the same fate. The hardships of your journey should not end with you; they should become fuel to spark systemic change.

As financial expert Dave Ramsey writes, *"When thinking about a legacy, invest in something people will forever identify you with"*. That could be talent development, institutional leadership, a foundation for social justice, or simply being known as the person who always lifted others up.

The Zulus of South Africa have a proverb that has helped me to create my future credo. It goes like this: *"Umuntu ngumuntu ngabantu"*, meaning: *"A person is a person through persons"*. We need each other to grow. Kindness in words and deeds create more kindness and confidence in human beings. Also, life's most persistent and urgent question, said Martin Luther King, Jr. is: *"What are you doing for others?"* This is a personal question for individuals to answer. For immigrants, you must have gone through hardship in your country of origin, and now that you are breathing fresh air in a foreign country, you should consider mobilizing forces to put an end to poverty and illiteracy. You will be remembered for this.

WHY THINKING BEYOND YOUR FAMILY MATTERS

Legacy becomes truly powerful when it extends beyond your immediate circle. It is easy to only think of your spouse, children, or extended family, but that is just the beginning. A visionary legacy is one that includes:

- Your community of origin,
- Your adopted community,
- Future immigrants who will walk the path you have walked.

Imagine if every immigrant committed to improving the lives of not just their own families, but ten others. The ripple effect would be profound.

This kind of thinking requires humility and purpose.

It demands asking not just, *"What do I want my children to have?"* but also, *"What kind of world do I want them to inherit?"*

WHAT YOU WILL NOT BE REMEMBERED FOR

Let us be honest: no one will talk about how expensive your car was at your funeral. No eulogy will celebrate how many designer clothes you wore or how lavishly you spent at weekend parties. Such things fade the moment you do.

But you will be remembered for the lives you touched, for the doors you opened, for the courage you showed in starting anew in a foreign land, and the wisdom you shared as you climbed upward.

THE FINAL CHAPTER IS YOURS TO WRITE

Every immigrant is writing a story - some more public, some more quiet, but all significant in their own way. The final chapters of those stories should be about more than personal gain; they should be about lasting change.

No matter your profession, your income, or your status, you have something valuable to leave behind - your reputation, your integrity, your service to others. Legacy is not what you leave to people, it is what you leave *in* them.

CONCLUSION: BUILD WHAT TIME CANNOT ERASE

To think like an immigrant at this level means to think beyond today. It means recognizing that your journey, your struggles, and your successes are not just yours. They are part of a larger narrative - one of resilience, contribution, and continuity.

Legacy is not about being remembered by many; it is about being remembered *meaningfully* by those you influence. Build something that outlives you. Build something that others can build upon. That is the highest calling of the immigrant journey - and the greatest measure of success.

THINKING LIKE AN
IMMIGRANT 108:

WILLINGNESS TO START FROM ZERO

A well-known proverb tells us that *"slow and steady wins the race"*. This timeless wisdom emphasizes the power of perseverance and consistent effort over time. Success, it teaches, is not always the result of speed or shortcuts, but of patience, resilience, and a willingness to grow steadily. For many immigrants, this lesson is more than a saying - it becomes a necessary mindset for survival and success in a new land.

When arriving in a new country, it is common to aspire for rapid financial progress, perhaps even aiming for a job with a paycheck that has many zeros. However, the reality often demands a different path: one that begins not at the top, but at the very beginning. The concept of "Thinking Like an Immigrant 108" centers on this very idea - the willingness to *start from zero*.

STARTING SMALL: THE FOUNDATION
OF LASTING SUCCESS

One of the most powerful attributes of successful immigrants is their readiness to begin with humble steps. If the skills they brought from their home country are not in demand or recognized in their new environment, they don't hesitate to pivot. Instead of resisting change or clinging to past expertise, they choose to learn new skills, adapt to the local context, and rebuild their identity in alignment with new opportunities.

This approach is rooted in a philosophy of self-help and incremental growth. Rather than chasing quick success or mimicking the paths of others, these individuals take a measured approach—first observing, then acting. They prioritize integration over instant gratification and seek to understand the culture, economy, and expectations of their new society before making major life decisions.

THINKING BIG: VISION GROUNDED IN REALITY

Successful immigrants do not allow themselves to be swayed by unrealistic financial projections or emotional impulses. They are deliberate in their decision-making. Initially, they may defer large investments or major moves until they have developed a deeper understanding of the society they now live in.

Once grounded, they begin to think big - but this thinking is informed by experience, not fantasy. They identify challenges, explore viable opportunities, and set long-term goals. This balance between humility and ambition allows them to navigate their new environment with both caution and confidence.

LEARNING FAST: ADAPTABILITY AS A KEY ASSET

However, starting small and thinking big are not enough without the third critical element: learning fast. Adaptability is the hallmark of immigrant success. The world is constantly changing, and immigrants often find themselves needing to absorb new information quickly - whether it is language, legal systems, workplace culture, or industry-specific knowledge.

Those who thrive are often those who are not too proud to learn from any available source - whether it be past experiences, the successes and failures of fellow immigrants, or the wisdom of native-born citizens. They understand that clinging to old habits or assumptions may hinder their progress, and they are willing to ask hard questions, challenge their own beliefs, and make necessary adjustments.

PROGRESSIVE GOALS AND SUSTAINABLE GROWTH

This process involves setting progressive goals - small, manageable objectives that build momentum over time. Rather than placing all their hopes on one venture or dream, successful immigrants diversify their efforts, ensuring that each step forward is grounded in something they can control or directly influence.

Ancient Chinese philosopher Lao Tzu once said, *"Great acts are made up of small deeds"*. This aligns with the approach of strategic immigrants who invest first in themselves, in their education, in networking, and in understanding their environment. Over time, these small actions compound to yield significant results.

Similarly, Confucius reminds us that *"It does not matter how slowly you go as long as you do not stop"*. The journey may be long, but persistence pays off. A desire to get rich quickly can be misleading - and even destructive. Sudden wealth, if not built on a foundation of discipline and knowledge, can vanish just as quickly. In contrast, wealth built through hard work and patience tends to be sustainable and meaningful.

CONCLUSION: FROM SURVIVAL TO SIGNIFICANCE

Ultimately, the lesson of "Thinking Like an Immigrant 108" is not merely about financial success. It is about embracing a mindset of growth, humility, and continuous learning.

Starting from zero is not a sign of failure, it is an act of courage and foresight. Those who are willing to begin again, adapt, and evolve are those who carve a meaningful and lasting path in their new society.

In our next theme, we will explore the idea of teachability - a trait that is deeply connected to learning fast and building a life of lasting success.

THINKING LIKE AN IMMIGRANT 109:

TEACHABILITY

"Thinking like an immigrant" means embracing a mindset of continuous growth. Success, for immigrants and anyone else, is not a destination – it is a journey that demands constant learning, self-awareness, and humility.

For many immigrants, especially those who have already achieved a measure of success, there is a subtle danger: becoming contented or complacent. When respect, recognition, or financial stability is attained, it is tempting to slow down. But true success calls for more. It requires a commitment to keep growing - socially, mentally, spiritually, and professionally.

WHY TEACHABILITY MATTERS

Teachability is the ability to remain open to new knowledge, perspectives, and ideas - even after achieving success. It is the willingness to learn from others, to ask questions, to accept feedback, and to make necessary changes in our lifestyle. Two philosophics about learning: "*Once you stop learning, you start dying*" attributed to Albert Einstein, and "*The illiterate of the 21st century will not be those who cannot read and write, but those who cannot learn, unlearn, and relearn*", attributed to Alvin Toffler, emphasize the importance of lifelong learning and adaptability in a rapidly changing world. Those who are teachable recognize that they do not know everything, and that learning never ends.

Successful immigrants do not rest on their past achievements. Instead, they use the respect they have earned as a platform to grow further and help others. Their growth is intentional - they grow on purpose and for a purpose, knowing that who they become affects their relationships, opportunities, and future success.

Five Ways to Stay Teachable

1. *Overcome the "destination disease":*
   • Many people stop learning once they have reached a goal. But real growth means realizing there is always more to learn. If you stop growing, you stop learning. And if you stop learning, you stop truly living.
2. *Move past the "success syndrome":*
   • Success can sometimes become a trap. It is easy to look at past achievements and feel satisfied. But teachable people focus on future goals, not past trophies. They ask, *"What is next and how can I grow further?"*
3. *Avoid shortcuts:*
   • Growth takes time and effort. There is no easy road to meaningful success. Be willing to invest in the process, even when it is difficult. Anything worthwhile is uphill - there is always a price to pay for lasting success.
4. *Let go of pride:*
   • Pride can block learning. No matter how much you know, there is always more to learn. A teachable person is humble enough to say, "I don't know", and eager enough to ask, "Can you teach me?"

5. *Learn from mistakes:*

- Everyone makes mistakes. The key is not to repeat them. A teachable person reflects on their experiences, learns from their failures, and avoids paying the price twice for the same error.

Teachability is the ability to learn from the perspectives and experiences of others while being open to new ideas and information. Self-discipline and diligence have already been discussed in this book as fundamental characteristics of successful people.

THE ROLE OF HUMILITY IN GROWTH

In addition to teachability is the invaluable quality of humility. Humble people are not shy about taking advice and are therefore teachable. Because they know they are not always right, they never stop learning. They are constantly asking for feedback and are willing to change where necessary.

Teachability is deeply tied to humility. Humble people know they are not always right - and that is exactly what makes them lifelong learners. They ask for feedback, they listen, and they are willing to adapt. Humility allows them to grow without ego getting in the way.

In earlier parts of this book, we emphasized the importance of self-discipline and diligence. These traits remain essential. But teachability, the ability fueled by humility, completes the picture. It turns ambition into wisdom and transforms talent into lasting impact.

THE POWER OF TEACHABILITY: REAL-LIFE IMMIGRANT STORIES

To think like an immigrant is to embrace a mindset of perpetual growth. Immigrants often arrive with limited resources but abundant determination, viewing every challenge as an opportunity to learn and evolve. This mindset is not just about survival, it is about thriving through teachability. Here are people who displayed attitude of teachability:

1. KATYA ECHAZARRETA – FROM McDONALD'S TO SPACE

At seven, Katya Echazarreta immigrated from Mexico, facing language barriers and academic challenges. Despite working multiple jobs to support her family, she obtained her B.S. in Electrical Engineering at UCLA where she received the prestigious Regents and Jack Kent Cooke Foundation Scholarships. She also received a full scholarship to pursue a master's degree in electrical engineering at Johns Hopkins University. She began her career at NASA's Jet Propulsion Laboratory and has worked on 5 NASA missions including the Perseverance Rover and Europa Clipper. In 2022, she became the first Mexican-born woman to fly to space with Blue Origin, demonstrating that teachability and perseverance can defy expectations (Gamillo, 2024).

Katya's story is a great lesson for immigrants. The message, which is clear and loud, is that the only limits in our life are those we impose on ourselves. Imagine a young girl without proficiency in English language breaking barriers to be recognized by NASA. Our limitations are often self-imposed.

As Henry Ford rightly said, *"Obstacles are those frightful things you see when you take your eyes off your goal"*. Limitations are temporary, and with determination and perseverance, we can overcome them. We have the power to break free from these limitations and achieve greatness. It is all about changing our mindset and believing in ourselves.

2. SEKOU CLARKE –
BUILDING AN EMPIRE FROM HUMBLE BEGINNINGS

Born and raised in Kingston, Jamaica, Sekou Clarke did not plan to become one of Orlando's top immigration attorneys, but that was exactly what happened. He came to the United States as a student at the University of Florida on a track and field scholarship. As a student, Sekou pursued a passion for justice and advocacy. After earning his law degree, he founded The Sekou Clarke Law Group, expanding it across multiple countries. His commitment to learning and adapting led to a 30% revenue increase during the COVID-19 pandemic and the creation of a Business Immigration Incubator to mentor fellow immigrants.

Sekou is popularly referred to as a fierce defender of justice, who commits himself to:

"Closing the gap between privilege and access, empowering those who have been denied opportunities... We understand the challenges faced by immigrants and those who have suffered unjust injuries, and we support them as warriors in their pursuit of justice. With compassion and resilience, we work tirelessly to ensure that every individual, regardless of their background, receives the fair treatment, compensation, and

support they deserve. Together, we strive to build a society where each person defines their own right to life, liberty, and the pursuit of happiness" (The USA Reporter (2024)

If Sekou Clarke can do it, you can! Just believe in yourself and get the ball rolling.

3. MARIA TELLERIA – MERGING CULTURES FOR INNOVATION

Maria Telleria came to the United States when her father, an engineer and sales executive in the automotive industry, transferred from Mexico to Detroit, Michigan. Language was her first challenge, but that was easily taken care of when her parents enrolled her in schools with dual language instruction. She was only 14 years old when she came to the US and adjusting to American culture was excruciating. As a child, Maria's father encouraged her to fix things with him around the house. He also arranged tours of manufacturing facilities he visited on sales calls to satisfy her curiosity.

Between Maria's junior and senior year in high school, she spent six weeks on the MIT campus at a summer program designed to introduce minority students to engineering and entrepreneurship. She enjoyed the hands-on experience, which led her to apply and be accepted to MIT. Maria earned a bachelor's degree, a master's degree, and a Ph.D. in mechanical engineering at MIT. Through her research, she saw great possibilities in building robots for situations other than assembly lines at manufacturing plants. She co-founded a company that bridges technological innovation with cultural understanding, illustrating how embracing diverse perspectives fosters creativity and success (Anderson, 2023).

4. JULISSA ARCE –
FROM UNDOCUMENTED TO WALL STREET

Julissa Arce, born in Taxco, Mexico, immigrated to the United States with her family at age 11 as an undocumented immigrant. She studied English and sailed through high school programs and a degree in Finance from The University of Texas at Austin. She rose through the ranks at Goldman Sachs, becoming a vice president, while navigating the complexities of living as an undocumented person in the US. After becoming a US citizen in 2014, she transitioned to advocacy, becoming a writer, speaker, and social justice advocate, particularly for immigrant rights. She co-founded the Ascend Educational Fund, a scholarship and mentorship program for immigrant students (Cardenas, 2022).

5. FLAVIA SANTOS –
OVERCOMING ADVERSITY TO LEAD

Flavia Santos Lloyd's journey from homelessness and undocumented status to becoming a successful immigration lawyer exemplifies resilience and teachability. In July 2016, she formally opened the Santos Lloyd Law Firm. It started as just her; then a part-time paralegal joined. Her firm, Santos Lloyd Law Firm PC, now employs forty staff members, reflecting her dedication to continuous learning and empowerment (Connolly, 2023; Harvard 2024).

Do you need more real-world stories? No, that was enough. These stories underscore that teachability is not just about acquiring knowledge, it is about the willingness to learn from every experience, adapt to challenges, and persist in the face of adversity.

By adopting an immigrant mindset, we can transform obstacles into stepping stones toward success.

FINAL THOUGHT

Success is not a place you reach and stop. In other words, success is not a destination. It is a process of *becoming*. By staying teachable, you ensure that your journey continues - upward, forward, and with purpose.

Thinking like an immigrant 109 means developing an attitude of continuous growth. Immigrants, especially successful ones, must be conscious of the danger of contentment or complacency with what they have achieved. If their success gives them influence and respect, they should think about capitalizing on the respect they have earned and continue to grow socially, mentally, spiritually and professionally.

Growth determines who we are, who we are attracted to, and who we are attracted to determines the degree of our success(es) in life. Immigrants who want to maximize their potential must determine to grow on purpose for a purpose. To grow on purpose, they must remain teachable, knowing that success is a journey and not a destination.

Teachability is the ability to learn from the perspectives and experiences of others while being open to new ideas and information. Self-discipline and diligence have already been discussed in this book as fundamental characteristics of successful people. In addition to these qualities is the invaluable quality of humility. Humble people have the ability to take advice and are, therefore, teachable. Because they know they are not always right, they never stop learning.They are constantly asking for feedback and are willing to change where necessary.

Thinking like an Immigrant 110:

Using available resources

Immigrants are often seen as underdogs - people who arrive in new countries with minimal resources, limited networks, and countless challenges. And yet, across generations and continents, immigrants have proven that success is not always born of privilege. Instead, it is often built on grit, resourcefulness, and the wise use of whatever is available. Thinking like an immigrant at this stage means embracing the power of modest beginnings and rejecting the myth that only the wealthy or highly educated can make a difference.

One of the most powerful reminders of this principle comes from Theodore Roosevelt, who often quoted his friend Squire Bill Widener: *"Do what you can, with what you've got, where you are"*. These words hold special weight for immigrants who are sometimes tempted to believe that their lack of money, citizenship status, language proficiency, or formal education is an insurmountable barrier. In reality, success does not always require extraordinary tools, just an extraordinary mindset.

Overcoming the myth of "Not Enough"

In today's hyper-competitive world, it is easy for immigrants to fall into a dangerous trap: the belief that you must have a college degree from a top university, millions of dollars in investment capital, or some rare technical skill to succeed. This belief paralyzes too many newcomers, especially those who feel marginalized or left behind.

But history and stories of highly successful immigrants tell a different story.

Just as fighting forces do not need weapons of mass destruction to win a war, immigrants do not need perfect circumstances to make a lasting impact. Think of how guerrilla fighters defeat larger armies using agility and adaptability. Think of David as recorded in the Christian Bible who was able to defeat Goliath with a simple sling and a shepherd's staff. Similarly, immigrants must learn to turn limitations into leverage points. Victory is often won through strategy, consistency, and relentless determination.

A real-world example that illustrates the power of using limited resources effectively is the story of Ruth Simmons, the first African American president of an Ivy League university. Raised in a poor family in segregated Texas, Simmons faced daunting obstacles - poverty, racial discrimination, and a lack of access to elite education. But she did not let those circumstances define her future.

Simmons maximized what she *did* have: a deep love for learning, an unwavering work ethic, and a small but supportive community. She earned a scholarship to Dillard University, a historically black college, and eventually a Ph.D. from Harvard University. Despite humble beginnings, her consistent use of available resources helped her shatter ceilings and become a trailblazer in American higher education. Her story demonstrates that success is less about what you start with and more about how you use it.

THE IMMIGRANT TOOLBOX

Many immigrants arrive with more tools than they realize. You may not have formal credentials, but perhaps you have:

- Bilingual ability, which can be an asset in many workplaces.
- A strong work ethic, cultivated through years of hardship.
- Cultural intelligence, which allows you to connect with diverse communities.
- Survival instincts, which teach you resilience and creative problem-solving.
- A desire to succeed, which, when paired with humility and consistency, can open surprising doors.

The truth is that these tools are often more valuable than any certificate. While education and money can certainly help, they are not the only currencies of success. Resourcefulness and integrity often go much further.

AVOIDING THE BLAME GAME

Another danger immigrants must guard against is the temptation to engage in blame game - blaming the host country for its bureaucracy or discrimination, blaming their home country for its corruption or failures, or blaming circumstances for lack of progress. While these frustrations may be valid, they should never become excuses for inaction.

Instead, immigrants must focus on what is within their control. Blaming others will not pay your bills, raise your children, or build a future. But taking action - even small, consistent actions - will. Whether it is starting a side hustle, enrolling in a night class, or simply learning the local language one word at a time, the key is to begin with what you have.

Sometimes we underestimate what we have while millions of people are jealous of what we have and itching to be like us.

RESOURCEFULNESS IN ACTION

Consider the many immigrant entrepreneurs who started businesses with very little resources:

- A Somali refugee in Minnesota who began a food truck and turned it into a national halal food brand.
- A Latin American immigrant who started cleaning houses and eventually opened her own cleaning agency employing dozens of others.
- A West African father who drove taxis by day and studied coding by night, ultimately landing a job in tech.

None of these stories began with million-dollar investments or Ivy League degrees. They began with the decision to make the most of what was available.

BEING AN EXAMPLE FOR THE NEXT GENERATION

Immigrants must also realize that how they use their resources sets an example for the next generation. Children watch how their parents handle adversity, how they pursue goals, and how they treat others. When you show that success can be built with limited means, you teach your children resilience, confidence, and humility.

Your story becomes a blueprint. It tells them: You don't need to wait for the perfect moment. You don't need to be rich or famous. Start now. Use what you have. That, in itself, is a legacy.

As Maya Angelou once said, *"Try to be a rainbow in someone's cloud."* Even if you cannot change your whole world today, you can still be a force for good in someone else's life. And often, when you begin uplifting others, your own circumstances begin to shift for the better.

TRANSFORMING SMALL RESOURCES INTO BIG IMPACT

At its core, *Thinking Like an Immigrant 110* is about perspective. Instead of focusing on what you lack, shift your focus to what you can do. Every resource - no matter how small - can be transformed with vision, discipline, and effort. Start where you are:

• If you have time, invest it in learning.
• If you have energy, use it to serve others.
• If you have a small income, save and plan wisely.
• If you have a story, share it to inspire others.

Great things often come from modest beginnings. But greatness requires action.

CONCLUSION: MAKE THE MOST OF THE JOURNEY

The immigrant journey is not an easy one. But embedded within its challenges are countless opportunities to rise. The secret lies not in what you lack, but in how you use what you already possess.

Whether it is your voice, your mind, your hands, or your heart - use them. Stop waiting for ideal circumstances or outside permission. History remembers those who took small steps in uncertain conditions and still moved forward.

As Roosevelt wisely said: *"Do what you can, with what you've got, where you are."* And let your journey be proof that even limited resources, when used with courage and consistency, can produce an extraordinary life.

FINAL REFLECTIONS TO SECTION II:

CHOOSE GROWTH OVER COMFORT

After reflecting on the ten different ways of thinking like an immigrant, one truth becomes abundantly clear: success in a new land is not accidental - it is strategic, deliberate, and deeply personal. It is born not from perfect conditions, but from a commitment to grow in the face of imperfect ones.

If you still find yourself uncertain about where to begin, what direction to follow, or how to navigate the unknowns of life as an immigrant, take to heart the timeless advice of motivational speaker Jim Rohn:

"Don't wish it were easier, wish you were better.
Don't wish for fewer problems, wish for more skills.
Don't wish for less challenge, wish for more wisdom".

This mindset is the essence of the immigrant spirit. It reminds us that we are not powerless. We are not defined by the systems that exclude us, or by the limitations of our starting points. We are defined by how we rise to meet our circumstances - with courage, creativity, and resilience.

WE ARE LIVING IN CHALLENGING TIMES

Our generation of immigrants faces unprecedented challenges - economic uncertainty, rapid technological change, geopolitical shifts, rising nationalism, and sometimes even hostility from the very societies we try to contribute to.

These are not the same circumstances our grandfathers or even our fathers faced. And with hope and good decisions, they are not the challenges our children and grandchildren will inherit.

What does this mean for humanity, particularly the current generation of immigrants? It means we are standing at a turning point. The decisions we make now - how we respond to adversity, how we invest in ourselves and our communities, how we choose to think - will shape not only our futures, but also those of our descendants. The power of positive thinking, combined with focused, purposeful action, may be the most important resource we possess in navigating this moment.

ADAPTATION, NOT ASSIMILATION ALONE

A key theme across the ten chapters of this Section is adaptability. Immigrants must remain alert to changing immigration laws, economic opportunities, and social expectations in their new countries of residence. Rules and systems are constantly evolving. So too must your strategy.

This does not mean abandoning your roots. It means learning how to live with dual awareness - honoring your heritage while skillfully adapting to the culture of your adopted country. It is about finding a healthy balance between two worlds. Neither must dominate; both can enrich you. But this balance requires mindfulness and maturity. It means recognizing when ancestral habits serve you, and when they hold you back.

In choosing not to elevate one culture over the other, you create space for the richness of both to thrive within you.

This is the quiet strength of the immigrant identity: being able to walk comfortably in more than one world and contribute meaningfully to each.

LEARN FROM THOSE WHO
HAVE WALKED BEFORE YOU

Another essential step is to learn from those who have succeeded. Every immigrant community has its trailblazers - those who came before you, faced similar obstacles, and found ways to overcome them. Their stories offer not just inspiration, but practical lessons. Learn how they built businesses, navigated complex legal systems, educated their children, and gave back to both their host and home countries. These are the principles discussed in the next Section of this book, and they are well worth studying.

Assimilation - understood not as the erasure of your identity, but as *cultural literacy* and functional integration - is an important part of this journey. When you learn how your new society operates, and participate fully in it, you gain access to greater social capital, economic mobility, and personal security. More importantly, you contribute to a more inclusive, integrated society.

WHAT YOU FOCUS ON SHAPES YOUR REALITY

One of the most powerful tools immigrants have is focus. Where you direct your attention determines your internal landscape. If you fixate on discrimination, bureaucratic delays, or cultural alienation, you will quickly become discouraged. But if you focus on opportunities, relationships, learning, and self-improvement, the road becomes clearer and wider. This is not about denial - it is about discipline. Discipline over your mind. Your emotions.

YOUR DAILY CHOICES.

No country on earth is perfect. Your country of origin was not perfect. If it had been, you likely would not have chosen to leave. So, rather than romanticizing what you left behind or resenting what you have come into, choose to *build something meaningful in the present*. Be deliberate in your gratitude. Be intentional with your energy.

As the saying goes, *"Energy flows where attention goes"*. If you want to experience progress, keep your eyes on progress. If you want to grow, invest time in growth.

KNOWLEDGE OR WISDOM? CHOOSE ONE

The more I think about my immigrant experiences, the more I have more to share. But for the sake of space, let's close the discussion of this Section with a final thought from Sandra Carey: *"Never mistake knowledge for wisdom. One helps you make a living; the other helps you make a life"*. This distinction is particularly relevant for immigrants. Many arrive in their new country with professional degrees or academic knowledge that are undervalued, even ignored. It can feel frustrating and demoralizing. But wisdom -- born of experience, humility, and inner strength - can never be taken from you.

Knowledge can get you a job, but wisdom will help you build a future. Wisdom will tell you when to speak and when to listen. When to wait and when to act. When to fight and when to walk away. It will help you make decisions that protect your dignity, preserve your relationships, and give purpose to your journey.

So, choose wisely. Choose courage over comfort. Choose learning over stagnation. Choose contribution over complaint. Choose legacy over lifestyle. Choose wisdom over mere knowledge.

FINAL WORDS: YOU ARE THE ARCHITECT OF YOUR FUTURE

Ultimately, "thinking like an immigrant" is not just about surviving the hardships of migration. It is about thriving despite them. It is about becoming the architect of your own life - building with whatever materials are available, refusing to accept mediocrity, and daring to believe in a future that is better than your past.

Whether you are just beginning your immigrant journey or are years into it, the ten principles explored in the next Section serve as guideposts. They do not guarantee an easy path, but they illuminate a meaningful one.

Success, fulfillment, and legacy are possible for you, not because the road is smooth, but because *you are willing to walk it*. Step by step. Day by day. Thought by thought.

My mother-in-law, Ursula Cole, once told her daughter in my presence, "Don't measure the size of the land by just looking at the land. Start building and then you will see how big the land is." As you move forward, remember this: you do not have to have it all to begin. Just begin with what you have. And never underestimate where it can lead.

Section III

Principles of Highly Successful Immigrants

INTRODUCTION TO SECTION III

In life, there is no final defeat nor ultimate victory - success is a continual journey, not a static destination. There is no point at which we can declare ourselves "sufficiently successful." As the author Michael Scott wisely observed, *"The day we stop learning is the day we die."* This sentiment encapsulates the spirit of success for many immigrants, who understand that growth is a lifelong endeavor. Success, then, is not merely about reaching a set point, it is about the persistence to keep moving forward, no matter the setbacks.

In this context, we can argue that every immigrant, wherever they have settled, has achieved success in one form or another. The very act of leaving their homeland, navigating the challenges of securing an immigrant visa, and embracing the uncertainty of a new life is a success worth recognizing. Yet, for many immigrants, this initial success is merely the beginning. They aspire to continue succeeding - not just today, but far into the future, driven by a tireless ambition to achieve even more.

That said, despite their hard work, many immigrants still feel they have not fully "arrived". There are times when their path remains unclear, when the challenges seem insurmountable, or when they struggle to see the "light at the end of the tunnel". Such feelings are natural, especially when the road to success is filled with obstacles that test both patience and resilience.

At the heart of this journey there is a crucial factor: *attitude*. Some immigrants face setbacks due to negative beliefs that can undermine their confidence.

Self-doubt, a lack of faith in their own abilities, a tendency to give up when confronted with adversity, or a pervasive pessimism can erode the persistence required for success. However, one thing is clear: most immigrants are fighters. They do not give up easily. Their diligence, resilience, and relentless pursuit of their goals are qualities that set them apart. These traits are the foundation of their success, regardless of the setbacks they face along the way.

This Section forms the cornerstone of this book. It provides a roadmap for contemporary immigrants, offering valuable insights into the principles and habits that highly successful immigrants have adopted. By studying these practices, newcomers can identify the behaviors and mindsets that are instrumental in achieving their dreams. Learning from those who have walked this path before them not only helps immigrants overcome the challenges of their current journey but also lays the groundwork for a future defined by growth and accomplishment.

The importance of this exercise cannot be overstated. Emulating the habits of successful individuals allows immigrants to adopt positive routines that significantly contribute to both personal and professional development. This, in turn, promotes consistency, discipline, and productivity - three pillars that are vital for long-term success. Moreover, these habits cultivate a positive mindset, which is essential when navigating the complexities of building a life in a new country.

By understanding and incorporating the values and behaviors of those who have succeeded before them, immigrants can chart their own path to success. These principles include learning from past experiences, managing resources effectively, embracing failure as a learning opportunity, developing a strong work ethic, committing to lifelong learning, setting clear and measurable goals, mastering time management, and cultivating resilience in the face of adversity.

Successful immigrants live by these principles. They are guided not just by ambition, but by a set of practical, time-tested ideologies that help them thrive in the face of uncertainty. In the following section of this book, we will explore twenty-five of these guiding principles, offering actionable steps that can inspire and equip today's immigrants to reach their fullest potential.

PRINCIPLE OF SUCCESS #1

SUCCESSFUL IMMIGRANTS UNDERSTAND LIFE BACKWARD BUT LIVE FORWARD.

To understand life backward but live forward, let us start the discussion with the real-life experience of Lamine Amadou, an immigrant in the United States.

TRUE LIFE STORY #1 - LAMINE AMADOU: FROM STRUGGLE TO SUCCESS

Lamine Amadou was born into a humble family where even daily meals were uncertain. His parents, though struggling financially, placed immense value on education and worked tirelessly to see him through secondary school. For Lamine, education was more than a goal - it was a lifeline out of generational poverty.

His fortunes changed when he won the Diversity Visa Lottery - a moment he saw as divine intervention. Arriving in the United States, Lamine carried with him the weight of past hardships but also a fierce determination to change his destiny. He committed himself to academic excellence, not only to uplift himself but to break the cycle of poverty and illiteracy in his family.

Yet, life in the U.S. brought new challenges. Lamine soon realized that being an immigrant and a person of color came with its own struggles - discrimination, marginalization, and a constant reminder of his outsider status. These experiences echoed the tribal and ethnic discrimination he had known in his homeland. Despite his achievements, he often felt held back by the very identity he had hoped would no longer be a barrier.

But Lamine refused to be defined by either past or prejudice. He reminded himself of his purpose - to create a better life and to rise above the limitations once imposed on him. Choosing hope over hardship, he sought guidance from fellow immigrants who had succeeded against the odds. Their advice was clear: stop lamenting the barriers and start building bridges. Invest in your skills. Adapt. Evolve.

Embracing this mindset, Lamine immersed himself in continuous learning - gaining new qualifications, acquiring trades, and enhancing his professional abilities. He understood that true success was not a destination but a journey of relentless growth.

Today, Lamine is thriving. His story is one of resilience, transformation, and unwavering focus. From the dusty paths of his village to the opportunities of a new land, he has crafted a life of purpose and pride. And now, he stands not just as a success story, but as a source of inspiration to others who arrive with nothing but hope - and the will to persevere.

Life is complicated. It is a journey that can be challenging but also fun and exciting. What is certain is that no one knows how life is going to unfold or end. We know when and where we were born, but we cannot foresee how, when and where we will die.

The decision by immigrants to emigrate to a foreign country exemplifies the philosophy that whereas life can only be understood backward, we must endeavor to live forward. Immigrants can only make sense of the experiences or events that pushed them to leave their indigenous homes, but they cannot predict their future in a new country. Successful immigrants understand the complexity of their lives, especially as it involves leaving loved ones behind and moving to a foreign country that they know very little about.

Many people emigrate to a foreign country to escape hardship, which may be the result of religious persecution, political oppression, poverty and economic decline, among other adversities. On arrival in a new country, the behavior of immigrants is often driven by prior experiences in their countries of origin. This is a good thing. Immigrants should never forget their roots while building a new life in a foreign land. Whether their past experiences were good or bad, they should learn from them but not allow them to impede their progress.

Successful immigrants constantly reflect on the past, learn from and rectify previous errors and thus prepare themselves for the future. Letting go of our past misfortunes and failures allows us to experience something new and promising.

Many immigrants focus on their bitter past experiences to a fault. I have met immigrants who deny their homelands, swearing never to ever return to or visit their countries of

THINK LIKE AN IMMIGRANT

origin. Others discard their native names and adopt European names. Though marriage outside one's ethnic or racial group is not wrong, some immigrants deliberately marry individuals of other ethnicities or races as expressions of anger against their ancestral roots and as a means to erase past melancholic experiences. These immigrants tend to forget that it was prior bad experiences that motivated them to emigrate in search of better opportunities.

There is nobody or any country without a bitter past. It just boils down to how you use those experiences to your advantage. This is precisely the point made by Maya Angelou when she said, *"I have great respect for the past. If you do not know where you've come from, you don't know where you're going"*[9]. I can add to that by saying if your feet could speak, you would understand where you came from and where you are going.

Things make sense in retrospect, but life continues forward. Many people are haunted by the poor choices they made in the past, but, while this is okay, we should not allow these choices to determine how we live in the future. When we succeed in any endeavor, we tend to stop learning, whereas when we fail, we continue searching for answers to the problem. We learn from failures and not from success. Therefore, rather than bowing to our mistakes, failures, or bad habits, we should learn from them. "Mistakes," argued Sophia Loren, *"are part of the dues one pays for a full life"*[10].

Learning from our past mistakes allows us to have a fresh start every day; it offers us the potential to be better than we were in the past.

---

9   Ruth Nina Welsh, "Inspiration from Maya Angelou". Ruth Nina Welsh, July 14, 2024, https://www.beyourowncounsellorandcoach.com/inspiration-from-maya-angelou.

10 "Sophia Loren Quotes about Mistakes", AZ Quotes, accessed March 29, 2025, https://www.azquotes.com/author/9042-Sophia_Loren/tag/mistake.

Successful immigrants know how to carve unique paths to find happiness, success, wealth, meaningful work and whatever else they desire in life. They are also good at revisiting and learning from their past as key step to forging forward and adapting to a competitive world. Successful immigrants do not allow their past misfortune to control their future. Rather, they channel their pains, negative emotions, and disappointments into productive initiatives.

I am not aware of anyone whose life is devoid of pain and suffering, or who has succeeded without a previous negative experience. Children with powerful parents sometimes suffer bullying by classmates while there are rich people who were college dropouts or who grew up in poverty-stricken environments. Nonetheless, the latter still forged ahead, determined to enlarge their capacity and expand their mind without being deterred by past experiences. Successful immigrants overcome difficulties by using past negative experiences as fuel for creating the future they long for rather than wasting time in complaints and finger pointing.

INSIGHT

The idea of "understanding life backward but living forward" is rooted in three powerful philosophies that have positively impacted people, sometimes without them even realizing it. These philosophies are eloquently expressed in the following quotes: Søren Kierkegaard famously said, *"Life can only be understood backwards, but it must be lived forwards"*.

A similar sentiment is captured by Albert Einstein, who advised, *"Learn from yesterday, live for today, hope for tomorrow"*. Though expressed from different perspectives, Steve Jobs echoes a comparable truth when he reflects, *"You can't connect the dots looking forward; you can only connect them looking backwards".*

All three of these statements acknowledge a shared truth: we each have a past. I have mine, you have yours, and we all have collective histories that shape who we are today. Our past experiences are mirrors that reflect the decisions we made - or did not make - and reveal the impact of those choices on our lives. Whether those choices were good or bad, we are ultimately responsible for them. It is up to us to examine our past actions, correct our mistakes where possible, learn from them, and equip ourselves to face the unpredictable challenges of the future.

The uncertainty of the future is inescapable. This makes it necessary to trust our instincts and our wisdom. While we may not be able to undo every past mistake, we can learn from them and ensure we do not repeat the same errors. It is crucial to prepare for the future, as it is the space where we will eventually reside, live, and grow. By understanding where we have been, we can make better choices moving forward, increasing our resilience and our ability to navigate what lies ahead.

In the end, living forward does not mean ignoring the past; rather, it means learning from it, adapting, and using that knowledge to guide our journey into an uncertain future. The future may be unpredictable, but the lessons of the past are the tools we need to shape it with purpose and intention.

PRINCIPLE OF SUCCESS #2

SUCCESSFUL IMMIGRANTS ARE PURPOSE-DRIVEN

"God created us on purpose, for a purpose". These words, spoken by Pastor Olumide Ogunjuyigbe at Jesus House DC in 2024, continue to resonate deeply with me. If God created humanity with intent, then it follows that our lives must also be guided by purpose. For immigrants especially, this guiding purpose often makes the difference between mere survival and lasting success.

PURPOSE GIVES IMMIGRANTS DIRECTION

In 1999, I met a young English woman in Ferney, France, who had moved there to pursue her studies. Despite the language barrier and cultural adjustments, she remained undeterred. When I asked why she had chosen to study in a country where she did not speak the language fluently, her answer was striking: her career demanded fluency in a second European language, and mastering French would open new doors. She had a clear and compelling "why", which helped her persevere through challenges. Her story highlights a timeless truth - when your actions are anchored in purpose, adversity becomes more manageable.

Immigrants must ask themselves a foundational question: Why am I leaving my home country? Whether it is for better educational opportunities, financial growth, safety, freedom, or to reunite with family, every migration story is driven by a core reason - a personal "why".

This "why" serves as a compass, pointing toward the destination of their dreams and giving direction when the path gets rough.

KNOWING YOUR "WHY" FUELS RESILIENCE

Life in a new country comes with inevitable setbacks - cultural shock, rejection, job market challenges, and loneliness. For those who are purpose-driven, these obstacles are not dead ends but detours. The "why" becomes an inner reserve of strength, reminding immigrants of the reason behind their sacrifices.

Purpose instills focus. It keeps successful immigrants grounded and motivated to rise above temporary failures. As George Washington Carver aptly noted, *"Ninety-nine percent of the failures come from people who have the habit of making excuses"*. Those who lack purpose often blame circumstances or others. In contrast, purpose-driven immigrants own their journey. They do not hide behind excuses. They learn, adjust, and keep moving forward.

PURPOSE AND PLANNING GO HAND IN HAND

Purpose without planning is like a ship without a sail. Immigrants who succeed do not just dream - they act. They set goals, develop action plans, and pursue them with discipline. Their aspirations may include attaining higher education, building a business, supporting extended family, or leaving a legacy. Regardless of the goal, they understand that failing to plan is planning to fail.

Effective goal setting involves more than listing desires. It requires defining short-term and long-term objectives, measuring progress, and being ready to adapt when plans collide with reality. Life is unpredictable, but those with clearly defined goals stay anchored through the storms.

CREATIVITY AND RESILIENCE: TOOLS OF THE PURPOSE-DRIVEN

Purpose-driven immigrants are often the most creative. They think outside the box and craft new solutions to unexpected problems. They challenge norms, innovate, and find ways to stand out. But creativity alone is not enough - resilience must accompany it.

Success rarely comes on the first try. Thomas Edison famously said, "*I never once failed at making a light bulb. I just found ninety-nine ways not to make one*". That mindset defines successful immigrants. They are not afraid to try again. They see failure not as a verdict but as part of the process.

Resilience, discipline, and emotional intelligence are all crucial traits in the pursuit of success. These qualities enable immigrants to rebuild when plans fall apart and to keep striving when hope seems dim.

PURPOSE IS POWER

A life without purpose is a life adrift. It is easy to get lost in routine or to be swayed by challenges when there is no clear vision guiding your actions. Purpose brings clarity. It informs decisions, fosters accountability, and generates meaningful results.

Purpose-driven immigrants do more than improve their own lives - they impact the communities around them.

They build bridges, inspire others, and contribute to their new homes in lasting ways. Their vision often extends beyond personal ambition; they aim to uplift others and leave behind a legacy greater than themselves.

Do you want to achieve a happy and successful life? Then listen to Albert Einstein who said, *"If you want to live a happy life, tie it to a goal, not to people or things"*. Immigrants who embrace this wisdom know that their purpose is what sustains them. It fuels their ambition, supports their efforts, and brings fulfillment.

FINAL THOUGHTS

Emigration is more than crossing borders, it is a journey of transformation. To succeed, immigrants must understand why they made that leap. A well-defined purpose is the foundation for all achievements. It sharpens focus, strengthens resolve, and brings meaning to every step of the journey.

If you are an immigrant - or planning to be one - know this: your purpose is your power. It is what will help you rise when you fall, push through uncertainty, and achieve what once seemed impossible. Keep refining it, stay committed to it, and let it guide you into a future filled with promise and impact.

PRINCIPLE OF SUCCESS #3

SUCCESSFUL IMMIGRANTS TAKE
CALCULATED RISKS

In the context of emigration, calculated risk refers to the conscious decision to leave one's home country after carefully weighing the potential benefits against the possible challenges and uncertainties. Immigrants who take calculated risks understand that success is not guaranteed, but they evaluate factors such as economic opportunity, political stability, safety, and long-term goals before making the move. Rather than acting impulsively, they choose to stepinto the unknown with preparation, strategy, and a sense of purpose.

Every immigrant success story is a study in courage, resilience, and above all, calculated risk. Risk is often mischaracterized as recklessness. The difference between success and failure often lies in the ability to take calculated risks, that is, actions taken with forethought, preparation, and a realistic assessment of potential gains and losses.

Migration, whether driven by choice or necessity, involves bold steps into the unknown. It is not merely a change of geography, it is a leap of faith into unfamiliar languages, cultures, economies, and legal systems. Yet, time and time again, immigrants have shown that when risk is balanced with reason, vision, and adaptability, the results can be transformational.

It is contended that a calculated risk-taking is the cornerstone of immigrant success - economically, socially, and personally - and offers data, life experiences, and examples to show why and how immigrants should embrace it.

In every era and on every continent, the most transformative human journeys begin with a leap into the unknown. Immigrants - people who leave behind their homes, languages, and familiar customs in search of something better - stand as some of the most audacious actors in this ongoing human drama. At the heart of their bravery lies not recklessness but a discipline of calculated risk-taking. This quality separates those who merely survive migration from those who thrive because of it.to reunite with family, every migration story is driven by a core reason - a personal "why".

MIGRATION ITSELF: THE ULTIMATE
CALCULATED RISK

To migrate is to engage in one of the oldest and most audacious human acts. Leaving one's home, often permanently, demands more than mere hope. It demands strategy, research, sacrifice, and the willingness to embrace failure and resilience alike. As author Tony Robbins once said, *"Change happens when the pain of staying the same is greater than the pain of change"*.

According to the International Organization for Migration (IOM), over 20,000 migrants died crossing the Mediterranean Sea between 2000 and 2023. In the first quarter of 2023 alone, 441 migrants perished at sea. These individuals did not act without consideration; rather, they weighed the certainty of danger, poverty, or persecution in their home countries against the uncertainty of the journey ahead.

They took a grim, calculated risk, believing that the possibility of a better life for themselves and their families was worth the risk.

I remember taking a less dangerous risk but no less significant in my early twenties. After graduation from secondary school and could not secure admission to a university in my country of origin, I worked and saved all the money I earned to travel to the United States of America (USA) for higher education. After a few years of working and saving money, I was able to pay one year school fees to secure admission to the university in the USA. That was a risky plan because I had no sponsor or rich parents to guarantee financial support while in the USA. Despite the risk aforethought, I went to the USA believing that if other foreign students were surviving, I would.

On arrival, I studied hard to maintain a high-grade point average (GPA) to qualify for grants or any form of financial aid that was available to foreign students. That was a calculated risk, carefully orchestrated toward achieving my educational objective. As Mark Zuckerberg once said, *"The biggest risk is not taking any risk... the only strategy that is guaranteed to fail is not taking risks"*. If I did not take the risk or were afraid of being deported for lack of ability to meet the financial obligations, I would probably not be writing this book today.

Another risk I took was to travel to the United States of America without any knowledge of the culture and immigration policies of the country. I was not scared about the differences in culture. The good part of my decision to emigrate to the USA was that English was the language of instruction and I would not have to learn a new language before starting my studies.

The other risks that haunted me throughout the period I stayed in the USA as a student was leaving behind my loved ones and promising career opportunities in my home country to begin life anew in the United States of America. But I went to the USA with the intention to hustle, doing menial jobs the native-born citizens were not willing to do. I studied hard to deserve a grant to finance my education and achieve my educational objective. In less than ten years in the USA, I earned a JD in Law and a PhD in Government/Public Administration. Thinking about this today, the risk was painful at the beginning but sweet at the end. Let us dissect this statement:

1. Based on my experience, risk "… can be painful at the beginning" for the following reasons:
   - *Fear of the unknown*: When we take a risk - like moving to a new country, starting a business, or changing careers - we often leave behind safety and certainty.
   - *Immediate costs*: Risks can involve financial loss, failure, rejection, or criticism.
   - *Emotional strain*: There may be stress, self-doubt, or fear during the early stages of a risky decision.

For immigrants, this could mean homesickness, job insecurity, language barriers, or starting at the bottom of the social ladder.

2. risk "… can be painful at the beginning "…but sweet at the end."
   - *Success and reward*: If the risk pays off, the results can be life-changing - more freedom, better income, education, or a higher quality of life.

- *Personal growth*: Even if things do not go perfectly as planned, taking a risk often builds resilience, confidence, and valuable experience.
- *Fulfillment*: The satisfaction of overcoming fear and achieving a goal is deeply rewarding.

For example, I worked hard in my country of origin, denied myself good things that money could buy to be able to emigrate to the US for higher education, but eventually I graduated, got a high-paying job as a diplomat with the World Health Organization, and lived a better life with my family.

Today when I remember the difficulties I encountered to get higher education, it reminds me that discomfort is often the "gate fee" to something better. Like planting a seed, the beginning is uncertain and messy - but if nurtured, it can lead to a bounty harvest. Calculated risk requires patience and courage upfront, but the payoff can be worth far more than the initial pain.

In sum, the lesson from my experience which contemporary immigrants should learn from is that taking a risk often involves short-term discomfort, uncertainty, or sacrifice - but if the risk is wisely planned and executed, it can lead to long-term gain, success, or fulfillment.

HISTORICAL AND CONTEMPORARY EXAMPLES OF CALCULATED RISK IN IMMIGRANT SUCCESS

To buttress the discussion so far made, here are real world examples of people who had the courage to embark upon a journey that others dreaded:

Example 1: Elon Musk

Born in South African, Elon Musk moved to Canada at age 17 and later to the United States. He studied at the University of Pennsylvania before co-founding PayPal, SpaceX, and Tesla. Each of his ventures involved immense risk, both financial and reputational, but Musk's decisions were data-driven and strategically planned. Today, he is the world's richest person with a net worth of $423 billion as of June 2025 earth. His journey demonstrates how calculated risk can lead to monumental success.

Example 2: Indra Nooyi

Indra Nooyi, born in India, came to the United States to attend Yale School of Management. After graduation, she took a risk by switching career paths and moving into corporate America. She worked at Boston Consulting Group; joined Motorola, 1986; moved to Asea Brown Boveri, 1990; joined PepsiCo as strategist, 1994; became the CFO of PepsiCo, 2000. Eventually, she became the CEO and President of PepsiCo, proving that immigrants who take educational and professional risks can rise to top positions in foreign societies

Example 3: José Andrés

Spanish-born chef José Andrés came to the U.S. and transformed the food and philanthropy industries through his culinary ventures and World Central Kitchen. He risked time, capital, and reputation but did so with a strong mission and calculated plans. His impact during crises like Hurricane Maria in Puerto Rico is a testament to the power of risk with purpose.

José Andrés, a Spanish born chef, came to the United States of America as an immigrant. From a carefully planned career in culinary, he made a significant impact on American cuisine with his innovative and authentic Spanish dishes. He transformed the food and philanthropy industries through his culinary venture, humanitarian efforts, particularly the creation of World Central Kitchen. He is the owner and chef of ThinkFoodGroup, which oversees over thirty restaurants around the world. He risked time, capital, and reputation but did so with a strong mission and calculated plans. His impact during crises like Hurricane Maria in Puerto Rico is a testament to the power of risk with purpose. His World Central Kitchen has been instrumental in providing food aid to displaced and injured and hungry Israelis and Palestinians in Gaza, risking losing his staff in an Israeli airstrike. His dedication to providing aid without political agenda has been recognized by people all over the world, highlighting his role as a philanthropist.

Example 4 – This author's personal experience: From Fear to Fortune

In 1975, I left a high-paying job in Nigeria and boarded a flight to the United States with no scholarship, no family waiting, and no cultural familiarity. I took the risk not because I knew I would succeed but because I had done the math. The declining educational environment in Nigeria offered no long-term security. I gambled on the promise of the U.S. educational system, worked long hours to support myself, and eventually earned advanced degrees. That journey shaped everything I am today. Had I stayed, out of fear, this book - and the life I have built - might not exist.

Beyond business, education is another key area where immigrants take calculated risks. Many arrive in their host countries and immediately pursue degrees, certifications, or vocational training - often while working multiple jobs and raising families. The tuition is high, the cultural adjustment steep, and the return on investment uncertain. But many succeed.

PHILOSOPHICAL AND ETHICAL REFLECTIONS

Risk is not just an economic or personal issue - it is also ethical and philosophical. Choosing to risk one's life or status for a better future is a profound moral choice. It reflects a deep human desire for freedom, dignity, and agency. As Ralph Waldo Emerson noted: *"All life is an experiment. The more experiments you make the better"*.

CONCLUSION

To succeed as an immigrant is to embrace uncertainty with clarity, determination, and vision. Every major step—whether leaving home, starting over, or chasing opportunity in unfamiliar territory—is an act of calculated risk. These choices are not made blindly; they are shaped by careful thought, informed by past experiences, and fueled by the desire for something greater. Calculated risk is what transforms fear into movement and uncertainty into possibility. For immigrants, it is not a reckless gamble, but a courageous strategy—one that turns hope into progress and dreams into reality.

PRINCIPLE OF SUCCESS #4

SUCCESSFUL IMMIGRANTS CONTINUALLY REINVENT, RETOOL & RESKILL THEMSELVES!

Real Life Story #1

James Ekanem was one of my interviewees, a successful architect in his country of origin, Nigeria. Due to economic turmoil, he decided to emigrate to the United States, where he hoped to make good use of his skills. He was certain that as an architect with 25 years' experience, he would not struggle to find a job. As an architect, he should not have had difficulty finding a job, but he had challenges because of his foreign degree and non-American practical work experience. The type of houses he designed and built in his country of origin were different from houses built in the United States. Designing and building wooden houses with interior partitioning and drywall sheets were new to him. In Nigeria, most houses are built with bricks.

Construction companies in the United States acknowledged James's talents and were willing to offer him a job and an opportunity to sharpen his knowledge in the American home-building industry. But that was predicated upon James agreeing to reskill/retool himself by taking courses in construction from a local community college.

However, James did not like the idea of going back to school. His friends, including myself, familiar with the American labor market, advised him to go back to school for at least one year to sharpen his knowledge in architectural designing, the American way. But our advice fell on deaf ears. At 42, James felt it was demeaning to return to the classroom with students as young as his.

Our alternative advice was for him to change his career, but he also thought he was too old to change a career. He did not return to his country of origin but remained in the United States - a defeated soul. He refused all counseling to retool himself in a community college to meet the demands of employers in the United States. He chose driving an Uber rather than going back to school. Although driving an Uber gave him enough money to meet his basic family needs, he could not forgive himself for abandoning his architectural career in Nigeria. Though he successfully relocated to one of the most advanced countries in the world, relying on GPS instructions to earn a living as an Uber driver was not worth losing the profession for which he had trained so hard.

Real Life Story #2

A young lady college graduate, Ime Okon, met a young man during their National Youth Service (NYSC) deployment. After two years of dating, they decided to get married. Ime's parents were rich enough to hire someone to do household chores.

This meant that Ime grew up not knowing how to perform most daily common household chores, including preparing meals. She exhibited timidity in public gatherings, sometimes to the chagrin of her fiancé. To her credit, she did recognize her shortcomings and decided to reinvent or reskill herself before the wedding. She read books on interpersonal relationships, marriage, family, parenting and cooking. She solicited the assistance of her mother and her fiancé's mother to teach her how to be an ideal traditional wife, which also meant sharpening her cooking skills.

Ime's intent was to undergo significant transformation in various aspects of her life, with the goal of creating a new and improved version of herself. Her mother and future mother-in-law offered her significant guidance to help improve her behavior, habits, methods of speaking and overall mindset. These pre-marital preparations helped Ime achieve and maintain a happy marital relationship with her husband, children and in-laws.

THE POWER AND NECESSITY OF SELF-REINVENTION

Reinventing ourselves means becoming a better, more refined version of who we are. It begins with introspection, a deep and honest examination of who we were, who we are now, and who we aspire to become. This reflective journey requires that we assess our values, strengths, limitations, habits, and aspirations. At the heart of this process lies self-awareness: the ability to observe our own thoughts, feelings, and behaviors, as well as how others perceive us.

This foundational skill is essential for personal growth and development.

Among immigrants, those who achieved great success, often do so because they are quick to recognize when they are on the wrong path - whether it is an unfulfilling career, an unhealthy relationship, or a stalled professional journey. They are attuned to their own progress and understand when they are not advancing fast enough to meet their ambitions. What sets them apart is their willingness to pivot. They adapt, recalibrate, and reshape their professional plans to align better with their evolving goals.

Self-reinvention does not always mean starting from scratch. Sometimes, it involves sharpening our intellectual edge or upgrading our technical skills. Other times, it means changing careers, rethinking work habits, or even transforming key aspects of our personality. What it always entails, however, is a rejection of complacency. Regardless of our current level of success, we must recognize that there is always room to grow. Today's accomplishments can be the foundation for tomorrow's greater achievements.

Ambitious, goal-oriented individuals often feel the pull toward reinvention when they realize their peers have surpassed them professionally. In such moments, we are faced with two broad choices:

1. Accept our limitations and remain in our comfort zone, or
2. Rise to the challenge, close the gap, and actively work to improve ourselves in our field.

The first option appeals to those who are contented with routine and the familiarity of the known. But the second option demands courage and effort. It means replacing old "parts" in our mental and emotional operating system - learning new skills, adapting to new tools, and embracing change. In today's fast-paced, technology-driven world, this kind of proactive reskilling is no longer optional; it is essential.

CONTINUING EDUCATION – SELF-RESKILLING & RETOOLING

This is especially true for immigrants from countries with fewer technological and economic resources. When newcomers to more advanced economies recognize the need for reinvention early, they are better positioned to find their niche, compete effectively, and secure well-paying, meaningful employment. Reinvention is not just a strategy for success - it is a survival skill in competitive global environments.

The journey begins with self-knowledge: a clear-eyed assessment of our strengths, weaknesses, and areas for improvement. As Alvin Toffler noted, *the key to thriving in the future is the ability to learn, unlearn, and relearn.*

195

Reinvention means updating our personal "software" by acquiring new capabilities, shedding outdated beliefs, and evolving into the person we aspire to be. However, this journey often requires stepping out of our comfort zone and starting anew - an intimidating prospect for many. Yet, with determination, effort, and persistence, transformation is not only possible but inevitable.

Sadly, some immigrants fail to reinvent themselves because they remain tethered to traditional values or cultural mindsets that are incompatible with their new environment. Their reluctance to adapt becomes a barrier to progress. A good example is James Ekanem, discussed above, who had the courage to leave his home country in search of better opportunities. Yet, once abroad, he clung so tightly to his old habits and ways of thinking that he failed to adapt and ultimately missed the chance to become the successful architect he had the potential to be.

True self reinvention requires accepting who we are today while making decisions based on growth rather than fear. Many people let fear or limiting beliefs guide their actions, convincing themselves they have fewer opportunities simply because they are immigrants, outsiders, or newcomers. But fear-based choices stifle potential. Growth, on the other hand, is rooted in courage, positivity, and belief in possibility.

Think of the lion that dares to hunt an elephant, or the mosquito that slips past palace guards to feed on the king's blood - both driven not by size or power, but by an unshakable willpower. Similarly, those who embrace courage and optimism can break free from limitations and reinvent themselves, no matter how daunting the path may seem.

The key to self-reinvention lies in continuously confronting our fears and anchoring ourselves in our core values. Successful individuals - immigrant or not - are those who make full use of their intellect, emotional intelligence, and determination. They do not wait for the world to change; they change themselves to meet the world.

It is important to remember that intellectual ability is not static. Left unchallenged, it diminishes over time. We must keep it sharp by surrounding ourselves with intellectually curious and inspiring people. We should read widely, attend seminars, seek mentorship, and most importantly, apply what we learn. Knowledge is most powerful when it is used.

As the elders in my Nigerian hometown often say, "*If you climb a fruit tree and are too afraid to step on the branch, you will never reach the ripest fruit*". In other words, fear holds us back from the greatest rewards in life. If you truly want to reinvent yourself, the first step is self-discovery - focusing not on what you fear, but on what you hope for and believe in.

Ironically, the best time to reinvent yourself is often when things are not going your way. Difficult circumstances force us to reassess, recalibrate, and redirect our energies. Many fear the past will repeat itself, but we are not history - we are human beings with the capacity to change, to grow, and to carve new paths forward.

Reinvention is not only possible; it is a necessary part of becoming who we are meant to be.

Principles of success #5

Real Life Story #3

I learned from my last job as a diplomat that self-protection is the best protection. The organization or country that you represent in a foreign country cannot protect you remotely.

By the same token, self-motivation is the most effective motivation. Your employer can double your end of the year bonus so that you may work harder moving forward, but the bonus alone will not motivate you. You must not only love what you do; you must also commit to improving yourself to work better daily. That is the habit of highly motivated people.

Asuquo Dankwa, one of my interviewees, said it took him 10 years to get a visa to enter the United States. "Now that I am here," he said, "absolutely nothing is impossible for me." That sounds like someone who knows why he came to the United States, not allowing himself to be held back by regrets or mistakes from the past. Be your own motivator. You have the power to do it. Do it today!

Successful immigrants are among the most highly motivated individuals in the world. Motivation - the inner force that breathes life into goals and fuels perseverance - is what drives them to overcome daunting challenges and achieve success in unfamiliar environments. I agree with Paulo Coelho that *"When we strive to become better than we are, everything around us becomes better too."* This is a powerful reminder that personal growth doesn't just transform us—it radiates outward, lifting the people, places, and possibilities in our lives.

Immigrants often leave behind the familiarity of home to pursue uncertain opportunities in foreign lands. They confront obstacles ranging from language barriers to cultural dislocation, economic hardship, and emotional strain. Yet, many rise above these challenges. What powers this rise? A unique blend of motivation, persistence, and resilience.

THE POWER OF PURPOSE AND PERSISTENCE

At its core, motivation answers a vital question: *Why do we do what we do?* For immigrants, the answer is often the pursuit of a better life - for themselves and their families. This strong sense of purpose is what sustains them when progress is slow or setbacks arise. While talent and education are valuable, it is motivation, strengthened by willpower, self-control, and discipline, that truly drives long-term success.

Motivation and habit work hand in hand. As motivational speaker Jim Rohn said, *"Motivation is what gets you started. Habit is what keeps you going."* Repetition breeds habit, and habit sustains us - even when our motivation dips. Successful immigrants understand this dynamic. They create systems and routines that reinforce their goals and push them forward.

Unlike those who abandon their dreams at the first sign of failure, successful immigrants persist. They are grounded in a mindset shaped by discipline, clarity of purpose, and an unwavering drive to improve. They understand that neither their home countries nor their new environments will hand them success; they must earn it.

A PERSONAL REFLECTION

Having spent two-thirds of my life as an immigrant, I have come to understand this reality deeply. Two forces have shaped my journey: fear and the desire to improve. The fear of stagnation, of wasted potential, coexisted with a fierce determination to grow. I have often viewed myself as a living book - studying, reflecting on what I do daily, and learning from the stories of other immigrants to discover what fuels success.

One critical insight I have gained is the value of willpower. While dreams give us vision, willpower turns that vision into action. It is what sustains motivation and transforms intention into accomplishment. Every successful immigrant I have met exhibits this trait. They do not just hope - they act consistently and deliberately.

COURAGE, DISCIPLINE, AND THE IMMIGRANT EDGE

It takes extraordinary courage to leave one's home and start over elsewhere, often without support or certainty. This bold leap requires more than bravery; it requires purpose-driven motivation. Many immigrants are further fueled by the awareness that they have been given a rare opportunity - to start anew. They honor that opportunity by going the extra mile, taking risks, and doing the hard work others may avoid.

In my own life, this motivation sparked an early ambition to become a writer. I admired authors who shaped minds and moved hearts. In secondary school, I began collecting articles, imagining one day I would write my own. That dream turned to reality when a visiting economics professor asked me to contribute an article to a book he was editing. At first I felt intimated, but summed up courage to research and write an article that was published while I was still a graduate student (Schofield, 1984). That experience ignited a lifelong habit of writing - a page a day, rain or shine.

Though life often disrupted my routine, I never abandoned it. Writing became more than a hobby; it became a reflection of my identity and motivation. Along the way, I learned that the road to success is not linear, that is, it's full of ups and downs, and setbacks, underscored by periods of slow progress. It is filled with twists and setbacks. The key lies in how we adapt and keep moving.

MOTIVATION FOR THE FUTURE

In a fast-changing world, motivation is not optional, it is essential. The challenges our forefathers faced are different from ours, and those who come after us will face even more complex ones. For today's immigrants and future generations alike, success will depend on the ability to stay motivated, adaptable, and disciplined.

Ultimately, motivation is what sets successful immigrants apart. It is the engine that powers courage, fuels action and sustains habit. It turns adversity into growth and opportunity into achievement. And it is this force - quiet, persistent, and powerful - that drives them to not only survive but thrive.

Principles of success #6

Successful immigrants are ambitious

Real Life Story #4

*In 1971, I secured a clerical job with a United
Nations (UN) organization in Brazzaville, Congo.
The salary and opportunity for professional growth
were more promising than what I had when I worked
in my country of origin, Nigeria. I took the job
and worked from April 1971 to August 1975 when
I resigned and emigrated to the United States to
further my education. My colleagues criticized my
decision and called me all kinds of names, including
ostentatious, pompous and over-ambitious.*

*In retrospect, I am inclined to think that I was
ambitious, but not over-ambitious. My colleagues
warned me that after my education, I would not
earn as much money in my home country as I had
earned as an international civil servant. But I was
not deterred. The more I was criticized, the more
I was driven to pursue a higher education. My
colleagues almost succeeded in discouraging me,
especially when I realized that I was relocating to
a foreign country without sponsorship.*

*Defying all odds, I moved to the United States,
passed through three institutions of higher education
in nine years, and eventually earned MA, JD, and
PhD degrees.*

When I returned to Nigeria, call it destiny, I secured another diplomatic status job with the UN organization that I left. The colleagues who tried to discourage me from initially leaving the organization and furthering my education were still there as "support staff." Some of them were assigned to my unit to work under my supervision. Ambition is not a dirty word.

AMBITION: THE HIDDEN ENGINE OF IMMIGRANT SUCCESS

Throughout this book, success will be examined from multiple angles - personal, professional, educational, and even spiritual. But one question underpins them all: *Can anyone truly be successful without ambition?* I strongly believe the answer is "No!"

Success is not accidental; it is intentional. It is born from a powerful internal force – *ambition* - that propels individuals toward goals with relentless energy. Ambition is the fuel that drives people to overcome adversity, take bold risks, and commit themselves to rigorous personal development. For immigrants in particular, ambition is more than just a motivating idea; it is a lifeline, a compass, and a survival tool.

THE DECISION TO EMIGRATE: AMBITION IN ACTION

I left my home country in 1975, driven by a burning desire to improve my life through education and skill enhancement. This was not a decision made lightly. It required courage, sacrifice, and, above all, ambition. I had a vision of a better future - one where I could develop personally and professionally in ways that were not possible in my native land.

That vision sustained me through the uncertainties of emigration, the cultural adjustments, and the criticisms I faced from friends and colleagues. It was not money, connections, or luck that gave me the strength to persist, it was ambition.

Ambition without action, however, is nothing more than fantasy. True ambition demands hard work, planning, and the ability to seize available opportunities. For immigrants, every step forward - whether it was learning a new language, enrolling in school, or applying for jobs - is guided by ambition and made real through persistent action.

Healthy vs. Unhealthy ambition

Ambition, like fire, can be either a source of warmth or destruction. It is crucial to distinguish between *healthy* and *unhealthy* ambition.

Healthy ambition is grounded in reality. It is the kind of drive that propels individuals to set attainable goals, build sustainable careers, and seek out personal growth without harming others. Healthy ambition inspires immigrants to study at night while working during the day, to master a new language in adulthood, or to start small businesses against daunting odds.

Unhealthy ambition, on the other hand, often stems from unrealistic expectations or comparisons with others. Applying for positions without the necessary qualifications, aiming for instant success, or ignoring ethical boundaries are all examples. Such ambition often leads to disappointment, damaged self-esteem, and wasted effort. As immigrants, it is vital to set goals that are challenging but achievable; goals that stretch us without breaking us.

AMBITION IN HISTORY: REAL-WORLD EXAMPLES

History is rich with stories of ambitious individuals who changed the world - not despite their failures, but because of them. Consider Alexander Fleming, who discovered penicillin after numerous failed attempts. His ambition did not just change his life, it saved millions. Or think of Thomas Edison, who reportedly failed over 1,000 times before successfully inventing the light bulb. Rather than seeing failure as defeat, he famously said, *"I have not failed. I've just found 10,000 ways that won't work."*

Then there is Elon Musk, born in South Africa, who emigrated first to Canada and then to the United States. His ambition led him to co-found PayPal, revolutionize transportation with Tesla, and aim for Mars with SpaceX. These ventures began as dreams - but were executed with unwavering ambition and relentless effort.

Even in the world of sports, we see ambition personified in individuals like Giannis Antetokounmpo, a Nigerian-Greek immigrant who rose from poverty in Greece to become one of the NBA's most celebrated players. His story is not just one of talent - it is a testament to ambition, sacrifice, and resilience.

THE IMMIGRANT ADVANTAGE: A UNIQUE DRIVE

Studies consistently show that immigrants often outperform native-born citizens in terms of business creation, educational attainment, and homeownership. Why? Because many immigrants arrive with an unshakable resolve to succeed. For them, failure is not a dead end but a detour.

According to the National Bureau of Economic Research (NBER), immigrants are nearly twice as likely to start a business as native-born Americans. The ambition that brought them across oceans and borders becomes the same ambition that drives innovation, job creation, and economic growth.

Even when faced with systemic challenges - language barriers, discrimination, limited social networks - immigrants often use these obstacles as motivation rather than deterrents. Their ambition does not waver; it intensifies.

AMBITION AS A MORAL IMPERATIVE

Ambition is not merely a personal trait; it is a moral imperative. Steven Pressfield writes, *"Ambition, I have come to believe, is the most primal and sacred fundament of our being... Not to act upon that ambition is to turn our backs on ourselves and on the reason for our existence."* This profound statement resonates deeply with the immigrant journey.

Ambition is what wakes us up early and keeps us up late. It is what pushes us to take night classes, save relentlessly, and resist the temptation to settle for mediocrity. It is what drives us to create better lives for our children. It is not selfish, it is purposeful.

Ambition, in its healthiest form, leads to service. The most successful immigrants often give back: they mentor, they hire, they advocate, and they inspire others to believe in their own potential.

FAILURE, RESILIENCE, AND GROWTH

Failure is not the opposite of success; it is part of the process. Every successful immigrant has encountered failure.

What sets them apart is their refusal to allow failure to define them. As Winston Churchill (or perhaps someone else) once said: "Success is not final, failure is not fatal: it is the courage to continue that counts."

Resilience, fueled by ambition, turns setbacks into setups for comebacks. Each failed job interview teaches a lesson. Each rejection refines a strategy. Over time, this process leads not only to personal growth but to professional breakthroughs.

CONCLUSION: THE IMMIGRANT'S COMPASS

Ambition is the immigrant's hidden compass. It guides their thoughts, decisions, and actions in unfamiliar territory. It helps them rise above economic hardship, language challenges, and cultural isolation. Without ambition, their journey would lose direction; with it, they are capable of incredible transformation.

As you read this concluding section, ponder on Steve Maraboli's aphorism: *"You were put on this earth to achieve your greatest self, to live out your purpose, and to do it courageously."* Do you agree? Ambition is the courage to pursue that purpose, no matter the odds.

To be successful, whether you are an immigrant or not, you must be relentlessly ambitious. Success is not handed out; it is earned. It is found at the intersection of hard work, persistence, and inspired ambition.

Let ambition be your guide. Not the loud, boastful kind, but the quiet, resolute kind that works diligently in the background, pushing you forward, even when the world says you cannot.

PRINCIPLES OF SUCCESS #7

SUCCESSFUL IMMIGRANTS ARE OPTIMISTIC

Real Life Story #5

Adama Daniel grew up watching his parents verbally and physically fighting about almost everything. The instability in the family affected him and his sibling. Adama attributed this problem to poverty, particularly scarcity of staple food items and lack of money to pay for other essential items such as school fees and clothing. He loved his parents and hated seeing them quarrel all the time.

Adama knew his father would not have money to support him in the university. After his secondary school education, he migrated to a neighboring country, rented a shop, and started wholesale business. He was optimistic that if he worked hard in his wholesale business, the future would be better. He also aspired to return to school for higher education after his business had become profitable.

Adama set himself in motion despite obstacles. He spent five years "grooming" his business, establishing contacts with suppliers and surrounding himself with hardworking youths. In sum, Adama did not like his life as it was; therefore, he tried to make it a little better through entrepreneurship.

He was successful in terms of financial returns in his business, which led him to return to school to further his education. He sent money to his parents regularly and constantly thanked them for seeing him through secondary school.

Adama's determination is worthy of emulation by other immigrants. As Helen Keller once said, "The true test of a character is to face hard conditions with the determination to make them better."[11]

OPTIMISM: THE QUIET STRENGTH BEHIND IMMIGRANT SUCCESS

Optimism is more than mere positive thinking—it's a powerful mindset rooted in hope, resilience, and a steadfast belief in a better future. It's the inner assurance that, no matter the obstacles or uncertainties, things will ultimately work out for the best. For immigrants, optimism isn't just helpful—it's essential. Uprooting one's life, leaving behind the familiar, and beginning again in an unfamiliar land demands a deep belief in the possibility of growth and transformation. That belief, fueled by optimism, often becomes their most valuable asset. As Helen Keller wisely said, "Optimism is the faith that leads to achievement. Nothing can be done without hope and confidence." For immigrants, these words couldn't be more true.

THE IMMIGRANT'S LEAP OF FAITH

The decision to emigrate is a profound act of faith - faith in a better future, in unseen opportunities, and in one's capacity to adapt and thrive.

---

11 "Helen Keller Quotes on Optimism...," The American Foundation for the Blind, accessed April 17, 2025, https://afb.org/about-afb/history/helen-keller/helen-keller-quotes/helen-keller-quotes-optimism.

People do not leave their homeland to chase illusions; they leave because they believe something better awaits them. This belief, often unshakable even in the face of adversity, reflects optimism in its purest form.

No immigrant can afford to make such a life-altering decision unless they are optimistic. Why would anyone take such a significant risk, invest resources, and endure the hardship of cultural adjustment if they had no faith in the outcome? Optimism is the invisible suitcase many immigrants carry with them - one that contains hope, determination, and a vision for the future.

THE IMMIGRANT'S LEAP OF FAITH

Optimists are not blind to hardship. Instead, they see challenges as part of the journey. Successful immigrants do not deny the difficulties of life in a new country - language barriers, credential recognition issues, racism, or employment discrimination. But they frame these difficulties as temporary setbacks, not permanent states. Even the most miserable day holds, for them, the promise of a better tomorrow.

For example, many refugees and asylum seekers arrive in host countries with little to nothing, yet many go on to become business owners, professionals, or community leaders. The Somali-American community in Minnesota, the Vietnamese diaspora in California, and the Iranian diaspora in Canada all demonstrate what happens when optimism meets opportunity.

These stories are a testament to what psychologists call *"learned optimism,"* a term coined by Dr. Martin Seligman. It refers to the ability to train the mind to view challenges as changeable and solvable.

Immigrants who succeed tend to adopt this mindset either consciously or through cultural and familial socialization.

A LESSON IN OPTIMISM: THE 2008 OBAMA ELECTION

A personal story highlights this dynamic. In 2008, as Barack Obama campaigned for the presidency, I observed two groups of college students divided in their belief about his chances to win the election. One group, the optimists, believed firmly that Obama could win despite centuries of racial oppression and discrimination against African Americans. The other group, the pessimists, doubted America's readiness to elect a Black president.

Both groups wanted Obama to win, but only one believed it was truly possible. And when he did win, many pessimists were shocked, even regretful that they had not supported him more actively. Some admitted that they had not voted at all, thinking it would be a waste of time. This hesitancy is emblematic of how pessimism can paralyze action, while optimism fuels participation, engagement, and change.

OPTIMISM VS. PESSIMISM:
A PSYCHOLOGICAL PERSPECTIVE

Winston Churchill once said, "*A pessimist sees the difficulty in every opportunity; an optimist sees the opportunity in every difficulty.*" This quote elegantly distinguishes the two mindsets. Optimists do not deny problems - they recognize them but also believe they are surmountable. Pessimists, on the other hand, often perceive barriers as permanent, and their lack of confidence leads them to withdraw from life's challenges.

From a psychological standpoint, excessive pessimism is associated with learned helplessness, a state where individuals feel their actions have no impact. Immigrants who fall into this mindset often struggle to progress. They become overwhelmed by systemic challenges or setbacks and may blame external circumstances - real or imagined - without taking proactive steps to improve their situation.

By contrast, research shows that optimistic people have better physical health, lower levels of stress, greater persistence in goal attainment, and more satisfying social relationships. These are all critical elements for immigrant success.

THE DALAI LAMA AND THE
BALANCED VIEW OF OPTIMISM

The 14th Dalai Lama (not the 54th, for clarity) offers a nuanced view: *"Optimism doesn't mean that you are blind to the reality of the situation. It means that you remain motivated to seek a solution to whatever problems arise."* This perspective is crucial. Blind optimism can lead to unrealistic expectations and disappointment, just as chronic pessimism can lead to paralysis and defeatism. The goal is not to deny reality, but to maintain faith in one's ability to shape it.

Immigrants must balance hope with strategy. An overly optimistic individual who refuses to plan, acquire new skills, or adapt culturally, may find themselves disillusioned. Conversely, the immigrant who sees hardship as inevitable and insurmountable will fail to capitalize on the very opportunities that motivated their journey.

SOCIAL NETWORKS:
THE OPTIMISM FEEDBACK LOOP

Social environments play a vital role in shaping optimistic or pessimistic outlooks. Immigrants who surround themselves with positive, forward-looking individuals are more likely to adopt similar mindsets. They benefit from encouragement, practical support, and shared success stories.

On the other hand, pessimistic networks tend to reinforce negative thinking. Immigrants who dwell in circles of cynicism - where conversations are dominated by complaints and hopelessness - often internalize those sentiments. They may begin to view their new environment as hostile, success as unattainable, and failure as inevitable.

Thus, immigrants must be intentional in choosing their social networks, mentors, and role models. Optimism, like pessimism, can be contagious.

Closing Thoughts:
Cultivating an optimistic immigrant mindset

We are all, at different times, both optimists and pessimists. Mood, circumstances, and even biology influence our outlook. But we can make a conscious decision to cultivate optimism as a tool for growth.

My advice to immigrants is simple but profound: choose optimism, even when it is difficult. Discard regret, self-doubt, and negative self-talk. Focus on your progress, however modest it may seem. Celebrate every milestone. Remind yourself that the journey is long but meaningful.

Optimism is not about ignoring reality. It is about seeing reality and choosing to believe that with time, effort, and persistence, you can improve it. It is about betting on yourself, even when the odds seem steep.

Success as an immigrant is rarely a straight line.

It is a series of hills and valleys, victories and setbacks. But if you carry optimism with you - quietly and consistently - you will find that each valley is followed by a climb upward, and each small win leads to a larger triumph.

Principle of success #8

Successful immigrants are time conscious

Real Life Story #6

Ada Chukuma, a middle level civil servant, was not time conscious in her country of origin. Apparently, being time conscious was not part of the culture of her home country. She was accustomed to arriving at her office late and leaving before closing time. She did not have to explain to anyone why she was coming to the office late. After years of going late to the office, it became a habit, which she carried into other aspects of her everyday life.

As the saying goes, "Nothing is permanent." She now resides in one of the Global North countries where punctuality is valued. However, she has not stopped going to work late and has subsequently been fired twice for her habitual lateness. She has also lost income as a result of not clocking in on time at the workplace.

Time is arguably the most valuable, yet most fragile resource we possess. It cannot be paused, saved for later date, or recovered once lost. For immigrants - individuals who have taken bold steps to restart life in a new land - mastery of time is not optional; it is vital. Time consciousness is not simply about punctuality; it is a mindset, a discipline, and a skill that separates successful immigrants from those who struggle unnecessarily in their host countries.

THINK LIKE AN IMMIGRANT

Renowned psychiatrist, Dr. M. Scott Peck, once said, *"Until you value yourself, you will not value your time. Until you value your time, you will not do anything with it."* This truth resonates deeply within immigrant communities. Immigrants who succeed tend to see time as a non-renewable asset, guarding it fiercely and spending it with intention and clarity. Every person, regardless of nationality, social status, or economic condition, has access to 24 hours, 1,440 minutes and 86,400 seconds each day. The difference lies in how each individual uses this fixed deposit of time.

THE STRATEGIC USE OF TIME: A HALLMARK OF SUCCESS

Immigrants who flourish in their host countries understand that time is not just money - it is life itself. They prioritize their goals, plan their days with precision, and eliminate distractions. Take, for example, Indra Nooyi, the Indian-born former CEO of PepsiCo, who emigrated to the United States and rose to become one of the most powerful women in global business. Nooyi was known for her rigorous time management skills - balancing her roles as a mother, student, and executive through meticulous planning and self-discipline.

Similarly, Elon Musk, though often associated with innovation and risk-taking, is also an immigrant (born in South Africa) whose approach to time is legendary. He splits his week into five-minute blocks, demonstrating the extraordinary degree of control he exerts over his schedule. Musk's time discipline is not coincidental - it is foundational to his success.

TIME MANAGEMENT IS A TRANSFERABLE SKILL - CULTURE IS NOT

One of the most common pitfalls immigrants face, especially those from parts of the Global South, is importing cultural habits that are incompatible with the time-sensitive, results-driven ethos of their new countries of residence. A glaring example of this is the notion of "African time," which refers to a flexible, and often mindless, approach to timekeeping. While it may be socially accepted in some home cultures, this attitude can be catastrophic in Western societies where punctuality is not only expected but deeply respected.

I recall an instance while representing the World Health Organization at a high-level meeting involving UN agencies and an African head of state. The head of state arrived nearly two hours late and casually remarked, *"Un petit retard à un rendez-vous, c'est ne pas trop mal."* Translated, *"A little lateness to a meeting is acceptable."* The comment, meant to minimize the delay, deeply offended several Western diplomats, and undermined the credibility of the delegation. Unfortunately, this incident illustrates a common attitude that many immigrants unwittingly carry with them.

In highly structured societies like the United States, Germany, or Japan, being late to a job interview, medical appointment, or business meeting is not interpreted as casual - it is perceived as disrespectful, irresponsibility, and unprofessional. Immigrants must understand that adaptation means more than just learning a new language or cuisine - it includes abandoning cultural practices that hinder integration and success.

REAL-LIFE EXAMPLE: UBER AND THE
ECONOMICS OF TIME

Consider my neighbor, Nicole Alfred, a Haitian immigrant and Uber driver. Nicole begins her day at 6:00 AM and works until she has earned $200 in net income, often by early afternoon. She could drive more, but she sets a clear financial goal tied to her available time. Unlike others who spend unstructured hours hoping for random returns, Nicole's strategy is driven by discipline and planning. She exemplifies the maxim that time is money, but only if used wisely.

Her story underscores a key point: immigrants who treat time as a commodity can structure their lives for both financial gain and personal fulfillment. Those who squander time - through excessive phone calls, endless social media browsing, gossip, or procrastination - often find themselves merely surviving rather than thriving.

TIME MANAGEMENT IS A SKILL, NOT A GIFT

Good time managers are not born, they are made. Immigrants who succeed often develop this skill through trial, error, and eventually, deliberate practice. Effective time management involves:

- Setting clear priorities (e.g., work, education, family)
- Creating daily routines and schedules
- Eliminating distractions, for example:
  - *Chatty workplace*: can interrupt focus on the job and lead to missed deadlines.
  - *Communication overload*: dealing with personal and unofficial emails and messages can fragment the attention of workers, thus

delaying execution of essential tasks
- *Social media*: obsession with the Internet and social media can divert workers' attention from performing important tasks.

- *Procrastination*: this is the disease suffered by many workers. Delaying completion of tasks often leads to longer work hours and missed deadlines.
- Delegating or outsourcing non-essential tasks
- Regular self-evaluation

By identifying and addressing these distractions, individuals can improve their time management skills and overall productivity. Workers, native-born and immigrants alike, are advised to think about these guidelines not as habits of convenience, but as strategies for survival and upward mobility in competitive societies. As the management expert Peter Drucker wisely said, "Time is the scarcest resource and unless it is managed, nothing else can be managed." Immigrants who understand this quickly learn that success depends not only on hard work but on smart time allocation.

FAILURE TO MANAGE TIME COULD LEAD TO FAILURE IN LIFE

The stakes of poor time management are high. Missing an interview, showing up late for work, or failing to meet a deadline can mean losing a job, damaging your reputation, or even facing deportation in extreme cases. Excuses such as "Sorry, I was on African time," are not just ineffective - they are insulting, if not harmful. Employers, clients, and institutions in host countries have little patience for cultural explanations of tardiness.

Moreover, immigrants who fail to adjust their attitudes toward time often end up clustering with others who share the same mindset - creating feedback loops of mediocrity, stagnation, and mutual excuses. These networks tend to reinforce complacency rather than challenge one another toward excellence.

TIME: A "CURRENCY" THAT CANNOT BE SAVED OR RECYCLED

While money can be earned, borrowed, or inherited, time cannot. Each of us receives 24 hours per day - no more, no less. The world's richest person cannot buy a second more than a street vendor in Lagos or a student in Montreal. The late poet Carl Sandburg puts it best:

> *"Time is the coin of your life. It is the only coin you have, and only you can determine how it will be spent. Be careful lest you let other people spend it for you."*

Unlike money, which fluctuates in value and is unequally distributed, time is universal. And yet, its value depends entirely on how we use it. As such, immigrants must see time not just as a calendar unit, but as a moral and economic obligation.

FINAL ADVICE FOR IMMIGRANTS

To every immigrant, particularly those arriving from cultures where time is loosely interpreted: Do not import attitudes that conflict with the value systems of your host country. When it comes to time, leave your old habits at the border. Adopt the time discipline of your new society. It may seem rigid at first, but it is one of the fastest routes to trust, respect, and success.

Avoid the indecisiveness that leads to wasted hours.

Avoid blaming external forces for your lateness or procrastination. Take responsibility for your schedule, your goals, and your life. Whether you are applying for a job, running a business, or attending school, your respect for time will always be one of your greatest assets.

In the end, success is not accidental. It is the byproduct of intentional living, of making every minute count, and of aligning your time with your priorities. Immigrants who understand this will not only survive - they will excel.

PRINCIPLES OF SUCCESS #9

SUCCESSFUL IMMIGRANTS HAVE POSITIVE ATTITUDES

Real Life Story #7

Dr. Gibson Johner graduated from a top medical school in the United States with a specialization in surgery. He aspired to work in a well-equipped hospital located in a diverse, multiethnic city. However, his expectations were not met. Instead, he was assigned to a small-town hospital serving a population of just two thousand people. Unofficially, he learned that this decision was influenced by his immigrant status. As part of his H-1B visa agreement, he had committed to serve wherever he was needed.

Initially disappointed, Dr. Johner felt that the posting did not offer an environment where he could fully realize his potential. Still, he adopted a positive mindset, reasoning that "a bird in the hand is worth two in the bush." Determined to make the most of the situation, he committed himself to working collaboratively with the hospital staff to transform the small facility into a center of excellence.

Thanks to his skill, dedication, and positive attitude, words of Dr. Johner's surgical success quickly spread beyond the local community to neighboring counties. Within five years, the rural hospital expanded to meet the growing demand from patients both near and far. Dr. Johner's reputation flourished, and he came to view what once seemed like a setback as a hidden opportunity.

His story is a powerful testament to the truth of Pastor Charles Swindoll's words: "Life is 10% what happens to you and 90% how you react to it".

THE POWER OF POSITIVE ATTITUDE
AMONG SUCCESSFUL IMMIGRANTS

One of the defining traits of successful immigrants is a consistently positive attitude. These individuals exhibit optimism, resilience, and a deep sense of gratitude. They believe in their own potential and maintain confidence in their ability to succeed, even in unfamiliar environments. As author Walter John once wisely stated, "For success, attitude is equally as important as ability." This maxim highlights a profound truth: while skills and knowledge are crucial, our disposition toward life and its challenges often determines the trajectory of our success.

Though the link between attitude and ability may not be immediately evident, the reality is that our mindset directly influences how we communicate, collaborate, and contribute - whether in a new cultural setting, a workplace, or within a broader community. Our attitude shapes how we tackle everyday responsibilities and respond to both adversity and opportunity. In essence, attitude is the silent architect of success, failure, and personal fulfillment.

Consider the example of Gibson Johner, a healthcare professional who dreamt of working in a state-of-the-art urban hospital. When circumstances placed him instead in a rural setting, he could have easily succumbed to disappointment. Yet, with a grateful heart and a positive mindset, he embraced the new environment. That experience not only deepened his professional skills but also laid the foundation for a more fulfilling career. This case illustrates how perspective - not just circumstance - drives growth.

RESPONDING TO LIFE'S CHALLENGES WITH POSITIVITY

Life is inherently unpredictable. It presents a constant flux of highs and lows, triumphs and setbacks. A positive attitude allows us to transcend limitations and maintain hope when things do not go as planned. In my personal experience, I have learned to respond to disappointment not with regret, but with reflection. I accept setbacks as a natural part of life's journey, learning from my mistakes and looking ahead with renewed energy. This approach has helped me remain resilient and proactive rather than bitter or defeated.

WINNING ATTITUDE

A winning attitude does not ignore failure; it learns from it. It resists the pull of self-pity and pessimism and embraces growth. While negativity tends to stifle creativity and hope, a positive outlook nurtures the courage to persevere. However, attitude alone is not enough. It must be coupled with action. We must take conscious steps to correct unproductive behaviors and make choices that lead to growth and progress. Many personal and professional frustrations stem from inappropriate behavior patterns, and by choosing constructive responses, we can break the cycle of defeat.

CULTIVATING RESILIENCE IN A NEW ENVIRONMENT

Immigrants often face circumstances beyond their control: language barriers, cultural adjustments, discrimination, or economic hardships. Some individuals remain stuck in these difficulties, allowing them to define their experience. Others, however, rise, fueled by resilience, a sense of purpose, and a belief in better days ahead.

It is easy to become discouraged in the face of failure. But one effective strategy to combat this is to study and emulate those who have succeeded under similar conditions. Successful immigrants often share common habits, e.g., they invest in self-development, build strong support systems, stay open to learning, and, most importantly, maintain an unwaveringly positive outlook.

A positive attitude fosters adaptability and builds emotional resilience. It helps immigrants navigate new systems with hope rather than fear and motivates them to pursue their goals with determination. It also encourages community building, which is vital in unfamiliar environments.

SELF-WORTH, HAPPINESS, AND THE ENERGY WE PROJECT

Positive people tend to be not only more successful but also contented with what they have. Their sense of happiness is internally generated rather than dependent on external circumstances. This internal positivity enhances self-worth, reinforces motivation, and fosters meaningful relationships. Immigrants who cultivate a healthy self-image are more likely to contribute positively to society, collaborate effectively with others, and serve as role models within their communities.

This call to action is a reminder that attitude is not passive, it is a deliberate choice backed by action and intention.

THE IMPACT OF MINDSET ON SOCIAL INTEGRATION AND PROGRESS

Media personality, Oprah Winfrey, once remarked, *"The greatest discovery of all time is that a person can change their future by merely changing their attitude."* This insight is especially meaningful for immigrants seeking to carve a new path. A positive mindset helps newcomers adapt more readily to their host country, overcome cultural barriers, and find purpose even amid initial setbacks.

Too often, some immigrants fall into the trap of the "three C's" - comparing, complaining, and criticizing. Disappointed by the pace of progress, they may externalize blame and adopt a victim mentality. This approach not only hinders personal growth but also leads to poor decision-making and disconnection from their new environment. A more empowering approach is to focus on the "bird in hand" - what one already possesses - and to build upon it with hope and initiative.

LESSONS FROM ROLE MODELS AND POP CULTURE

Even in unexpected places, such as professional wrestling, we can find valuable life lessons. The WWE trio known as "The New Day" - Kofi Kingston, Xavier Woods, and Big E - champion the "Power of Positivity." Their mindset teaches that resilience, sportsmanship, and a refusal to succumb to envy or defeat are essential ingredients for success. Whether they win or lose, they maintain a healthy attitude and take responsibility for their performance. This is a useful metaphor for immigrants and anyone striving to thrive in a competitive environment.

THE VALUE OF CONSTRUCTIVE THINKING

Constructive thinking focuses on solutions and inner strength rather than external limitations. It frees us from the trap of comparison and fosters humility and appreciation for diversity. Through positive thinking, we become more aware of our strengths and open to learning from others. Rather than resisting failure or criticism, we learn to use them as tools for self-improvement.

It is also important to note that positivity does not guarantee universal acceptance or rewards. Others may attempt to impose their expectations or values on you. In such moments, hold fast to your identity and personal vision. Your goal should not be to become what others want you to be, but to realize the best version of yourself.

CONCLUSION: CHOOSE THE PATH OF POSITIVITY

In summary, attitude is a powerful determinant of how immigrants - and indeed, all individuals - navigate the challenges and opportunities of life. A positive attitude promotes personal development, fosters resilience, improves relationships, and fuels the journey toward long-term success. As Israelmore Ayivor aptly puts it:

> *"Nothing good stands without the right attitude. You may know how to do it, but if the attitude is negative, all you can say is 'I could have done it.'"*

Let us then choose to live with the power of positivity. Let us focus on what is possible, rather than what is missing. In doing so, we not only empower ourselves but inspire others to rise above adversity and strive for their highest potential.

The final takeaway is a quote attributed to Ernest Agyemang Yeboah:

> *If you think the world is full of darkness, let us see your light. If you think the world is full of wickedness, let us see your goodness. If you think people are acting wrongly, let us see your right action. If you think people don't know, let us see what you know. If you think the world is full of uncaring people let us see how you care about people. If you think life is not being fair to you, let us see how you can be fair to life. If you think people are proud, let us see your humility. We can easily find fault and we can easily see what is wrong, but a positive attitude backed by a right action in a true direction is all we need to survive in peace and harmony in the arena of life.*[12]

Life is unpredictable, full of unexpected twists and turns that can catch us off guard at any moment. We cannot always control what happens to us—be it challenges, failures, or sudden changes—but we can control how we respond. That is why it's essential to be armed with a positive attitude. A positive mindset helps us stay resilient in difficult times, find solutions instead of dwelling on problems, and maintain hope when the future is uncertain. It doesn't mean ignoring reality, but rather choosing to face it with strength, optimism, and the belief that better days are always possible.

---

12 "Ernest Agyemang Yeboah Quotes," Goodreads, accessed April 26, 2025, https://www.goodreads.com/quotes/7725669-if-you-think-the-world-is-full-of-darkness-let.

Principle of success #10

Successful immigrants are agents of change

Real Life Story #8

Ubong Elijah emigrated to the United Kingdom in 2005 to pursue higher education. His intention was to return to his country of origin after his education. He was from a country blessed with crude oil deposits and planned to return to use his acquired skills to serve his country. After graduating with an MSc in petroleum engineering, other immigrants and classmates pressured him to remain in the UK to work. His income would be much higher than what he would earn if he returned to his home country. Ubong settled down, got married, and then sought and obtained residency in the UK.

He joined an association made up of members of his ethnicity, which met once a month to discuss how they could help each other in a foreign country. At these meetings, he found out that many immigrants, despite their education, could not find jobs and, therefore, could not afford three meals a day in the UK, the island nation that colonized and exploited the resources of their home country for centuries. He vowed to work to change the situation. His compatriots mocked him and wondered how he was going to change the situation.

He established a non-profit organization, mobilizing both immigrants and citizens to work together to serve those in need in their community. He obtained funding from philanthropists and local council authorities.

Within two years of operating his non-profit organization, Ubong ran and got elected to represent the county in his Borough. His social and political activism brought him closer to major political leaders and business owners. With his influence and support, many hardworking immigrants were able to secure funding to start businesses. His influence also reduced unemployment rate and discrimination in his community

IMMIGRANTS AS CATALYSTS FOR SOCIO-ECONOMIC VIBRANCY AND POLICY REFORM

Immigration has always been more than just a demographic phenomenon; it is a powerful force for economic development, cultural transformation, and social innovation. Immigrants not only seek to improve their own lives and those of their families but often become key players in revitalizing communities, initiating grassroots change, and influencing public policy in profound ways.

This essay explores how immigrants, through active engagement in socio-economic life, become change agents in their host societies. We analyze this from public policy, psychological, and educational perspectives, focusing on how immigrants drive transformation, advocate for inclusive policies, and shape vibrant and resilient communities.

IMMIGRANTS AND SOCIO-ECONOMIC RENEWAL, ENTREPRENEURSHIP AND ECONOMIC GROWTH

One of the most visible and quantifiable ways immigrants contribute to their new communities is through entrepreneurship. In cities like Dayton, Ohio, and Buffalo, New York, immigrant business owners have been instrumental in revitalizing once-declining neighborhoods. In Buffalo's West Side Bazaar, immigrants from Burma, Ethiopia, Peru, and Sudan have started restaurants, boutiques, and service centers - bringing life to previously abandoned commercial areas. These businesses not only meet local demands but also create jobs, generate tax revenues, and attract cultural tourism.

According to a 2023 report from the Connecticut Institute for Refugees and Immigrants, immigrants account for about 20% of the state's workforce and nearly 25% of all business owners - despite making up just 15% of the total population. Their combined economic contribution amounts to over $1.6 billion annually. Across the United States, similar patterns emerge: immigrants are twice as likely as native-born citizens to start a business, helping to fuel economic dynamism and job creation.

FILLING LABOR GAPS IN CRITICAL SECTORS

Immigrants are vital in sustaining essential sectors such as healthcare, agriculture, construction, and technology. In many urban centers, immigrant nurses, doctors, and aides form the backbone of the healthcare system. In rural towns, immigrants are helping sustain farms and meatpacking plants that would otherwise face labor shortages.

Their presence ensures the continued functioning of essential services and supports food security and public health.

Moreover, their educational backgrounds - particularly among refugees and high-skilled immigrants - add value to STEM fields. Immigrants are often overrepresented in graduate programs and innovation-driven industries, contributing significantly to scientific research, technology development, and education.

PSYCHOLOGICAL PERSPECTIVE: IMMIGRANTS AS RESILIENT CHANGE MAKERS: FROM ADAPTATION TO EMPOWERMENT

Immigration requires immense psychological resilience. Navigating new languages, legal systems, and cultural expectations can be overwhelming. Yet, those who succeed often do so by developing a strong sense of self-efficacy. This internal belief that one can influence outcomes becomes a powerful engine for social participation and leadership.

Psychologists define "psychological empowerment" as the process by which individuals gain control over their lives and a critical understanding of their environment. Empowered immigrants are more likely to participate in civic life, mentor others, and contribute to collective goals. This empowerment is often expressed through community organizing, participation in local governance, and volunteerism.

ROLE MODELING AND INTERGENERATIONAL TRANSFORMATION

The psychological journey of the immigrant does not end with survival or success.

Many successful immigrants intentionally serve as role models within their communities. They motivate others, especially younger generations, to believe in their potential, to persevere through hardship, and to engage constructively in society.

The story of Ubong Elijah, who began his professional career in a rural hospital instead of the urban center he had hoped for, is a powerful illustration. Rather than viewing the rural placement as a setback, he embraced it with humility and optimism. Over time, he became a community leader and a changed agent, transforming local healthcare services while developing a reputation for compassion and competence. His psychological resilience translated into systemic change.

EDUCATIONAL CONTRIBUTIONS AND TRANSFORMATION
CULTURALLY RESPONSIVE EDUCATION

In schools across America, immigrant students bring linguistic diversity, cultural richness, and global perspectives. However, without the right educational frameworks, these assets may be underutilized or even stigmatized. Culturally responsive teaching - pedagogical approaches that affirm students' backgrounds while promoting academic excellence - has proven effective in engaging immigrant learners.

Teachers like Keishia Thorpe, a National Teacher of the Year recipient, have been lauded for their work with immigrant and refugee students. Thorpe's educational model emphasizes belonging, identity affirmation, and rigorous standards. Her students not only achieve high academic results but also develop strong leadership skills that they carry into broader society.

EDUCATION AS A PLATFORM FOR CIVIC ENGAGEMENT

For many immigrants, education becomes the foundation for broader community involvement. Schools often serve as community hubs where parents network, share resources, and begin their civic journeys. Through Parent-Teacher-Associations (PTAs), school board involvement, or adult English as a second language (ESL) classes, immigrants start engaging with local institutions, fostering democratic participation and social cohesion.

IMMIGRANTS INFLUENCING PUBLIC POLICY: GRASSROOTS ADVOCACY AND POLICY CHANGE

Immigrants are not passive beneficiaries of policy; they are increasingly shaping it. Organizations like CASA de Maryland (a Latino and immigration advocacy-and-assistance organization based in Maryland), Pilsen Neighbors Community Council, and RAICES (in Texas) advocate for policies affecting immigrant communities, from language access to housing rights and education.

CASA de Maryland led a successful campaign to implement a statewide law requiring reasonable access to government services for individuals with limited English proficiency. This kind of advocacy transforms lived experiences into policy wins, demonstrating that immigrants can shape systems to be more equitable and inclusive.

In Chicago, the Pilsen Neighbors Community Council has used civic organizing to improve public services, secure educational investments, and influence local political agendas. Immigrant-led movements in Illinois have helped pass driver's licenses for undocumented residents, tuition equity laws, and sanctuary policies.

POLITICAL REPRESENTATION AND SYSTEMIC INCLUSION

Immigrant participation is also evident in rising numbers of immigrant-origin leaders in public offices. From school board members to state legislators, these leaders bring unique perspectives that broaden policy discourse. In places like Minnesota, cities with large East African immigrant populations are electing Somali Americans to local office. Their advocacy has pushed issues like housing, police reform, and language access into the mainstream.

SOCIAL INTEGRATION AND COMMUNITY REVITALIZATION: CREATING WELCOMING, INCLUSIVE SPACES

Immigrants often take the lead in creating spaces that celebrate diversity and inclusivity. From cultural festivals and public art installations to community centers and food cooperatives, immigrant-driven initiatives foster social cohesion.

In Philadelphia, public art projects like "Love and Liberation" use murals to honor immigrant stories and reclaim public space for celebration and dialogue. These efforts not only beautify the urban landscape but also challenge anti-immigrant narratives and promote intercultural understanding.

In New York, the Queens Night Market, run largely by immigrants, draws thousands weekly to sample international cuisine, art, and music.

Such events do more than entertain, boost local economies, connect people across cultures, and stimulate civic pride.

FAITH-BASED AND VOLUNTEER NETWORKS

Many immigrants build or join faith-based networks that offer not only spiritual support but also community services such as childcare, health clinics, and legal aid. These networks are especially crucial during crises, as seen during the COVID-19 pandemic, where immigrant-led groups mobilized rapidly to deliver food, PPE, and information in multiple languages.

By fostering a culture of mutual aid and social responsibility, immigrants lay the groundwork for healthier, more equitable communities.

OVERCOMING CHALLENGES: THE ROLE OF AGENCY AND VISION: FROM VICTIMHOOD TO AGENCY

The choice between being a victim of change or an agent of change is central to the immigrant experience. While some immigrants fall into despair or resentment, others make a conscious decision to adapt, lead, and uplift. This shift in mindset, from surviving to thriving, is where transformation begins.

Success stories often begin with personal discipline and resilience, but they blossom through collaboration, vision, and mentorship. Asking the right questions, e.g., "What can I contribute?" "Who can I work with?" "How do I build something lasting?" is key to becoming an effective agent of change.

FAITH, VALUES, AND INTEGRITY

As change agents, immigrants must also draw on deep moral resources. Whether rooted in religious faith, cultural traditions, or humanistic ethics, values such as honesty, gratitude, and empathy serve as moral compasses in navigating unfamiliar terrains. These values enable immigrants to model constructive behavior, reject victimhood, and inspire others.

CONCLUSION: A BLUEPRINT FOR FUTURE POLICY AND COMMUNITY DEVELOPMENT

Immigrants are not merely individuals adapting to a new land - they are essential architects of that land's future. Through entrepreneurial vigor, civic engagement, educational contributions, and moral leadership, they build bridges between past and future, self and society, local and global.

For public institutions, the message is clear: policies that integrate, support, and empower immigrants are investments in societal resilience and innovation. Cities and states that embrace immigrant talent, value diversity, and prioritize inclusion will be better equipped to face the challenges of the 21st century.

For immigrants themselves, the call is equally clear: step into the arena - not just to change your life, but to transform your world. Successful immigrants not only strive to improve themselves and the lives of their family members, but they also act as catalysts for change by participating in community development initiatives. You become an agent of change the moment you decide to do something to improve your lifestyle and inspire and influence others positively.

For most immigrants, the choice is between being an agent of change or a victim of change. If you choose the former, you must be prepared to channel all your energies, as Ubong Elijah did, towards building the new world you want to live in and not wasting your energy fighting the old world. Playwright George Bernard Shaw has said that *"Progress is impossible without change, and those who cannot change their minds cannot change anything."*[13] Therefore, no matter how difficult change may be, change is necessary for our growth.

---

13 "George Bernard Shaw Quotes," Brainy Quote, accessed April 28, 2025, https://www.brainyquote.com/quotes/george_bernard_shaw_386923.

PRINCIPLE OF SUCCESS #11

SUCCESSFUL IMMIGRANTS HAVE EMOTIONAL INTELLIGENCE SKILLS

Real Life Story #9

Branda Lopez is the headmistress of a private day school in a city comprising many racial groups. Parents - white, black, and Latino - in the city scramble to enroll their children in this school. Many parents refer to Branda Lopez, not as the headmistress, but as "the Latina."

Ms. Lopez is consistently under pressure by parents who are not Latino. This is because some of these parents accuse her of giving preference to Latino children in the admission process. There are no facts to corroborate this accusation even though Latino students constitute the highest number of students enrolled in the school. Ms. Lopez remains nonchalant as parents keep accusing her of favoritism and discrimination.

For the most part, conflicts between parents and the headmistress are emotionally driven. Parents wishing the best for their children allow emotions to overcome their sense of reasoning. They fail to recognize that white, black and brown children have equal rights to attend the school and Ms. Lopez has no control over the number of students admitted from various racial and ethnic groups.

THINK LIKE AN IMMIGRANT

On her part, the headmistress should have paid more attention to concerns expressed by parents seeking admission for their children.

Eventually, parents took the matter to the School Board, which determined that Ms. Lopez was not guilty of discriminatory practices in the admission process. The problem, however, escalated because Ms. Lopez lacked the emotional intelligence (EI) skills required to deal with the parents' complaints. Emotional intelligence is the ability to manage your own emotions while making the effort to understand the emotions of people around you. It involves self-awareness, self-regulation, motivation, empathy and social skills.

EMOTIONAL INTELLIGENCE: A KEY TO IMMIGRANT SUCCESS

Migration is one of the most courageous and life-altering decisions a person can make. Leaving behind the familiar environment in search of better opportunities, safety, or freedom is never easy. Immigrants often face a complex array of challenges - linguistic, cultural, economic, psychological, and social. To overcome these hurdles and build a fulfilling life in a new country, technical skills and academic credentials alone are not enough. What truly sets successful immigrants apart is a particular set of personal attributes, among which emotional intelligence (EI) stands out as one of the most critical.

At its core, emotional intelligence refers to the ability to recognize, understand, manage, and influence one's own emotions and the emotions of others.

The concept gained widespread attention through the work of psychologist Daniel Goleman, who identified five core components of emotional intelligence:

- self-awareness,
- self-regulation,
- motivation,
- empathy, and
- social skills.

While this concept applies to all human relationships, its importance is magnified in the immigrant experience, where adapting to a new social and cultural reality requires flexibility, resilience, and deep interpersonal sensitivity.

In this principle of success, we will explore why emotional intelligence is not just an asset but a necessary skill for immigrants to thrive. By drawing on both psychological and social perspectives, we will examine how emotional intelligence helps newcomers navigate the complexities of integration, establish meaningful connections, protect their mental health, and unlock professional and personal success.

DEFINING EMOTIONAL INTELLIGENCE IN A SOCIAL AND PSYCHOLOGICAL CONTEXT

Emotions are not simply fleeting feelings; they are essential to human survival and interaction. They inform our decisions, shape our relationships, and influence how we perceive the world. Psychologically, emotions are responses to significant internal or external events. Socially, they are the medium through which human beings connect and communicate. Emotional intelligence, therefore, can be viewed as the capacity to navigate this emotional landscape effectively.

From a psychological standpoint, emotional intelligence includes both intrapersonal skills (self-awareness, self-regulation, motivation) and interpersonal skills (empathy and social competence).

Socially, emotional intelligence plays a pivotal role in how we relate to others, particularly in complex, multicultural environments. In a new country, immigrants encounter unfamiliar customs, social norms, and communication styles. The ability to respond adaptively rather than react impulsively is a marker of high emotional intelligence.

A classic study by the Carnegie Institute of Technology found that 85% of financial success is attributed not to technical knowledge but to what it calls "human engineering," the ability to communicate, lead, empathize, and relate to others. These are all hallmarks of emotional intelligence. This insight is particularly relevant for immigrants who must build new social networks, navigate unfamiliar systems, and often re-establish their professional identities from scratch.

EMOTIONAL INTELLIGENCE AND SELF-AWARENESS: THE FIRST STEP TO INTEGRATION

Self-awareness is the cornerstone of emotional intelligence. It involves recognizing your emotional states, understanding your triggers, and being aware of how your emotions influence your behavior. Immigrants who cultivate self-awareness are better equipped to cope with the inevitable culture shock that comes with moving to a new country. They can recognize when they are overwhelmed, anxious, or homesick and can take steps to manage these feelings in constructive ways.

Self-awareness also encourages honesty and introspection. It allows immigrants to understand their strengths, weaknesses, and values, which is crucial in a new environment where they may need to redefine their roles in society. For instance, a skilled professional whose qualifications are not recognized in the new country may feel disillusioned. Without self-awareness, such disappointment can fester into frustration or bitterness. With self-awareness, however, that individual is more likely to adapt, retrain, or seek alternative opportunities while preserving self-esteem.

MANAGING EMOTIONS IN A NEW WORLD

The immigrant journey is emotionally demanding. From bureaucratic hurdles and job insecurity to social rejection and language barriers, the pressures can be relentless. Managing one's emotions, another core component of emotional intelligence, is not about suppressing feelings but regulating them to respond effectively to stress.

Emotional regulation helps immigrants remain calm under pressure, bounce back from setbacks, and avoid destructive behaviors such as anger, withdrawal, or denial. For example, an immigrant who is unfairly treated at work due to bias might feel justifiably angry. A reactive outburst could worsen the situation, while a person with emotional intelligence would acknowledge the anger, analyze the context, and respond strategically - perhaps by seeking support or reporting the incident through appropriate channels.

Managing emotions also supports mental health, which is often compromised in immigrant populations. According to numerous studies, immigrants are at a higher risk of anxiety, depression, and trauma-related conditions.

The ability to understand and manage one's emotional responses is a key factor in building psychological resilience.

EMPATHY AND CULTURAL SENSITIVITY: BUILDING BRIDGES ACROSS DIFFERENCES

Empathy - the ability to understand and share the feelings of others - is perhaps the most socially transformative aspect of emotional intelligence. For immigrants, empathy facilitates integration by enabling them to appreciate the perspectives and norms of the host culture. It also allows them to recognize and honor the emotional experiences of others who may not share their background.

Empathetic immigrants are more likely to form meaningful connections, not only within their ethnic or linguistic group but also with people from other communities. This openness reduces isolation and fosters inclusion. It also empowers immigrants to contribute to their new societies as bridges between cultures, mediating understanding and collaboration in workplaces, schools, and neighborhoods.

Moreover, empathy is a two-way street. When immigrants display empathy, they often receive it in return. This creates a cycle of mutual respect and trust, essential for reducing prejudice and promoting social cohesion.

MANAGING EMOTIONS IN A NEW WORLD

The immigrant journey is emotionally demanding. From bureaucratic hurdles and job insecurity to social rejection and language barriers, the pressures can be relentless. Managing one's emotions, another core component of emotional intelligence, is not about suppressing feelings but regulating them to respond effectively to stress.

Emotional regulation helps immigrants remain calm under pressure, bounce back from setbacks, and avoid destructive behaviors such as anger, withdrawal, or denial. For example, an immigrant who is unfairly treated at work due to bias might feel justifiably angry. A reactive outburst could worsen the situation, while a person with emotional intelligence would acknowledge the anger, analyze the context, and respond strategically - perhaps by seeking support or reporting the incident through appropriate channels.

Managing emotions also supports mental health, which is often compromised in immigrant populations. According to numerous studies, immigrants are at a higher risk of anxiety, depression, and trauma-related conditions. The ability to understand and manage one's emotional responses is a key factor in building psychological resilience.

EMPATHY AND CULTURAL SENSITIVITY: BUILDING BRIDGES ACROSS DIFFERENCES

Empathy - the ability to understand and share the feelings of others - is perhaps the most socially transformative aspect of emotional intelligence. For immigrants, empathy facilitates integration by enabling them to appreciate the perspectives and norms of the host culture. It also allows them to recognize and honor the emotional experiences of others who may not share their background.

Empathetic immigrants are more likely to form meaningful connections, not only within their ethnic or linguistic group but also with people from other communities. This openness reduces isolation and fosters inclusion. It also empowers immigrants to contribute to their new societies as bridges between cultures, mediating understanding and collaboration in workplaces, schools, and neighborhoods.

Moreover, empathy is a two-way street. When immigrants display empathy, they often receive it in return. This creates a cycle of mutual respect and trust, essential for reducing prejudice and promoting social cohesion.

SOCIAL SKILLS: THE CURRENCY OF OPPORTUNITY

In any society, relationships are the bedrock of opportunity. This is especially true for immigrants, who often start with limited professional and personal networks. Social skills - such as active listening, two-way communication, conflict resolution, and collaboration - are central to building these networks. They also help immigrants navigate the often unspoken social rules that govern behavior in their new environment.

Many immigrants face the temptation to remain within familiar social enclaves, only interacting with others who speak their language or share their background. While this can provide comfort and a sense of identity, it can also limit exposure to broader opportunities. Emotionally intelligent immigrants recognize the importance of stepping outside their comfort zones. By interacting with a diverse range of people, they not only improve their language skills and cultural knowledge but also gain access to jobs, services, and friendships that enrich their lives.

Networking is not merely a professional strategy - it is a survival skill. Whether finding housing, employment, childcare, or healthcare, immigrants rely heavily on the support and information that comes through personal connections. Emotional intelligence, particularly in the form of empathy, patience, and open-mindedness, makes it easier to forge these connections.

ISOLATION VS. INCLUSION:
THE EMOTIONAL COST OF DISCONNECTION

One of the gravest threats to immigrant success is social isolation. When immigrants feel excluded, misunderstood, or unwelcome, they may retreat inward, cutting themselves off from valuable resources and support systems. This isolation can lead to a range of negative outcomes, including depression, anxiety, substance abuse, sleep problems, and even physical health issues.

Some immigrants may unwittingly contribute to their own isolation by clinging only to familiar social groups or avoiding situations where they feel insecure. While these reactions are understandable, they can become self-imposed barriers to success. Emotional intelligence helps immigrants break out of this cycle. By managing fear and uncertainty, they can take social risks, initiate conversations, ask for help, and build bridges with others.

Inclusion is not just a policy goal for governments; it is an emotional state. When immigrants feel emotionally included, they are more likely to contribute positively to their communities, work environments, and civic life. Emotionally intelligent individuals are not passive recipients of inclusion; they actively create it through empathy, openness, and interpersonal skills.

EMOTIONAL INTELLIGENCE AND
PROFESSIONAL SUCCESS

In today's economy, technical knowledge alone is not enough. Employers value employees who can work well with others, adapt to change, and handle stress, all of which are underpinned by emotional intelligence. Immigrants who cultivate these skills stand out in the workforce. They are more likely to be promoted, respected, and integrated into organizational cultures.

Moreover, entrepreneurial immigrants - those who start businesses or community initiatives - rely heavily on emotional intelligence. They must inspire trust, manage teams, resolve conflicts, and connect with clients from diverse backgrounds. In this way, emotional intelligence becomes not just a survival tool, but a pathway to leadership.

CONCLUSION:
EMOTIONAL INTELLIGENCE AS A LIFELINE

The journey of immigration is a profound human experience marked by risk, resilience, and transformation. To succeed in this journey, emotional intelligence is not a luxury; it is a lifeline. It enables immigrants to understand themselves, navigate complexity, and build lasting relationships. It protects their mental health, enhances their professional prospects, and empowers them to contribute meaningfully to their new society.

In a world that is becoming increasingly interconnected and multicultural, emotional intelligence is not only crucial for immigrants but also for the communities that receive them. Societies that value emotional intelligence - through education, workplace training, and public policy - create spaces where diversity is not just tolerated but celebrated. Ultimately, the emotionally intelligent immigrant is not just someone who adapts to a new culture but someone who shapes it - bringing empathy, insight, and human connection to the forefront of social life.

PRINCIPLE OF SUCCESS #12

SUCCESSFUL IMMIGRANTS ARE POSITIVELY SELFISH

Real Life Story #10

In 2023, Edith Konte, an immigrant in France, received fifty-six phone calls from members of her family and friends in her country of origin, requesting money, clothing, computers, phones and all kind of other items they could not afford locally. Many of these items are what they wanted and not what they needed. Some of the things they asked for were things Edith would not think of buying for herself, even if she needed them, due to financial constraints. However, knowing the precarious economic situation in her home country, Edith never said no to any of these requests because she did not want members of her family to suffer. Many immigrants have the same mindset.

Edith worked two jobs in France to be able to support herself and her siblings. The intriguing aspect of this story is that when she prepared her monthly budget, her needs were at the bottom of the list. Which means she considered the needs of others above hers. Though she worked twelve to fifteen hours a day to earn more money, Edith lived from "paycheck to paycheck," which meant she would be unable to pay for her living expenses if she lost a month's income or if her income dropped.

She also had difficulty paying for her utilities and prescription drugs.

Edith's inability to balance her work-life brought disastrous consequences to her family. Her children were left to fend for themselves most of the time, and when she was sick, she found reasons not to see a doctor because she could not pay her hospital bills. Even when she did see a doctor, she could not pay for prescription drugs.

While anxiously laying on a hospital bed one day, Edith received a phone call from her brother asking for money. She had already spent a lot of money supporting his university education. It was then that Edith realized that if she really loved her family, she must remain alive by taking care of herself. The dead do not support the living. Essentially, Edith decided to adopt an attitude of positive selfishness. Before you assist others, it is important that you first take care of yourself.

THE POWER OF POSITIVE SELFISHNESS: A WAKE-UP CALL FOR IMMIGRANTS

Immigration is often romanticized - seen as the ultimate leap toward prosperity, freedom, and new opportunities. But behind the glossy postcards and smiling photographs lies a complex, emotionally taxing reality. For many immigrants, especially those who come from collectivist cultures where communal responsibility is ingrained, the pressure to give back to those left behind can be overwhelming. The moment an individual steps onto the soil of a so-called "developed" nation, a common assumption arises back home: *they have made it.*

Suddenly, the phone rings endlessly. Relatives ask for money for their children's school fees, medical bills, funeral contributions, food, and seed capital for businesses. Friends hint at personal struggles. Even distant acquaintances feel entitled to help, believing access to foreign currency equals financial abundance. This leads to a pattern of giving that, while noble on the surface, can quickly drain immigrants emotionally, financially, and spiritually. It is in this context that a new mindset must emerge - *positive selfishness.*

WHAT IS POSITIVE SELFISHNESS?

At first glance, the phrase "positive selfishness" may seem contradictory. In everyday parlance, *selfishness* has negative connotations, being egocentric, greedy, and unconcerned with the needs of others. But positive selfishness reframes this idea: it is the conscious act of prioritizing your own well-being, goals, and mental health without being destructive or cruel to others. If you have travelled by air recently, you will recall hearing an announcement by the crew before the plane takes off which sounds like this:

> *"If the cabin pressure changes, oxygen masks will drop from the panel above your seat. Pull the mask towards you to start the flow of oxygen. Place it firmly over your nose and mouth, secure the elastic band behind your head and breathe normally. Make sure to put on your own mask before assisting others."*

The key phrase in this announcement is: "Put on your own mask before assisting others." The crew is not saying one should not assist his/her child or aged mother sitting next to them. I interpret this to mean that "Self-care isn't selfish, it's

255

essential." You are not abandoning others; you are equipping yourself to serve them more effectively.

From a broader perspective, positive selfishness does not mean withholding help entirely from those in need. Rather, it means helping others in ways that do not harm your own life, your financial stability, or the well-being of your nuclear family. It is the realization that you cannot sustain others if you are running on empty. To practice positive selfishness is to say, "Yes, I care - but I also matter."

PERSONAL STORY: GIVING WITHOUT BOUNDARIES

In 2019, I received forty-eight separate phone calls from family members asking for money. Each request came with a compelling backstory - hospital bills, school fees, burial arrangements, start-up business capital, and food shortages. Out of love and a sense of obligation, I responded positively to most of them, remitting money regularly throughout the year.

Months later, while thinking about the help I had extended to others, I realized that only six out of the twenty recipients had acknowledged receipt of the funds. Others neither acknowledged receipt nor offer a word of thanks. None of the recipients ever phoned to ask me how I was doing or how I was able to support them. The emotional disconnect was glaring.

This finding left me discouraged and disillusioned. The act of giving, which should have brought joy and connection, felt instead like a drain on my spirit. I realized then that I was behaving like a hardworking elephant but eat like ants.

CULTURAL PRESSURES:
COLLECTIVISM VS. INDIVIDUALISM

Much of this pressure stems from the cultural expectations embedded in collectivist societies, where the success of one is seen as a responsibility to uplift all. In collectivist cultures - common in Africa, Asia, and Latin America - people are socialized to be generous, dependable, and sacrificial. Sayings like: *Umuntu ngumuntu ngabantu* in Zulu (South African) language, translated, "A person is a person through others," reflect this deep-rooted value system.

These words of wisdom reinforce my collectivistic cultural thinking, propelled me to send food aid to my village, Afaha Ikot Nkang, during the Covid 19 pandemic of 2019 through 2020. Because the pandemic generated food and hunger problems in my community, I sent food aid to the entire village periodically. The photos below capture some of the instances when I delivered food supplies.

PHOTO BY: CHARLES UDO UKO (2020)

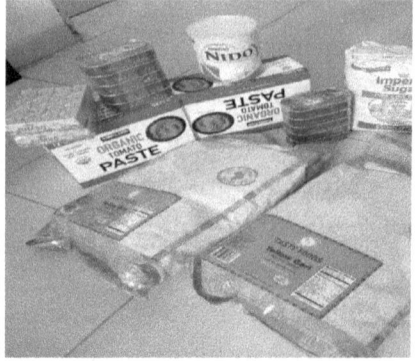

PHOTO BY: CHARLES UKO, DECEMBER 2024

By contrast, individualistic cultures - like those in the U.S., Canada, Germany, or the U.K. - prioritize personal goals, independence, and self-actualization. People are taught to be responsible for "putting on their own oxygen mask," and not worrying about others, at least in the short run. Immigrants moving from collectivist to individualistic societies often struggle with this cultural shift. They want to embrace the opportunities of their new lives but feel shackled by invisible contracts with people back home. Yet even in collectivist cultures, one must ask: at what cost?

WHY POSITIVE SELFISHNESS MATTERS

Positive selfishness helps immigrants set boundaries that protect their emotional, physical, and financial health. Without such boundaries, immigrants risk:

- Neglecting their nuclear families, especially spouses and children who live with them in the host country.
- Delaying their personal goals such as buying a home, going back to school to reskill or retool themselves, or starting a business.
- Burnout and resentment caused by over-extending themselves for people who may never reciprocate or express appreciation.

A man named Benjamin Chimana, an immigrant I spoke to in the course of collecting information for this book, embodies this conflict. He sent $50,000 to his nephew back home to start a small business. Not only was the nephew ungrateful, but he also insisted the money was not enough and falsely assumed Benjamin earned three times what he was asking for a month and, therefore, should have sent more money. Benjamin was saddened. He worked night shifts as a security guard while attending school during the day. No one ever sent him money. No one asked how he was coping.

This, sadly, is a familiar tale among immigrants. Many report that the only time their phones ring is when someone wants something. Emotional connection and concern for their well-being are often absent.

THE NEVER-ENDING CYCLE OF REQUESTS

Immigrants who send money frequently find that one request breeds another. You pay for your cousin's school fees, and soon you are asked to pay for his siblings' or support his parents. There is no endpoint. And unfortunately, helping without limits teaches people to expect help, rather than appreciate it. A friend once said, "The more you give, the more they assume you have to give."

This is the curse of generosity without boundaries - it fuels sense of entitlement rather than gratitude.

LEARNING TO SAY "NO"

Saying "no" does not make you a bad person. It makes you wise and calculated. You are not an ATM. You are a human being. You are allowed to rest, to save, to spend on your personal growth. Immigrants must learn to say:

- "I cannot help with that right now."
- "I have already committed my finances elsewhere."
- "This request doesn't align with my priorities at the moment."

Saying "no" is especially necessary when requests come from able-bodied adults who can support themselves. Support should empower people, not enable dependence.

YOU CANNOT POUR FROM AN EMPTY CUP

We often hear the saying, *"You can't pour from an empty cup."* Yet many immigrants act as though the contents of their cups are limitless, pouring until there is nothing left for themselves. This is unsustainable. Positive selfishness encourages immigrants to fill their own cups first - through rest, education, career advancement, emotional support, and family care. Once your cup is full, you can then give from a place of abundance, not obligation.

Think of it as a bank account: if all you do is withdraw, eventually you will go into debt. Positive selfishness ensures you invest in yourself first so that you have the stability to uplift others.

GOD, GROWTH, AND GIVING:
A BALANCED PERSPECTIVE

Many spiritual teachings support generosity, but they also support balance. In the Christian Bible, Psalm 128:2 reminds us: "*You will eat the fruit of your labor; blessings and prosperity will be yours.*" This suggests that we are meant to enjoy the rewards of our hard work not just transfer them to others.

Likewise, Martin Luther King Jr.'s famous question: "*What are you doing for others?*" need not exclude doing for yourself. Helping others is important, but not at the cost of your health, dreams, or family life.

APPRECIATION AND ENTITLEMENT

One of the most painful realities immigrants face is the lack of appreciation from those they help. When recipients show an attitude of entitlement instead of attitude of gratitude, it becomes emotionally exhausting. Over time, this imbalance can lead to bitterness or emotional withdrawal.

Philanthropist Brian Tracy once advised: "*Always give without remembering and always receive without forgetting.*" This wisdom holds - but only when giving is met with receiving, not expectation. If the people around you constantly forget your sacrifices, it is time to rethink your approach.

CONCLUSION: A HEALTHIER WAY TO HELP

Immigrants are some of the most resilient, generous, and hardworking individuals in the world. Their journeys often involve incredible sacrifice and determination.

But generosity should never be self-destructive.

Positive selfishness is not a betrayal of your roots. It is an evolution of your mindset. It means:

- Protecting your mental and financial health.
- Setting healthy boundaries.
- Helping selectively and wisely.
- Prioritizing your nuclear family.
- Refusing to enable dependency and entitlement.
- Building a life that you, too, can enjoy.

When you are whole, you can give more meaningfully. When you are stable, you can uplift others sustainably. Let your giving come from strength, not guilt. So, to every immigrant feeling torn between helping others and preserving themselves, I say

- You matter.
- Your peace matters.
- Your growth matters.
- You can still rise by lifting others - but only if you rise first.

Finally, "Live your life in such a way that you will be remembered for your kindness, compassion, fairness, character, benevolence, and a force for good who had much respect for life, in general." - Germany Kent

PRINCIPLE OF SUCCESS #13

SUCCESSFUL IMMIGRANTS ARE SELF-RELIANT AND SURROUND THEMSELVES WITH SUCCESSFUL PEOPLE

Real Life Story #11

Blessing Abebe and her husband emigrated to the United States to improve their career prospects. Both husband and wife were in the medical profession. They lived a good life in their country of origin, but due to political instability and insecurity of life and property, they decided to emigrate to a country they believed would be safer for them and their children. They came to the US to build on the successes they had achieved in their country of origin.

A few months after their arrival, they were able to secure jobs commensurate with their training and experience. In her daily interaction with her colleagues, many of whom shared her racial background, Blessing noticed that they spent a lot of time gossiping about their friends, other colleagues and even their spouses. At lunch breaks, Blessing tried to persuade these colleagues to talk about improving their productivity, rather than gossiping. She was not a snob; she just wanted to be in the company of forward-thinking people. But her colleagues stopped talking to her, accusing her of having a "holier-than-thou" attitude.

Blessing responded by building relationships across ethnic and racial lines with individuals from whom she could learn and exchange constructive ideas. Her new workplace peers had been in the organization longer than her and taught her new skills. She was not only a quick learner, but also thirsty for knowledge. Within two years of interacting with these new peers, she learned so much about the organization that she caught the attention of the management team. As a result, she was promoted to a supervisory role and was tasked with overseeing the work of those colleagues who had labeled her as "holier-than-thou."

Immigration is often a journey of courage, uncertainty, and renewal. Many leave their home countries in search of better opportunities, safety, or personal growth. Yet only a fraction of immigrants realize the full promise of their new environment. One of the most underrated but powerful factors behind this disparity is the company they keep. As the saying goes, *"Show me your friends, and I will show you your future."* This simple yet profound truth highlights the importance of relationships in determining not only one's trajectory but also the quality and sustainability of their success.

THE POWER OF ASSOCIATION: WHY SURROUNDING YOURSELF WITH SUCCESSFUL PEOPLE SHAPES YOUR DESTINY

This essay explores why successful immigrants - and indeed, all high achievers - are intentional about the people they surround themselves with. Through educational insight, philosophical reflection, real-life examples, and advisory notes, we unpack why success is often a team sport and how choosing the right team is critical to winning in life.

THE PSYCHOLOGY OF INFLUENCE

Human beings are inherently social creatures. From the moment we are born, we learn by mimicking those around us. Psychologist Albert Bandura, in his social learning theory, argued that people learn behaviors through observation, imitation, and modeling. This means we are deeply shaped by our environment, especially the people within it.

When immigrants land in a new country, they are in a period of high cognitive and emotional plasticity. What and who they surround themselves with can determine whether they rise or stagnate. If they find themselves among people who are driven, goal-oriented, and optimistic, they are more likely to adopt similar attitudes. On the contrary, if they settle into communities that nurture apathy, fear, or mediocrity, these mentalities can quickly take root.

This principle is not limited to psychology. In the field of neuroscience, research has shown that "mirror neurons" in our brains fire both when we perform an action and when we observe someone else performing it. This underscores how deeply we internalize the behaviors of those around us, consciously or not.

PHILOSOPHICAL FOUNDATIONS: MAN AS A SOCIAL ANIMAL

The ancient Greek philosopher, Aristotle, described man as a "zoon politikon" - a social animal. He believed that humans realize their full potential only within the context of community and mutual development. This notion suggests that isolation is detrimental not only to personal growth but also to moral and intellectual maturity.

Immigrants often face the temptation to retreat into solitude, especially when dealing with cultural barriers or early failures. However, successful immigrants push beyond these discomforts and intentionally build networks of purpose-driven individuals. They seek community not just for comfort but for growth.

Consider the Stoic philosophy as well. Marcus Aurelius, a Roman emperor and philosopher, emphasized the importance of rational companionship. He wrote, *"The soul becomes dyed with the color of its thoughts."* That includes the thoughts shared and modeled by those around us.

EDUCATIONAL PERSPECTIVE: LEARNING THROUGH ASSOCIATION

Formal education teaches concepts, but experiential learning, much of which occurs through associations, is equally, if not more, powerful. Mentorship, peer learning, and group accountability are all educational models grounded in interpersonal interaction.

Take, for example, the story of Blessing Abebe above, a case in point of a high-achieving immigrant who inspired her colleagues by modeling excellence and positivity. Her proactive attitude did not just propel her forward; it created ripples that uplifted those around her. Such individuals are natural educators, not in the traditional classroom sense, but in the powerful school of life.

Successful immigrants recognize that proximity to success breeds success. They often join professional networks, mentorship groups, or community organizations where learning is informal but impactful.

These arenas provide not only opportunities but also inspiration and constructive feedback - tools more valuable than any textbook.

ADVISORY LENS: HOW TO CHOOSE
THE RIGHT PEOPLE

Many immigrants (and even natives) struggle with loneliness and a lack of direction. In such times, it is tempting to accept any form of companionship - even if it is toxic or limiting. But as Dan Peña wisely said, "Show me your friends and I will show you your future". That is why one must be deliberate about relationships. Here are actionable strategies to curate your circle:

- *Define your values and goals*. You cannot choose the right people if you do not know where you are going. Write down your short and long-term goals. Then people seek who either embodies those goals or support them.
- *Be observant.* Not everyone who smiles is your friend. Look at people's actions, habits, and patterns over time. Are they ambitious, honest, and consistent?
- *Engage in value-adding conversations.* Test relationships by engaging in deeper discussions. Do these people challenge your thinking, support your growth, or just flatter you?
- *Diversify your circle.* Do not surround yourself with clones of yourself. Find people from different backgrounds, industries, and experiences who can broaden your perspective rather than engaging in homosocial reproduction.

- *Be the kind of person others want to learn from.* Before seeking successful friends, ensure you are cultivating habits that attract such individuals. Like attracts like.

The strategies offer guidance on choosing the right people to build meaningful and growth-oriented relationships, especially for immigrants and those feeling isolated. It emphasizes being intentional about your social circle, as the people around you influence your future. Key strategies include: defining your values and goals, observing people's actions over time, engaging in meaningful conversations, diversifying your network, and becoming someone who attracts high-quality connections.

REAL-LIFE EXAMPLES OF SUCCESSFUL IMMIGRANT NETWORKS

Across the globe, there are stories of immigrants who transformed their lives by aligning with the right people:

- *Elon Musk*, born in South Africa, became one of the world's most influential entrepreneurs. Musk credits much of his success to networking with visionaries in Silicon Valley. His associations led him to PayPal, Tesla, and SpaceX.
- *Indra Nooyi*, an Indian immigrant who became the CEO of PepsiCo, often talked about how strong mentors and supportive colleagues influenced her trajectory in the corporate world.
- *Hamdi Ulukaya*, founder of Chobani Yogurt and originally from Turkey, built a multi-billion-dollar business in the U.S. He credited part of his success to forming a circle of trust with employees and advisors who shared his passion and work ethic.

These examples prove that success is never a solo project. The right people make the impossible achievable.

THE IMPORTANCE OF SELF-RELIANCE AND DUE DILIGENCE

While building a strong network is crucial, successful immigrants never abdicate responsibility for their own lives. They understand the balance between dependence and self-reliance.

As President Ronald Reagan famously stated during nuclear treaty negotiations, *"Trust, but verify."* Immigrants must exercise the same wisdom in their relationships. While someone may appear successful or helpful, it is essential to evaluate whether their values align with yours.

Additionally, you are your own best partner. Practice self-coaching, self-reflection, and continuous learning. Read biographies of successful immigrants, attend webinars, join relevant forums, and stay updated with trends in your field.

Remember, being alone is not the same as being lonely. Solitude can be a source of strength when used to deepen your self-awareness and sharpen your vision.

SOCIAL INTEGRATION AND THE POWER OF COMMUNITY

Community integration is another pillar of immigrant success. Often, successful immigrants are deeply involved in civic life; they volunteer, start initiatives, or join neighborhood associations. This involvement not only boosts their visibility but also deepens their connection to the host country.

If you cannot find supportive individuals within your immediate environment, consider:

- Joining professional associations related to your career.
- Becoming part of online communities that align with your goals.
- Volunteering in areas that matter to you.
- Starting a mastermind group or support circle.

These efforts do not just expand your network; they expand your perspective and influence.

CONSTRUCTIVE FEEDBACK VS. COMFORT TALK

One of the most harmful tendencies is surrounding oneself with people who only affirm your existing beliefs and behaviors. While encouragement is vital, so is accountability. Seek people who:

- Offer constructive criticism even when it is uncomfortable.
- Question your decisions to help you think more critically.
- Hold you accountable to your goals.
- Celebrate your wins genuinely, without envy.

Comfort talk might feel good, but truth talk is what propels you forward. Growth requires tension - the kind that stretches you into new dimensions.

SUCCESS IS HOLISTIC

Merriam-Webster defines success as a "favorable or desired outcome." But what is "favorable" depends on one's values. For some, it is financial freedom. For others, it is raising children in a safe environment or contributing meaningfully to society. Regardless of your definition, one principle stands firm: who you associate with will either move you toward that goal or away from it.

Success is not a product of luck or background alone. It is a reflection of choices we make, especially the choice of who we let into our mental, emotional, and professional space.

CONCLUSION: BUILD YOUR TRIBE WITH PURPOSE

We always need people to encourage us, and they do not need to be popular or have advanced education. The most important factor is that they possess an exceptional drive and are dedicated to achieving excellence. You can find them if you diligently and intentionally look for them. Think about the people whose words of encouragement have lifted you up and brought out the best in you, or after a setback, helped you get back on your feet. Surrounding yourself with mediocre and uninspiring individuals can lead to failure. Successful immigrants are successful because they network actively, establish vital relationships and surround themselves with achievers who support their goals.

In summary, the journey to success, especially for immigrants, is a complex and often difficult path. But one thing is clear: you cannot walk it alone. Whether through mentors, friends, colleagues, or role models, the people around you will shape your thinking, behavior, and ultimately your outcomes.

Surround yourself with people who challenge, uplift, and inspire you. Be humble enough to learn, wise enough to choose, and brave enough to let go of toxic relationships. Cultivate your own mind to become someone others want to learn from - and watch how your tribe grows.

Your success starts with one critical choice: *who are you walking with!*

PRINCIPLE OF SUCCESS #14

SUCCESSFUL IMMIGRANTS ARE SELF-DISCIPLINED

Real Life Story #12

I am a diabetic, which means my blood sugar levels are too high. I became aware of my condition in my early forties, just after I secured a diplomatic job that offered many opportunities to enjoy life's pleasures. However, amidst this abundance, my personal physician advised me with more "don'ts" than "dos." As a diabetic, I was told to avoid alcohol and starchy foods. My doctor warned that long-term alcohol consumption could lead to excessively high blood sugar levels and result in medical complications, such as disturbances in fat metabolism, nerve damage, and eye disease.

As a diplomat with access to a wide variety of alcoholic beverages at discounted prices and having been raised in Africa where starchy foods like pounded yam and rice are staples, it was challenging for me to resist these foods and alcohol. However, to maintain my health, I made a conscious effort to avoid them. This decision also meant skipping many diplomatic functions, and when I did attend, I opted for sugar-free soft drinks instead.

At home, my wife was initially frustrated that I would not eat our traditional starchy foods.

Gradually, she reduced the amount of food in her cooking and eventually stopped preparing some of them altogether. I faced a choice: either continue drinking alcohol and eating starchy foods, which would lead to an early death, or abstain from both and live a long, healthy life. Now, in my eighties and living healthily with type 2 diabetes, I realize I would not have reached this age without my self-discipline.

Building a meaningful life abroad begins with developing two foundational traits: adaptability and self-discipline. Adaptability allows you to adjust to new environments, systems, and cultures, making daily life manageable in unfamiliar territory. But it is self-discipline that ultimately determines whether you grow, thrive, and build something lasting. A better life isn't defined by possessions—what's in your closet, your storage unit, or the next item on your wishlist. It's defined by the kind of person you become and the integrity you cultivate along the way. The transformation from who you are today to who you aspire to be hinges on your capacity for self-discipline.

WHAT IS SELF-DISCIPLINE?

Self-discipline is the ability to regulate one's emotions, thoughts, and behavior in the face of temptation, distraction, or adversity. It is doing what needs to be done, when it needs to be done - regardless of your emotional state or external pressures. In essence, self-discipline is a form of self-mastery. It involves the consistent practice of habits and choices that align with long-term goals over immediate gratification. Often used interchangeably with terms such as willpower, self-control, determination, and persistence, self-discipline is what keeps people on course.

It empowers us to resist negative impulses, maintain focus, and persevere through difficult times. This quality becomes particularly vital for immigrants, who must often rebuild their lives from scratch in an unfamiliar environment.

THE POWER OF SELF-DISCIPLINE: A CRITICAL INGREDIENT FOR IMMIGRANT SUCCESS

Immigrants face unique challenges that demand an extraordinary level of discipline. These include navigating a new language, overcoming cultural barriers, managing financial instability, adapting to new laws and systems, dealing with social isolation, and often supporting family members both at home and abroad. In these situations, self-discipline becomes more than just a personal virtue - it becomes a survival skill.

Self-discipline distinguishes us from those who lack it. Our behavior, whether in public or private, among family or at work, is observed by those around us. Every day, we risk becoming what others perceive us to be. However, with self-discipline and self-mastery, we can express to the world our true selves through our actions. If we do not conduct ourselves properly, we risk allowing others to label us in ways that are hard to change.

Self-discipline teaches us the importance of self-mastery and self-control, reminding us never to take anything for granted. It guides us in choosing what we want in the present while also considering our future desires. Maxwell Maltz, the author of *"Psycho-Cybernetics: A New Way to Get More Living out of Life,"*[14] states that "The ability to discipline yourself to delay gratification in the short term in order to enjoy greater

---

14 Matt Hogan, "'Brian Tracy Quote on Delaying Gratification...," Movemequotes.com, accessed May 6, 2025, https://movemequotes.com/brian-tracy-quote-on-delaying-gratification.

rewards in the long term is the indispensable prerequisite for success." Self-discipline encourages us to reassess our current actions and decisions to ensure they align with our goals for future success.

Developing self-discipline is not easy, nor is it always enjoyable. The positive aspect of self-discipline is that it is a learned behavior rather than an innate trait. However, this also means that it is influenced by the culture of the society we live in. For immigrants in the United States, for example, adjusting to different cultural perspectives can pose challenges. Each immigrant arrives in the US with a unique story, which shapes their identity and worldview.

Immigrants who succeed are often those who understand that every choice counts. They refrain from wasteful habits, they work diligently even when unseen, and they maintain focus in the face of discrimination, loneliness, or economic hardship. In contrast, many who fail to thrive in a foreign land often struggle with consistency, time management, or falling into unhealthy coping mechanisms such as substance abuse, procrastination, or self-doubt.

PERSONAL REFLECTION

Without self-discipline - and the courage to avoid substances that could raise my blood sugar - I would not be writing this essay today. This is not a hypothetical scenario; it is my lived reality. Self-discipline has empowered me to prioritize my health, manage my emotions, and pursue my goals even in the face of personal sacrifice. The choices I have made - to refrain from alcohol, to follow a strict diet, to stay committed to personal growth - are all grounded in intentional self-discipline.

Self-discipline has allowed me to be in control of my future, not enslaved by fleeting desires. And this realization leads to one of the most powerful truths of all: YOU, and only YOU, are responsible for the quality of your life. As writer Bob Moawad so insightfully stated, *"The best day of your life is the one on which you decide your life is your own. No apologies or excuses. No one to lean on, rely on, or blame. The gift is yours - it is an amazing journey - and you alone are responsible for the quality of it."* This principle is especially relevant for immigrants who must take ownership of their decisions, actions, and outcomes.

CONQUERING THE SELF

Plato once said, *"To conquer oneself is the best and noblest victory; to be vanquished by one's own nature is the worst and most ignoble defeat."* This quote reflects the struggle that many face - not against external enemies, but against inner weakness.

Temptation is everywhere, particularly in countries where freedom and consumerism abound. Alcohol, gambling, unhealthy food, excessive screen time, and toxic relationships can derail even the most ambitious immigrant. The question is: how do you resist these temptations and stay true to your vision?

The answer to that question is simple but not easy: through *self-discipline.* Self-discipline allows us to delay gratification. It teaches us to prioritize long-term growth over short-term pleasure. It helps us make wise decisions in the present that will benefit our future. In doing so, it becomes the foundation of personal and professional success.

CAN SELF-DISCIPLINE BE LEARNED?

Absolutely, just like any other habit can be learned. Self-discipline is not a fixed trait; we are not born with it. Like muscle, it strengthens with use. Some individuals develop it early, through structured routines like doing chores, finishing homework, or following household rules. Others may grow up without much structure or guidance, and as a result, may struggle with discipline in adulthood.

But regardless of your background, it is never too late to learn self-discipline. All it takes is a strategy and commitment to practice. Start small. Create simple routines, such as waking up at the same time every day, organizing your workspace, or budgeting your income. Gradually, add more challenging goals such as completing a course, learning a new skill, or limiting your screen time. Over time, you will develop resilience and internal strength.

SELF-DISCIPLINE IN ACTION

Real-life examples of self-discipline are all around us, often hidden in the mundane. Acts of self-discipline include:

- Brushing your teeth before breakfast
- Dressing appropriately for work
- Wearing your seatbelt
- Avoiding texting while driving
- Turning off devices at bedtime
- Listening actively without interrupting
- Taking responsibility for mistakes
- Controlling your emotions during arguments
- Completing difficult tasks on time

- Respecting coworkers, neighbors, and community members
- Managing your finances and living within your means
- Practicing good health and hygiene habits
- Refraining from gossip, greed, and bigotry

These behaviors might seem small, but collectively, they reflect a disciplined mindset. They influence how others perceive you, and more importantly, how you perceive yourself. Every disciplined act reaffirms your control over your life.

IMMIGRANT IDENTITY AND PUBLIC PERCEPTION

As immigrants, we are always being watched by our neighbors, our coworkers, our children, and society at large. Our behavior, whether in private or in public, helps shape the narrative of what it means to be an immigrant.

When we behave with integrity, respect, and discipline, we uplift not only ourselves but our family and the entire community of immigrants. When we succumb to vice, dishonesty, or irresponsibility, we give others reason to judge or stereotype us.

Discipline helps us rise above these risks. It allows us to demonstrate excellence regardless of background or accent. It allows us to control the narrative of who we are, not based on origin, but on character.

ALIGNING PRESENT BEHAVIOR WITH FUTURE GOALS

Self-discipline also helps us align our present behavior with future aspirations. Maxwell Maltz, author of *Psycho-*

Cybernetics, wisely stated, *"The ability to discipline yourself to delay gratification in the short term in order to enjoy greater rewards in the long term is the indispensable prerequisite for success."* This statement is timeless and universal. Whether your goal is to become a homeowner, build a business, send your children to college, or simply live a dignified life, you must learn to sacrifice the unnecessary for the essential.

For me, managing my diabetes requires not just medication, but lifestyle changes. I declined sugary beverages and heavy meals, even when those meals were lovingly prepared by my wife, because I was focused on a larger goal: *health, clarity, and longevity.* Such sacrifices are not always fun, but they are necessary. And they become easier when you keep your eyes on the big picture.

THE ROLE OF CULTURE AND ENVIRONMENT

It is also important to recognize that discipline does not develop in a vacuum. It is shaped by the culture and environment around us. In the United States, for example, the culture is fast-paced, individualistic, and often focused on instant results. For an immigrant from a slow paced global-South country, this can be overwhelming.

Each immigrant brings with them a cultural identity shaped by family values, social customs, and previous experiences. Sometimes, these values may clash with the dominant culture, leading to confusion or a sense of alienation. In such situations, self-discipline helps maintain your internal compass. It helps you choose what to adopt, what to reject, and how to blend the best of both worlds.

Case Studies

There are several success stories of immigrants who have achieved success due to self-discipline. Here are some of the stories:

1. In the Real-Life Story # 12 above, I narrated my battle against diabetes. I am alive and strong today due to self-discipline. The struggle has been to keep A1c below 7. Anyone who is diabetic or knows someone with that condition knows the uphill battle to stay alive. Following medical advice requires self-discipline to avoid alcohol, sugar, and sweets during social gatherings is akin to resisting cultural regression - choosing a higher goal over short-term comfort. Managing a chronic illness takes daily discipline, just as integrating into a new society requires small, consistent efforts over time.

Whether it is refraining from indulgent food or resisting old mindsets, the common thread is intentional behavior change. This is the hallmark of successful immigrants.

2. Self-discipline moved Dr. Mo Ibrahim, a Sudanese, to the global stage. Born in Sudan, Dr. Mo Ibrahim emigrated to the United Kingdom (UK) for higher education. Despite cultural shock and financial constraints, he disciplined himself to humbly and diligently pursue his objective. He studied engineering by day and worked as a cleaner at night at the University of Birmingham, where he eventually earned a Ph.D. in mobile communications. Over time, his self-discipline led him to found Celtel,

one of Africa's most successful mobile networks. He later established the Mo Ibrahim Foundation to promote good governance in Africa. Dr. Ibrahim attributes his success not to genius, but to rigorous self-discipline and an uncompromising work ethic.

3. Daniela Varela immigrated from Peru to Toronto (Canada) as a teenager. She arrived speaking little English, failed her first semester in high school, and felt isolated. Her turning point came when a teacher encouraged her to journal every day and read English newspapers aloud at home. She did this for 18 months. Today, Daniela is a communications director at a multinational firm and often mentors young immigrants. *"Discipline changed my life,"* she says, *"I built fluency with flashcards and willpower."*

Daniela subscribed to her teacher's advice and read English newspapers for 18 months with a view to improving her proficiency in English language. Without doubt, it called for self-discipline and commitment to excellence to pull oneself out of the failing group.

4. Chinwe Eze – From Nigeria to Germany: Chinwe, a trained nurse from Nigeria, faced widespread discrimination when applying for nursing jobs in Germany. Instead of returning home or reacting with bitterness, she worked in a care home while teaching herself German every night. After three years, she passed the proficiency exams, earned new credentials, and was hired at a major hospital in Berlin. Chinwe says, *"Discipline didn't just change my career; it healed my heart."*

The lesson Chinwe Eze's story teaches us is that in every philosophy of human greatness, mastery of the self is considered the highest form of success. Greek philosopher Epictetus taught that happiness depends not on what happens to us, but on how we respond. Similarly, in immigrant life, what truly counts is how individuals respond to unfamiliarity, rejection, or setbacks - and that requires mental discipline.

5. Javed Akhtar story – Pakistan to Norway: In Pakistan, Javed was taught never to challenge elders or speak assertively. But in Norway's workplace culture, initiative and critical thinking were highly valued. His lack of assertiveness was seen as passivity. Realizing this, Javed enrolled in public speaking courses, observed his Norwegian colleagues, and began practicing direct communication. *"I didn't lose my culture,"* he says, *"I added to it."* Today, Javed is a successful engineer and team leader in Oslo.

Javed story shows how culture can enhance or impede progress. Culture is powerful - and so is the need to update it. When immigrants relocate, the habits, expectations, and assumptions that shaped them often need realignment.

KEY QUESTIONS FOR REFLECTION

At this stage, you understand why the book in your hand - *Think like an immigrant* - is worth reading. As you think about your journey, ask yourself the following questions:

1. Do I have the self-discipline to cope with the challenges of living in a new country?

2. Do I make choices that align with my long-term goals - or am I guided by convenience and impulse?
3. Do I surround myself with people who encourage growth, or those who hinder it?
4. Am I setting a positive example for my family and community through my daily actions?
5. What small changes can I make today that will lead to long-term improvement?

Answers to these questions will help you gain clarity in what you are doing, take ownership of your life journey, and ensure your daily choices align with the long-term success and fulfillment you seek in a new country.

CONCLUSION:
BECOMING THE PERSON YOU ASPIRE TO BE

At its core, self-discipline is not just about achieving success, it is about becoming the person you want to be. It is about choosing personal excellence over mediocrity, values over vanity, and purpose over pleasure.

For immigrants, self-discipline is more than a personal tool, it is a collective asset. It helps bridge the gap between where we came from and where we are going. It ensures that we not only survive but thrive in new environments. It helps us turn our stories into legacies worth telling.

Remember this wherever you find yourself: Your future is shaped by your daily habits. Your legacy is crafted by your discipline. And the person you become tomorrow depends on the choices you make and the actions you take today.

PRINCIPLE OF SUCCESS #15

SUCCESSFUL IMMIGRANTS ARE PATIENT

Real Life Story #13: Paul and Adiaha Akpabio

Paul and Adiaha Akpabio were married for fourteen years and lived a fulfilling life in their country of origin before they decided to emigrate to the United States. Like many others, they were drawn by the promises of freedom and the opportunity to realize their full potential through hard work. However, unlike those who come with unrealistic expectations, Paul and Adiaha were also grounded in the wisdom that the U.S. is not a paradise. They knew that building a better life in a foreign land would require hard work - and more importantly, patience.

With two young children in school and limited income, they faced challenges with grace. They worked harder than they had back home, managed their resources wisely, and endured the discrimination many immigrants encounter in the workplace. More importantly, they refused to succumb to frustration or regret.

When I met them at a local grocery store and asked how they were coping, Adiaha responded with a warm smile: "God has been faithful, and with God on our side, we will do well.

We know why we came here, and as the saying goes, a patient dog eats the fattest bone." Paul echoed her sentiment, adding, *"My brother, success is sweet, but we are not in a hurry. We are not taking shortcuts. My wife and I are taking online classes to prepare ourselves for greater opportunities. Pray for us."*

I answered unequivocally, "Amen."

The power of patience: A vital virtue for immigrant success. The above story is a compelling reminder that in the immigrant's journey, patience is not optional - it is foundational.

PATIENCE: A MISUNDERSTOOD STRENGTH

There is a common saying: *"Patience is a virtue."* But in today's fast-paced, "microwave culture," patience is often misunderstood as weakness or passivity. For many immigrants, the desire to succeed quickly leads to disappointment and stress when reality does not match expectations. Some even resort to shortcuts - cutting legal, ethical, or academic corners - that ultimately backfire.

Yet the reality is clear: real success requires real patience. Philosopher Jean de La Bruyère said, *"No road is too long to the man who advances deliberately and without undue haste; and no honors are too distant for the man who prepares himself for them with patience."* For immigrants, this means recognizing that the road to success in a new country is long, unfamiliar, and filled with roadblocks - but navigable with steady resolve.

The impatience trap: Wanting it all now

Many immigrants arrive with high hopes, inspired by stories of prosperity. But few see the years of behind-the-scenes effort it takes to get there. Some immigrants, unwilling to invest time in retooling their skills or education, seek "get-rich-quick" schemes or settle for unrecognized credentials. In desperation, some even turn to diploma mills - earning degrees that lack credibility and do not lead to real opportunities. These are "educated illiterates" immigrants compete with.

The consequences of impatience are often disappointing: years wasted, doors closed, and dreams deferred. As George Bernard Shaw once said, *"Two things define you: your patience when you have nothing, and your attitude when you have everything."* Without patience, both stages of life become dangerous: scarcity breeds bitterness, and abundance breeds arrogance.

Patience in practice:
Work, family, and personal growth

Patience is not limited to waiting, it is about how we wait. It is about attitude, emotional maturity, and deliberate restraint.

In The Workplace

Success rarely comes overnight. Immigrants who take the time to understand the system, invest in education, and work diligently tend to advance faster than those who jump from job to job seeking quick gains. I recall a recent graduate who told me he planned to change jobs frequently until he found one that "pays good money and feels right." I advised him to consider building experience and reputation first. Patience is often the price of stability.

In The Home

Many immigrant families suffer internal conflict due to impatience - between spouses, between parents and children, or even within oneself. Richard Needham once said, "*You don't just marry one person; you marry three: the person you think they are, the person they actually are, and the person they will become as a result of being married to you.*" Without patience, relationships collapse under the weight of unrealistic expectations.

In Parenting

Children test our limits. They grow at their own pace. An impatient parent might resort to harsh discipline or overlook the child's emotional needs. But a patient parent is a better listener, guide, and role model. Children learn patience by observing it in their parents.

PATIENCE WITH SELF: THE FORGOTTEN VIRTUE

We often tell others to be patient but forget to extend the same grace to ourselves. This is especially true for immigrants grappling with cultural shock, financial pressure, or a delayed sense of purpose.

Self-blame becomes easy when life feels stagnant. Some immigrants blame society, employers, their parents, or even God for their struggles. But the truth is: you made the decision to emigrate, and your success depends on your ability to be kind and patient with yourself as you adjust to the new environment.

Success does not come from panic or pressure.

It comes from consistency, learning, and staying the course, especially when results are not immediately visible.

Health benefits of patience

There is also a growing body of research showing that patience leads to better physical and mental health. A study by Schnitker and Emmons (2007) found that patient individuals report higher well-being, less depression, and stronger relationships. Impatient individuals, on the other hand, are more prone to stress-related health issues - such as ulcers, insomnia, headaches, and anxiety.

Moreover, patience correlates with *agreeableness*, a personality trait marked by compassion, generosity, and empathy. Patient individuals tend to have better social support, which is vital for immigrants adjusting to a new life.

Patience in daily life: Quiet strength

During one of my visits to McDonald's, I met a young immigrant flipping hamburgers to save money for his education. Despite impatient customers and the heat of the fryer, he wore a smile on his face and served each order with pride. Fascinated by his attitude, I returned a few days after just to speak to him and encourage him to maintain that disposition. His patience, even in discomfort, reflected his long-term mindset worth emulating.

He understood something many people do not, i.e., patience often involves enduring personal discomfort for future gain. Whether it is standing behind a hot oven or sitting through a night class after a long work shift, this kind of patience builds character.

BUILDING A SUPPORT NETWORK

If you want to thrive in a foreign country, surround yourself with people who embody the fruits of patience - kindness, empathy, wisdom, forgiveness, and generosity. These individuals are more likely to succeed, not just materially but emotionally and spiritually.

Success is contagious. It does not spread from person to person like a cold. Instead, through learning from and observing successful people around you, success spreads from one area of your life to another, creating a powerful momentum that can transform everything. Another benefit of building a support network is that you will be less lonely, more respected, and more socially fulfilled.

Patience also helps us forgive others' imperfections. It prevents us from cutting people off too quickly or misjudging intentions. Friendships, mentorships, and even job offers often blossom through consistent, patient effort over time.

THE LONG ROAD TO PARADISE

We often underestimate the length and depth of the journey to a better life. Some paths take years, not months. But the good news is that the fruit of patience is always sweeter than the spoil of haste.

Patience protects your health, preserves your integrity, strengthens your relationships, and allows you to navigate complex challenges without losing your way. As Kira Newman noted in her research, "*Good things really do come to those who wait.*" Those who are patient are not sitting idle; they are preparing, learning, growing, and becoming.

Final thoughts: A call to immigrants

To every immigrant reading this: Know that your dreams are valid, but your journey requires patience. The challenges you face today are not signs of failure but steps toward your future. Avoid the temptation to take shortcuts.

Instead, take heart in the knowledge that slow growth is strong growth.

In the words of Jean-Jacques Rousseau: "*Patience is bitter, but its fruit is sweet.*"

Choose to wait. Choose to work. Choose to grow.

And remember: "*The patient dog eats the fattest bone.*"

Principles of success #16

Real Life Story #14

Bakari Bontu came to the United States as a student. After his pre-medical education, he tried unsuccessfully to gain admission to medical school. His failure to gain admission was not due to his grades. Most public medical schools give preference to American citizens, which makes securing admission by international students difficult.

However, Bakari was not going to compromise his professional ambition because of rejection. He applied to other medical schools the next year and received more letters of regret. One of the schools offered him a place to study Physiology, which he accepted - not as a substitute for medical school, but to better prepare for it. In the final year of his MSc in Physiology, he applied to medical schools again. This time, he had the "good problem" of having to choose among three schools that offered him admission.

There are three lessons to learn from Bakari's story:

- Successful people are persistent and resilient in the face of challenges and setbacks. They embrace failures, learn from them, and use that knowledge as a steppingstone towards success.
- To realize their dreams, successful people are willing to try new things and confront uncomfortable situations. For example, Bakari agreed to study physiology even though this was not his planned future career. He used his study of physiology as a foot-in-the-door to medical school.
- The third lesson to be learned from Bakari's story is that his eventual success resulted from the adjustments he made in seeking admission to medical school.

One important lesson to learn from failure is to reflect on how you may be responsible for your own failure. In the case of Bakari, he did not carry out enough research to have a full grasp of what it takes to gain admission to medical school in the US. But he recognized his mistake and worked around it, and this contributed to his success.

Failure is often considered a "dirty word" across cultures. Ironically, while many people avoid any association with failure, successful immigrants tend to embrace it. Their inability to achieve certain goals in their home countries often becomes the catalyst for seeking better opportunities abroad. Those who make the bold decision to emigrate are typically aware of the obstacles ahead, yet they proceed, fully prepared to face failure and persevere through it if necessary.

Failure is often painful; however, the enduring regret of abandoning one's goals without achieving them can be far more agonizing.

As Vince Lombardi aptly states, *"Winners never quit, and quitters never win."*[15] Truly successful individuals demonstrate persistence and resilience in the face of adversity and setbacks. Thus, persistence is a fundamental component in the pursuit of success, while its absence frequently leads to failure.

THE IMPACT OF CONSISTENCY

Some immigrants often struggle more than others not because they lack talent or work ethic, but because they lack *consistency*. Whether talented or hardworking, without sustained effort, progress falters. Consistency is the key. In any endeavor, if you remain consistent, success becomes inevitable.

As Winston Churchill once said, *"Success is not final, failure is not fatal: it is the courage to continue that counts."*[16] Failure is simply a signal pointing us in a new direction, not a stop sign. Stop treating failure like a permanent red light. If you never fall, you will never understand the strength it takes to rise again. What truly matters is the courage to keep moving forward. To do this, you must believe in yourself and refuse to give up. While working hard and smart are both important, it is consistency and continuous effort - not raw strength or high intelligence - that unlock our full potential.

Many of the world's most successful individuals have faced repeated failures before achieving greatness.

15 "Vince Lombardi Quotes," Brainy Quote, accessed May 9, 2025, https://www.brainyquote.com/quotes/vince_lombardi_122285.

16 "Winston S. Churchill Quotes," Goodreads, accessed May 8, 2025, https://www.goodreads.com/quotes/3270-success-is-not-final-failure-is-not-fatal-it-is.

Henry Ford, for instance, went bankrupt several times before finally revolutionizing the automobile industry with the Ford Motor Company. Thomas Edison famously failed a thousand times before perfecting the modern light bulb, viewing each setback as a step toward success. Luther Vandross was booed off the stage at the Apollo Theater not once, but four times, yet he persevered to become one of the most iconic voices in rhythm and blues.

These stories remind us that failure is not a dead end, but a detour on the long road to success. As singer Elvis Presley once wisely said, *"When things go wrong, don't go with them."*[17] Instead, rise, refocus, and keep moving forward.

Some immigrants struggle with a mindset limited by fear - fear of failure, fear of embarrassment, and fear of the unknown. To them, everything feels too risky, and this hesitance can keep them from pursuing their dreams. Conversely, successful immigrants know that staying in the comfort zone is not a recipe for growth. Instead of running from fear, they confront it directly and use it as a tool for learning and progress. They see fear not as a barrier, but as a signal pointing toward growth opportunities. By understanding the roots of fear and recognizing that failure carries valuable lessons, they transform setbacks into steppingstones. Embracing this mindset brings them one step closer to turning their dreams into reality.

It is okay to fail. Those who think they cannot make a difference should remember one of my favorite aphorisms by the Dalai Lama: *"If you think you are too small to make a difference, try sleeping with a mosquito."*[18]

---

17 "'When Things Go Wrong,'" The Foundation for a Better Life, accessed May 8, 2025, https://www.passiton.com/inspirational-quotes/6489-when-things-go-wrong-dont-go-with-them.

18 "Unlocking Profit, Value, and Time in Your Business," Business Fitness, March 22, 2022, https://businessfitness.biz/small-businesses-can-make-a-big-difference.

Even something as small as a mosquito can disturb an entire palace and its royal residents. Size or background does not limit your power to make an impact.

Immigrants should take this to heart. Do not say, "I'm a foreigner," or "I don't speak perfect English, so I can't compete." Do not be intimidated by anyone or life's circumstances. If you emigrated to the US, you are in the "land of the free and the home of the brave," so be brave. Learn, grow, and believe that you belong and can thrive.

Believe in yourself. Never be afraid to fail. Do not waste energy trying to hide your failures, embrace them. Each failure is an opportunity to understand what went wrong, to grow, and to move forward stronger. Quitting out of fear of what others might think only stunts your growth. If you are afraid to fail, you are not ready to succeed. In the words of author Jack Canfield, *"Don't worry about failures, worry about the chances you miss when you don't even try."*[19]

What often separates successful immigrants from those who struggle is not luck or talent, it is relentless perseverance. They try again and again, no matter the setbacks. They understand that not every day will go as planned, but by combining motivation with unwavering enthusiasm, they create momentum. Success is not the absence of failure; it is the result of refusing to stop. *"You don't just fail once,"* Professor Dashun Wang says, *"You fail over and over."*[20] Success belongs to those who keep showing up, keep learning, and never stop believing in the possibility of a better future.

---

19 "Motivational Quote by Jack Canfield," Insight of the Day, accessed May 8, 2025, https://insightoftheday.com/motivational-quote-by-jack-canfield-03-30-2025.

20 "Why Do Some People Succeed after Failing, While Others Continue to Flounder?," Kellogg Insight, December 2, 2020, https://insight.kellogg.northwestern.edu/article/some-people-succeed-after-failing-others-flounder.

INSIGHT

Failure and disappointment are never easy to endure, yet they can sometimes become catalysts for growth and renewed optimism. I admire the determination of many immigrants who choose not to be defined by setbacks. Instead, they adopt powerful strategies to rise above adversity: they ignore limiting opinions, stay rooted in prayer and spiritual strength, confront their weaknesses through honest self-reflection, and boldly map out their futures. They also learn to distance themselves from people who bring negativity into their lives. These individuals understand that success is often a battle - one that may need to be fought more than once to be truly won.

PRINCIPLES OF SUCCESS #17

SUCCESSFUL IMMIGRANTS ARE NOT AFRAID TO START FROM ZERO

THE GIFT OF STARTING FROM ZERO: A PATH TO REINVENTION AND RENEWAL

Starting from zero is what most people dread because it is considered a setback. But what if I told you that starting from zero is not a setback? What if, instead, it is a doorway - a powerful opportunity to rewrite your story?

When immigrants arrive in a new country, they often leave behind more than just a location. They part with their careers, their credentials, their social networks, and even parts of their identity. Rebuilding life in an unfamiliar land is not only difficult, it can feel overwhelming.

Many of these individuals were accomplished professionals in their home countries: doctors, engineers, teachers, entrepreneurs. But upon arriving in their new home, they find that their qualifications are not recognized, their experience undervalued, and their career paths blocked by licensing barriers or unfamiliar systems. And so, they are faced with a daunting reality: they must start over.

THE POWER IN LETTING GO

A few years ago, I bought a dilapidated house and set out to refurbish it. As the repairs dragged on, costing more money and time than expected, it dawned on me that it would have been easier, cheaper, and more rewarding to buy land and build the house I truly wanted from scratch rather than renovating an old house.

This experience taught me an important lesson - one that applies beyond real estate. Just as it is challenging and costly to modify an old, crumbling property, it can be just as difficult to hold on to an outdated skillset, especially in a new country where the job market and cultural expectations are different. Sometimes, it is more profitable - personally and professionally -to start from zero and learn something entirely new.

Successful immigrants understand this. They are not afraid to recreate themselves, piece by piece, using the human and material resources available to them. They embrace change, let go of what no longer serves them. They not only have the courage to begin again. But they see reinvention not as a failure, but as a path to success.

THE COURAGE OF REINVENTION

Successful immigrants are not afraid to recreate themselves. They approach their new reality not with bitterness, but with vision. They enroll in new training programs, learn unfamiliar trades, and pursue opportunities outside their former comfort zones. This willingness to adapt is not a sign of failure; it is a mark of inner strength.

Today's job market is evolving at an unprecedented pace. For those who are willing to learn new skills or explore unfamiliar paths, there are countless opportunities regardless of age or previous experience. The key is having the courage to let go of what no longer serves you and the openness to start building again.

For anyone hesitant to begin again or embark on a new path, the life of Abraham Lincoln offers remarkable inspiration. Despite having minimal formal education, Lincoln enlisted in the US military and while in the service, pursued the study of law through diligent self-education. His determination led him to a career as a lawyer and later as a congressman. His journey, however, was not without setbacks. Lincoln campaigned for a seat in the US Senate and lost. Yet he did not allow that defeat, or his lack of academic credentials, to deter him. Just two years after that loss, he ran for the presidency, won, and ultimately became one of the most revered presidents in American history. His legacy proves that reinvention is not a detour; it is often the very road to greatness.

Lincoln's story is a powerful reminder of what can be achieved when one refuses to be defined by failures or limitations. Had he chosen not to persist, the course of American, and perhaps global history, might have been entirely different today. As Lincoln's story illustrates, success is rarely immediate, and the path towards it often includes failure. However, for those who possess the courage to persevere, the rewards at the end of the journey can be extraordinary.

CONFRONTING FEAR AND DOUBT

I once met an immigrant with tears in his eyes who asked me, "How do I start life all over again? How can I be sure I will succeed in a new career? What if I choose the wrong profession again?" These fears are not uncommon. Many immigrants are hesitant to try something new, paralyzed by the uncertainty of starting over. Putting myself in his shoes, I realized how easy it is to lose hope when life takes an unexpected turn. When everything you have worked for no longer holds value, the future can feel overwhelmingly uncertain.

Instead of delivering a traditional sermon about prosperity and good tidings to this downhearted individual, I decided to engage him in a simple memory game. I asked him to name one or two successful people he knew who had never experienced failure at any point in their journey. He could not name one. I then assured him that starting over is not a sign of failure; it is a mark of courage. It reflects the bravery to give oneself a fresh start, to believe in the possibility of renewal.

As our discussion unfolded, expressions on his face and body language began to change. Smiles slowly appeared on his face, signifying understanding of irrefutable truth that success often follows many failures. What truly matters is the willingness to keep going, to take one small step at a time.

Of course, no matter how intentional or careful we are in trying to reinvent ourselves, there will be missteps. There will be blunders. But those setbacks do not define us. They are part of the process, and they should never stop us from forging ahead.

The truth is every successful person, in anything, must have had to stop and reflect on his/her station in life and rather than being downhearted, begin again - many times, if need be, to achieve a goal. Starting from zero is not a shameful place. It is a place full of potential.

THE PSYCHOLOGY OF ZERO

We often imagine the worst-case scenario when facing change. Our minds are wired to avoid uncertainty, and so we become paralyzed by fear. The reality is that we can either be shaped by our fears or led by our hopes.

Fear of failure can distort our judgment, dampen our courage, and rob us of opportunity. But those who succeed are not those who never feel fear; they are those who choose to keep moving forward despite it. Winston Churchill captured it best when he said, *"Success is going from failure to failure without losing enthusiasm."* That is the spirit of perseverance, and it is what makes starting from zero such a powerful choice.

ZERO IS NOT NEGATIVE

Contrary to popular belief, zero is not always a negative number. In fact, zero is the beginning of everything. Mathematically, zero is neutral, but philosophically, it is possibility. The world's most powerful financial numbers - $100,000, $1,000,000 - are just digits with zeros. There is power in the idea of beginning. Starting from zero gives you the freedom to:

- Correct past mistakes.
- Shift into a more meaningful or relevant career.
- Upgrade your skills.
- Realign your values with your goals.

When one door closes, it does not mean the journey ends. It means a new journey begins, one that you can design on your own terms.

A CALL TO ACTION

To those who feel stuck, discouraged, or uncertain: do not be afraid of starting over. Start again with your eyes open, your heart steady, and your will intact. Use the resources around you. Reach out to others. Ask questions. Learn. Grow. Try. Fail. Try again.

If life has brought you back to zero, do not resist it. Embrace it. Because the opportunity to begin again is not punishment, but a gift.

CLOSING INSIGHT

Everyone fails. Everyone doubts. But not everyone chooses to keep going. Let it be said of you that you chose courage over fear, growth over comfort, and potential over pride.

Do not be afraid to start from zero because from zero, you can build anything.

Every human being has, at one time or another, experienced failure. It is part of what makes us human. Yet, it is this very experience, along with our ability to learn, think, create, and reflect, that makes us the most creative beings on the planet.

To protect ourselves from perceived danger, we often imagine the worst-case scenarios. In doing so, we inadvertently scare ourselves. This leaves us with a choice: to become victims of our fears and anxieties, or to move forward with courage. Fear of failure is a persistent companion - in the workplace, within our families, in our social circles, and in leadership roles. We fear abandonment, we fear not being good enough, and sometimes, we even fear success, especially if it threatens to isolate us or provoke envy. We live in constant negotiation with fear. But we must be vigilant, for fear of failure, if left unchecked, can drastically alter the trajectory of our lives.

I have met immigrants who, instead of saying "I can't," choose to face challenges with the mindset of "How can I tackle this problem?" Their determination reflects a deeper truth: success is not measured by the absence of failure, but by the courage to persevere.

What matters most is the courage to continue - not whether we will succeed or fail. What this means, essentially, is that success consists of going from failure to failure without loss of enthusiasm. No one celebrates failure and failure does not define a person. Failing to achieve your goal does not mean *you* are a failure; it simply means you have not succeeded yet.

Many well-known people started with nothing. In fact, it is a privilege to have the opportunity to begin again. When one door closes, be ready and willing to walk through another if it opens. If you find yourself starting over, do not fear zero. As any mathematician will tell you, zero is not negative; it is a new beginning.

Immigrants move across the world in search of opportunities to thrive. Why, then, should starting from zero be something to fear, especially if it leads you to your goals? Use the opportunity to correct past mistakes, change careers, or acquire new skills that will improve your competitiveness. In the end, do not be afraid to start from zero. After all, the six-figure salary that many chase as a mark of success is full of zeros.

PRINCIPLE OF SUCCESS #18

SUCCESSFUL IMMIGRANTS STRIVE FOR FINANCIAL FREEDOM

Real Life Story #15

Matthew and Dorcas were once small-scale traders in their home country. After winning the Diversity Immigrant Visa Lottery, they came to the United States in search of a better life. Though I didn't initially ask what "better" meant to them, it quickly became clear through our conversation that they were deeply concerned about the cost of living and relatively low wages—realities that sharply contrasted with their expectations. They spoke candidly about friends who had fallen into debt while chasing lifestyles they could not sustain, mistaking surface-level comfort for true prosperity.

What stood out most was Matthew's simple yet powerful statement: "To stay afloat, we have decided to cut our coat according to our size." In other words, they made a conscious decision to avoid spending money they didn't have—particularly through credit cards—and to reject the lure of living beyond their means. They saw the dangers of financial overextension and agreed, as a couple, to prioritize saving, and building credit.

Eventually, they invested in a home—not just as a place to live, but freedom from tenant-landlord imbroglio, and as a long-term asset that could be converted to cash if/when necessary. To them, real estate represented the first step to and a reliable path to financial peace.

In this piece, the terms *financial freedom* and *financial security* will be used interchangeably to refer to a state in which one has enough financial resources to cover basic needs, manage emergencies, and make life choices without being overly constrained by money. It means not living paycheck to paycheck, not drowning in debt, and not depending entirely on others or unstable systems for survival. Financial freedom gives people the ability to live with dignity and make decisions based on values rather than financial desperation.

Many people emigrate in search of freedom. But what kind of freedom? Most immigrants I've spoken with mention freedom of worship, freedom of expression, and the freedom to marry whom they choose. These are powerful and important liberties. Rarely, however, do they speak of *financial freedom.* Either they do not understand the significance of being financially free or they don't understand its significance.

In a foreign country, financial freedom is not just about comfort, it's about survival, autonomy, and stability. Without it, the very freedoms immigrants come seeking can feel hollow, overshadowed by anxiety, dependency, and the constant pressure to "catch up." But with it, individuals gain the ability to shape their own lives, pursue their goals, and weather the storms that inevitably come with starting over in a new land.

UNDERSTANDING FINANCIAL FREEDOM

Financial freedom does not mean being rich. It means being in control of your money instead of being controlled by it. As Kahlil Gibran once said, *"Life without liberty is like a body without spirit."* True liberty includes the freedom to make life choices without being paralyzed by financial constraints. For immigrants starting life afresh in a new country, financial security should be a central goal. Without it, even the most basic aspects of life - healthcare, housing, education, and retirement - become a constant struggle.

Unfortunately, many immigrants fall into the trap of conspicuous consumption soon after receiving their first paycheck/cheque. The temptation to "catch up" with others by buying the latest car, or taking lavish vacations can be overwhelming - especially after years of "living from hand to mouth" in their countries of origin. But outward displays of success often mask inward financial stress. When spending outpaces income, even a higher paycheck can lead to deeper debt.

WEALTH IS A TOOL AND NOT A STATUS SYMBOL

Money is not evil. What matters is how we use it. As Dave Ramsey explains in his book, Financial Peace (1992), *"Financial peace isn't the acquisition of stuff. It's learning to live on less than you make, so you can give money back and have money to invest."* The path to financial freedom involves self-discipline, strategic saving, and intentional living.

It is easy to believe that earning more is the answer to all our problems. But the real challenge is managing what you earn wisely.

Wealth, if handled poorly, brings stress, if handled wisely, fosters freedom. When immigrants confuse income with wealth, they risk becoming "wealthy on paper" or "successful" but trapped in debt, constantly working to maintain a lifestyle they cannot afford.

PRACTICAL STEPS TO ACHIEVE FINANCIAL SECURITY

I participated in a non-academic discussion with friends on this subject of financial security. A colleague said he was afraid of the aftermath of being financially independent because nothing is constant. If you are afraid you might not be able to maintain the lifestyle you have been enjoying since arriving in your new country of residence, practice the following:

1. *Live within your means*
   - Spend less than you earn. Avoid loans for non-essential items. Buying expensive things to impress others is a fast track to financial insecurity.
2. *Save and invest consistently*
   - Even small amounts add up over time. Treat saving not as deprivation but as an investment in your future peace of mind.
3. *Avoid consumer debt*
   - Borrowing money to buy depreciating assets - like flashy cars, designer clothes, or luxury vacations - is a dangerous habit. Always ask: "Is this purchase helping or hurting my future?"
4. *Improve financial literacy*
   - Read books, take classes, attend seminars, and talk to people who are financially secure. Learn from those who have successfully built wealth from the ground up.
5. *Stop comparing yourself to others*

- You do not know their income, their debt, or their stress level. Focus on your own goals, your own timeline, and your own financial plan.

6. *Plan for emergencies and retirement*
   - Life is full of unexpected expenses. A healthy emergency fund is one of the greatest stress relievers. Retirement will come - whether you are ready or not.

True financial freedom means having enough resources to make choices without being constrained by financial stress. The key is to live simply, avoid lifestyle inflation, and build enough financial security to reduce money-related stress without being consumed by materialism.

CHOOSE FREEDOM OVER FLASH

Many immigrants fall into the trap of borrowing to buy things they cannot afford. For example, some take out large loans for luxury vacations or Ivy League education when a more modest, debt-free option would serve them better. It is important to remember that you are not spending your money when you borrow - you are spending the bank's. And they will want it back with interest. Remember, relying on other people's money makes you a slave to the lender.

Successful immigrants understand this. They avoid unnecessary loans, purchase only what they can afford, and prioritize financial flexibility over short-term pleasures. By doing so, they escape the cycle of debt and give themselves breathing room for life's unexpected turns.

MONEY IS FREEDOM ONLY IF USED WISELY

As a retiree living on a fixed income, I often reflect on my own financial journey. There were times of doubt and struggle, and times I questioned whether true financial freedom was even possible. But resources like Dave Ramsey's book and his "Financial Peace" seminars reminded me: financial freedom is less about how much you make and more about how you manage what you have.

One key lesson that stuck with me is this: *Money does not change your character - it reveals it*. Every spending decision reflects what we value most. Wise spending helps us grow in self-discipline and align our money with our true priorities.

FINAL THOUGHTS: WHAT REALLY MATTERS

Financial freedom does not mean stockpiling wealth; it means making life decisions without the constant burden of financial stress. It gives you the ability to enjoy time with loved ones, pursue meaningful work, and face life's challenges with confidence.

Some may argue, "You can't enjoy life until you have achieved financial independence." That may be partly true. But if in the process of chasing wealth you neglect your health, family, or happiness, then what have you really gained?

So, the goal should be a balancing act - work hard, live intentionally, and save consistently. Build a life that honors your values, provides for your future, and gives you the freedom to choose - not just to survive.

In the end, highly successful immigrants are not those who earn more.

They are those who manage their money wisely, live within their means, downsize their quest for materialism, and build lasting financial security—one thoughtful decision at a time.

INSIGHT

The journey to financial freedom is long and requires continual, intentional growth in financial literacy. Make it a habit to read, learn, and surround yourself with the right people - those who can challenge and expand your understanding of money and wealth. Money exists to enhance our quality of life, not to consume it. Be careful not to fall into the trap of working endlessly or chasing income solely to pay off debts, especially at the expense of your health or your family. True financial independence is about more than just numbers in a bank account. It is about having the time and freedom to be present for the people who matter most.

Some might argue, "You can't enjoy time off or quality family time without first achieving financial independence, and that takes hard work." That is true. But what good is wealth if you are too burned out or disconnected to enjoy it? If you become rich but lose your family along the way, who will share in or inherit what you have built? It is a classic chicken-and-egg dilemma. So, what is the answer? Start by choosing your priorities wisely and pursue financial independence in a way that does not sacrifice what truly matters. Work hard but also live well. In the end, the wealth that counts most is measured not just in dollars, but in relationships, peace of mind, and time well spent.

Principles of success #19

Successful immigrants have an unquenchable thirst for knowledge

Real Life Story #16: A Tale of Two Sons

A father sent his two sons to the United States for higher education. Both had graduated with First Class Upper honors in their undergraduate studies back home. Motivated and ambitious, they were not pushed by parental pressure but driven by a deep desire to succeed. Encouraged by their dedication, their father made the significant decision to invest in their futures abroad.

Once in the U.S. - thousands of miles from home and family support - the two young men charted their own paths. Each found a well-paying job in his field of specialization. But while their educational backgrounds were similar, their attitudes toward personal growth and knowledge differed greatly.

One son actively sought to understand the nuances of American society - its work culture, technological advances, and interpersonal dynamics. He enrolled in online courses, attended workshops, and constantly upgraded his professional skills. The other, although equally intelligent, became complacent.

After work, he spent most of his free time watching movies and disengaging from professional development.

In time, the difference became stark. The son who continued to learn and adapt grew more emotionally and professionally stable. His relentless pursuit of knowledge helped him navigate challenges, seize opportunities, and gain the respect of his peers. His brother, though once equally promising, began to stagnate.

This story illustrates a powerful truth: successful immigrants are not necessarily the most intelligent or best educated - they are the ones who are most eager to learn. In this principle we will discuss why it is important for immigrants to be thirsty for knowledge and the kind of knowledge they need.

WHY KNOWLEDGE MATTERS FOR IMMIGRANTS

For many immigrants, the initial decision to move to a new country is sparked by knowledge: a desire to apply what they already know and to expand on it in a more promising environment. But success abroad requires more than carrying previous knowledge - it demands a commitment to learning new things as well.

Knowledge is the key that unlocks opportunity. It enables immigrants to adapt to new systems, compete in unfamiliar job markets, understand their rights, and contribute meaningfully to their communities. More importantly, it empowers them to create stability and achieve upward mobility, despite starting out in an entirely new context.

Immigrants who thrive are not passive recipients of opportunity; they are active seekers of it. Their unquenchable thirst for knowledge fuels progress. They do not wait for doors to open - they prepare for when they do. Like a deer panting for water in the desert, they pursue education, skill acquisition, and personal development with urgency and purpose.

WHAT KIND OF KNOWLEDGE IS NEEDED?

In a new country, immigrants must pursue multiple forms of knowledge including but not limited to:

1. *Cultural Knowledge*: Understanding the social norms, values, and communication styles of their new environment helps immigrants navigate relationships and avoid misunderstandings. This includes learning the unspoken rules of the workplace and broader society.

2. *Professional and Technical Knowledge*: Even with strong academic backgrounds, immigrants often need to "retool" or update their skills to match local market demands. This might involve getting certifications, learning new technologies, or understanding industry standards specific to their new country.

3. *Practical and Legal Knowledge*: From understanding immigration laws to financial systems, health care, and educational structures, practical knowledge is essential for making informed decisions and avoiding costly mistakes.

4. *Language Proficiency*: Strong communication skills in the dominant language are essential for both personal and professional success. Fluency opens doors to better jobs, stronger networks, and leadership opportunities.

5. Soft Skills and Emotional Intelligence: Adaptability, problem-solving, teamwork, and leadership - often underestimated - are crucial for career advancement and community integration.

KNOWLEDGE IS POWER AND FREEDOM

The value of knowledge cannot be overstated. It is more precious than gold because it multiplies opportunity, self-confidence, and personal agency. Futurist Alvin Toffler captured this perfectly: *"The illiterate of the 21st century will not be those who cannot read and write, but those who cannot learn, unlearn, and relearn."*

The ability to unlearn outdated assumptions or methods, and to adapt to new realities, is especially vital for immigrants. Holding on to obsolete knowledge or resisting change limits potential and stifles progress. On the other hand, those who embrace change and learning - regardless of age or background become resilient, innovative, and indispensable.

THE AFRICAN IMMIGRANT EXAMPLES

Despite facing barriers such as racial bias, discrimination based on their accent and national origin, or credential recognition issues, many African immigrants have risen to the top of their fields. According to Lorenzi and Batalova (2022), African immigrants are among the most educated immigrant groups in the U.S. even more so than some native-born Americans.

How do they achieve this? By investing in themselves. They update their skills, pursue higher education, and strategically position themselves for success.

318

They do not dwell on past achievements; instead, they adapt, invent, reinvent, retool, and reskill themselves constantly.

This pattern is repeated across immigrant communities. I have met individuals who arrived in the U.S. with no formal education, and through sheer determination and the pursuit of knowledge, became inventors, entrepreneurs, scholars, and even Nobel laureates.

THE COST OF IGNORANCE

Business owners recognize and reward employees who invest in personal and professional growth. These employees bring more value, take initiative, and are often promoted into leadership roles. Immigrants who prioritize learning stand out, and those who do not may find themselves stuck, frustrated, and overlooked.

Acquiring knowledge can be time-consuming, difficult, and costly. But the cost of ignorance is far greater. As the saying goes, *"If you think education is expensive, try ignorance."* Every missed opportunity, bad decision, or stagnant year can often be traced to a lack of knowledge and increases the chances of failure. You cannot afford to stop learning. The moment you stop learning, you stop progressing. Make the pursuit of knowledge and the development of new skills a lifelong habit, one that you cherish and prioritize.

FINAL THOUGHT: MAKE LEARNING A WAY OF LIFE

Would you rather take the long, sometimes costly, journey toward knowledge, or remain stuck in ignorance? In life, ignorance costs more than we realize. Successful people make learning a lifelong habit.

They read books, attend seminars, and surround themselves with people they can learn from. They are always looking for ways to gain a competitive edge. They are not contented with yesterday's knowledge because they know tomorrow demands more. For immigrants, this mindset is not just helpful, it is essential.

So, whether you are starting a new life abroad or already years into your immigrant journey, remember this: knowledge is your most reliable passport to success. Cherish it. Pursue it relentlessly. Let your thirst for learning define your path, and you will not only survive in a new land but thrive in it.

Principles of success #20

Real Life Story #17: Douglas Massey in Paris

Douglas Massey, a young and promising American professional, arrived in Paris to represent his company abroad. While technically proficient and highly capable in his field, he lacked cultural sensitivity and made little effort to understand the French way of life. He spoke no French and showed no interest in learning the language, choosing instead to socialize only with English-speaking expatriates.

One of Massey's most significant missteps involved his disregard of the French tradition of "la sieste" - a short rest (a nap) after lunch. Disregarding this cultural practice, he insisted that his team resume work immediately after eating. This cultural insensitivity led to growing resentment among his French colleagues, who responded with minimal effort and a lack of cooperation.

His refusal to engage with the local culture, both linguistically and socially, eventually undermined his professional role.

Disconnected from his team and ineffective in his duties, Massey was recalled to the company's home office and eventually lost his position.

Culture encompasses the social behaviors, customs, institutions, values, and beliefs of a group of people. It includes language, traditions, religion, norms, and collective knowledge passed down through generations. Culture is often deeply rooted in a particular nation, community, or ethnic group and shapes the way individuals perceive and interact with the world.

Cultural differences refer to the variations in these elements between societies. These differences can manifest in communication styles, social etiquette, family dynamics, work habits, attitudes toward authority, and even concepts of time and space. Understanding these distinctions is essential for anyone living or working in a culturally diverse environment.

WHY CULTURAL COMPETENCE MATTERS FOR IMMIGRANTS

For immigrants, adapting to life in a new country often requires more than legal status or employment. It demands cultural competence, which is:

The ability to understand, communicate with, and effectively interact with people across cultures.

Cultural competence is not about abandoning one's heritage; rather, it is about integrating new cultural norms in a way that enables full participation in society. Culturally competent individuals:

- Are aware of their own cultural worldview.
- Show respect for different cultural practices and beliefs.
- Possess knowledge of other cultural perspectives.
- Demonstrate willingness to learn, adapt, and empathize.

Without cultural competence, even skilled immigrants can struggle with integration. Conversely, those who actively build this capacity can thrive socially, professionally, and personally.

THE PATH OF INTEGRATION: BALANCING TWO WORLDS

Immigrants often live between two worlds - their country of origin and their new homeland. Successfully navigating these dual identities involves resocialization: adopting the norms and values of a new culture without losing connection to one's heritage. The story of Douglas Massey above illustrates a key point, i.e., technical skill alone does not ensure success in a cross-cultural environment. Respect, empathy, and willingness to adapt are equally essential.

In the United States, where cultural diversity is part of the national identity, immigrants are encouraged not to assimilate by erasing their background, but to integrate in a way that enriches the social fabric. The U.S. motto, *E pluribus unum* - "Out of many, one" - captures this ideal. However, achieving this unity requires active participation from both immigrants and the host society.

CULTURAL COMPETENCE IN A MULTI-CULTURAL NATION: THE AMERICAN EXPERIENCE

America's diversity is reflected in hyphenated identities such as African-American, Mexican-American, or Asian-American. These identities represent both heritage and American belonging. Cultural competence enables individuals, whether native-born or immigrant, to navigate this plurality with respect and understanding.

Rather than demanding uniformity, true inclusion values each culture's contribution. For this to work:

- Immigrants must show openness to new cultural norms.
- Host societies must make space for cultural expression and inclusion.

Together, these efforts create a society that is not only diverse but cohesive, where difference is seen as a strength, not a barrier.

INSIGHT:
CULTURAL DIVERSITY AS A STRENGTH

As immigration continues to shape high-income countries, cultural diversity should be viewed as a powerful resource. No culture is inherently superior to another. When approached with respect and openness, cultural differences can foster creativity, innovation, and social harmony.

Successful integration is a two-way street - a shared commitment by immigrants and host communities to listen, learn, and grow together. For immigrants, this means developing cultural competence, participating fully in their new society, and contributing to a more inclusive future.

In the end, cultural competence is not about losing who you are. It is about expanding your identity to include a broader understanding of humanity - one that allows us to move from being strangers to collaborators, from outsiders to community-builders.

PRINCIPLE OF SUCCESS #21

SUCCESSFUL IMMIGRANTS ARE PROFICIENT IN THE LANGUAGE OF THE HOST COUNTRY

Real Life Story #18

Language proficiency is one of the most critical factors influencing both where immigrants choose to go and how well they integrate upon arrival. Across the globe, colonial histories continue to shape migration patterns. For example, many individuals from former French colonies in Africa tend to migrate to France, while those from former British, Spanish, or Portuguese colonies often choose destinations where their colonial languages are still spoken. Language, once a tool of imperial power, remains a powerful influence on modern mobility.

Language is a vital means of communication, both verbal and nonverbal. As Nelson Mandela once said, "If you talk to a man in a language he understands, that goes to his head. If you talk to him in his language, that goes to his heart." This quote powerfully underscores that language is not just a tool, it is a bridge to connection, understanding, and belonging. It is also one of the most essential expressions of culture and identity.

Recognizing the importance of language, countries like Nigeria have introduced French into the national curriculum. Surrounded by francophone neighbors, Nigeria sees bilingualism as essential for regional trade, cooperation, and stability. This proactive approach underscores the value of language skills - not just for individuals, but for national development.

WHY LANGUAGE PROFICIENCY MATTERS

Proficiency in the language of the host country is crucial for immigrants as it significantly influences their integration, employment opportunities, and social mobility. Effective communication allows immigrants to navigate daily life, from understanding public transport to accessing healthcare and education. For instance, immigrants in Germany who master the German language tend to find jobs more quickly and participate more fully in society.

Language proficiency also enhances employment prospects. Employers often prefer candidates who can communicate clearly with colleagues and customers. In Canada, the government even emphasizes language training as part of its immigration integration programs. Without adequate language skills, immigrants may be limited to low-skilled jobs, regardless of their qualifications.

Moreover, speaking the host country's language fosters social inclusion. It helps immigrants build relationships with neighbors, participate in community events, and understand cultural nuances. For example, Spanish-speaking immigrants in the United States who learn English are more likely to engage in civic activities and education for their children.

The ability to speak the language of a host country is crucial for immigrants. It enables integration, fosters meaningful relationships, and allows participation in every aspect of society, from employment and education to healthcare and community life. Without it, communication becomes a daily challenge, and feelings of isolation or inadequacy may arise.

This truth is clearly illustrated in *"Principle of Success #20"*, where Douglas Massey's lack of French proficiency severely hampered his effectiveness in France. His professional struggles highlight how language barriers can limit even the most skilled individuals.

A PERSONAL STORY: LEARNING FRENCH IN CONGO

I experienced this firsthand when I accepted a position with the World Health Organization in Brazzaville, Congo. At the time, I did not speak French. Leading a team of monolingual French speakers was daunting. It became quickly evident that I needed to reinvent myself. I committed to learning French with purpose and discipline. Over the course of a year, I gradually became conversational in a blend of English and French, "Franglais," as some call it.

What truly helped me were my supportive colleagues. They saw my effort, empathized with my struggle, and encouraged me to practice. Their patience and persistence created an environment where I could grow. This journey taught me that language learning is not just about mastering grammar; it is about connection, humility, and shared respect.

Initially, receiving official documents in French was terrifying. I had to rely on junior staff for translation. Leading a team I could not confidently communicate with was exhausting.

At times, I feared my credibility was at risk. But in hindsight, the pressure to learn under those conditions was a gift. Today, I can confidently travel to any francophone country and engage meaningfully with the people I meet.

THE POWER OF LANGUAGE IN DAILY LIFE

Effective communication is the hallmark of successful people. Language allows us to share our stories and, more importantly, learn from others. I still vividly remember my first day at JFK Airport in New York. After a long flight, I urgently needed to "ease myself" or use the bathroom. I asked a customs officer where I could find a "toilet." He looked puzzled and did not seem to understand what I meant by "toilet." After a few awkward moments of verbal and nonverbal communication, he finally said, Oh, you mean a "restroom." I did not know what he meant by "restroom" either, but I followed his directions - which was, hand pointing at one direction, "Go straight, then turn left, you won't miss it." Lo and behold, I found exactly what I was looking for. In many parts of Africa, the term commonly used for the place where people relieve themselves is 'toilet,' whereas in the United States, it's more often referred to as a 'restroom.' This reflects regional differences in language and cultural expression. That small but unforgettable encounter reminded me always of the practical importance of understanding not only language, but also culturally acceptable local expressions.

LANGUAGE AND INCLUSION

Language shapes our identity. It allows us to express who we are, share our culture, and participate in civic life. For immigrants, language proficiency is a key to social and economic mobility.

It enhances job prospects, promotes access to services, and fosters a sense of belonging.

By contrast, poor language skills can become a barrier to achieving one's goals. They may limit employment opportunities, restrict access to healthcare or housing, and make it difficult to build relationships or participate fully in society.

THE ROLE OF LANGUAGE IN EDUCATION

As an educator, I have seen how language impacts learning. Some of my students are native speakers of French or Spanish, and studying in the United States posed a major challenge. They often struggled to articulate their thoughts and are sometimes ridiculed for their efforts by other students whose mother tongue is English. During discussion, I could tell they were thinking in their native languages and translating into English, which often diluted or distorted the message. To support them, I would translate key concepts into French and offering extra tutorials - steps that helped bridge the gap.

LANGUAGE IN A GLOBALIZED WORLD

We live in an increasingly multilingual and interconnected world. Today, fluency in multiple languages is an asset in the global job market. In the U.S., for example, bilingual candidates - especially those who speak English and Spanish - are in high demand. Being able to communicate with diverse populations makes one a more competitive and valuable employee.

Immigrants from Francophone, Hispanic, or Lusophone countries who arrive already speaking English often find it easier to integrate and access better opportunities.

Ideally, immigrants should begin learning the dominant language(s) of their destination country even before relocating. Multilingualism enhances not only employability but also cross-cultural understanding and community engagement.

INSIGHT: COMMUNICATION IS MORE THAN WORDS

There is an important caveat: speaking a language fluently is not the same as using it wisely. Successful immigrants understand that effective communication involves emotional intelligence. Words can either foster connection or cause division. How we speak matters as much as what we say.

As the old wisdom goes, perhaps we were given two ears and one mouth for a reason - so that we listen and hear more than we speak. Washington Irving once remarked, *"The tongue is the only tool that gets sharper with use."* With that in mind, immigrants should strive not only for fluency but also for discretion, empathy, and grace in their communication. As is written in the world's most read book, the Bible, *"Let no corrupt communication proceed out of your mouth, but that which is good for the use of edifying, that it may minister grace unto the hearers"* (Ephesians 4:29–32)

Language fosters a sense of belonging. It is through language that we define our identity, express and share our history and culture, learn about and defend our human rights, and participate fully in all aspects of society. For immigrants, the ability to communicate in the host country's language is one of the main drivers of successful social and economic integration. Proficiency in the local language enhances employability, opens doors to better-paying jobs, and facilitates upward mobility in the job market.

Conversely, a lack of language proficiency is a major barrier that prevents many immigrants from achieving their goals. It hampers communication, which is essential for building interpersonal relationships, and makes it challenging to access education, secure gainful employment, obtain medical care, negotiate housing, and feel a sense of adequacy and inclusion in society.

PRINCIPLES OF SUCCESS #22

SUCCESSFUL IMMIGRANTS PLACE A HIGH PREMIUM ON HONESTY AND INTEGRITY

Real Life Story #19

Victor Kamini traveled to the UK for higher education in corporate finance. After graduation, he was granted a visa to stay for practical training to gain experience before returning to his home country. Victor applied to many companies and finally secured a position in a small family-owned business.

The principal owner, influenced by the common stereotype that immigrants are untrustworthy, was initially hesitant about hiring Victor. Despite his concerns, he took a chance, offering Victor a one-year contract on probation and closely supervising his work. Victor quickly exceeded all expectations. His professionalism, adherence to rules and regulations, discipline, honesty, and punctuality impressed the owner. Victor became the "stone that the builders rejected" - a steadfast asset the owner had initially overlooked. He diligently monitored the company's financial health and provided expert advice on investing company funds. Over time, the owner began to trust Victor more, gradually delegating responsibilities and eventually appointing him as Senior Vice President.

Although the owner's biological children opposed this decision, the owner stood firm. The business was the legacy he wished to leave for his family, and he was confident that Victor - not his children - would ensure its success.

When the owner retired as CEO, he handed the company over to Victor, making him the new CEO. Victor's journey from a doubtful immigrant hire to the trusted leader of the company is a testament to integrity, hard work, and merit overcoming prejudice.

INTEGRITY: THE CORNERSTONE OF SUSTAINABLE SUCCESS

The foundation stones of lasting success are honesty, character, integrity, and loyalty. If you can close your eyes, examine yourself truthfully, and extend that honesty to others, you are already walking in integrity. For those seeking advancement, especially in unfamiliar environments, it is essential to remember that meaningful progress rarely happens overnight. Endurance, patience, intentionality, and diligence are key ingredients in any long-term success story.

Unfortunately, in many receiving countries, harmful assumptions persist about immigrants being untrustworthy due to perceived hardship they suffered in their countries of origin. These stereotypes often surface subtly in professional environments. Skilled individuals may be recruited based on their talents, only to be micromanaged or scrutinized more closely than the native-born citizens. This contradiction reflects a lack of trust and can be profoundly demeaning.

In some institutions, hiring immigrants is even discouraged based on unfounded biases.

Non-violent response to sins of assumption

The most effective response to such prejudice is not throwing blames or name calling, but quiet demonstration, such as, proving doubters wrong through commitment to excellence in all that you do, consistent integrity and professionalism in all responsibilities entrusted to you.

Honesty is not just a moral value; it is a universal strength. People are drawn to those who are trustworthy, who speak the truth, and who act with fairness, even when no one is watching.

As Thomas Jefferson said, *"Honesty is the first chapter in the book of wisdom."* In every endeavor, we collaborate with others, and people are far more inclined to work with someone who has a reputation for honesty. Transparency in words and actions builds the trust that sustains relationships, whether in personal life or in business.

Honesty is also a universal language. People can sense it across cultures and circumstances. However, while honesty is globally recognized, cultures may express or interpret it differently. This makes it essential for those (particularly immigrants) adjusting to a new cultural environment to reflect on how their own values align with those of the society around them.

Even in societies where corruption exists, honesty is still respected. Integrity, the quality of adhering to strong moral and ethical principles, remains a rare and valuable asset.

Employers and colleagues alike prefer to work with those who are consistent and trustworthy. As Warren Buffett once noted, *"In looking for people to hire, you look for three qualities: integrity, intelligence, and energy. And if they don't have the first, the other two will kill you."*

Likewise, Benjamin Franklin advised, *"Let no pleasure tempt thee, no profit allure thee, no persuasion move thee, to do anything which thou knowest to be evil… for a good conscience is a continual Christmas."*

Those who maintain their integrity can pursue their goals without sacrificing their values. They resist the temptation to submit false documents or manipulate systems. They live within their means, fulfill their family responsibilities, and honor their promises to clients, colleagues, and loved ones.

Integrity cannot be seen with the eye, but it is revealed in actions. It shows in how one behaves when no one is watching. It is what shapes character and determines the kind of person one becomes. Without it, even the greatest accomplishments are hollow. Success without integrity is, in truth, failure.

As George Washington once said, *"I hope I shall possess firmness and virtue enough to maintain what I consider the most enviable of all titles, the character of an honest man."* Integrity is not just a private virtue; it is a public responsibility.

In today's world - where suspicion and bias can still shape perceptions - upholding integrity is more important than ever. A single dishonest act can reinforce negative stereotypes and damage the credibility of many. This makes it all the more important to live with discipline and to act with moral clarity.

Dishonest shortcuts, whether through falsified documents, misrepresentation, or unethical behavior may bring short-term gain but often lead to lasting damage. Once credibility is lost, especially in legal or public records, the consequences can be severe and long-lasting. Integrity protects your freedom, your reputation, and your future.

'

PATH OF FAILURE VS PATH OF SUCCESS

There are two paths open to every individual: the path of failure, paved with blame, resentment, and deception; or the path of success, built on learning, integrity, connection, and purpose. The choice is always yours. And in that choice lies your power.

Highly successful immigrants choose the higher path. They reject the lure of easy shortcuts and instead commit to values that build true, lasting success. That is not all. These are people who surround themselves with others who uphold honesty and practice ethical behavior. When people know your intentions are genuine, i.e., when they see you living your truth, they are more inclined to respect and trust you. In leadership, this builds loyal teams. In business, it attracts dedicated customers. In life, it fosters meaningful relationships.

MORAL INTELLIGENCE: A KEY TO SUCCESS

Successful immigrants, or any individual, often possess high moral intelligence - an inner compass guided by integrity, responsibility, empathy, and forgiveness. Your actions, whether noticed or not, shape how others perceive and respond to you. Honoring your commitments, treating others with respect, and taking responsibility for your choices are all indicators of moral strength.

To build moral intelligence, reduce excuses, avoid blame, take full ownership of your behavior, and reject even "small" dishonesty. More importantly, be patient with others' shortcomings and practice forgiveness. Forgiving others frees you to move forward with clarity, unburdened by resentment.

INSIGHT

Integrity is the quiet commitment to tell ourselves the truth. Honesty is the courage to share that truth with others. Both are essential for anyone who aspires to live a meaningful and successful life.

The sacrifices required to uphold integrity can be difficult, but the cost of abandoning it is far greater. Integrity fuels long-term achievement and personal peace. Those who remain true to their values, even in the face of opposition or hardship, will ultimately thrive, not just professionally, but as human beings.

In a world full of shifting standards, let your life be defined by what does not change: your character, your values, and your commitment to do what is right.

Principles of success #23

Successful immigrants give to Caesar what belongs to Caesar

Real Life Story #20

Alfred Mandaba, a retired diplomat, relocated to the United States (US) after many years of distinguished foreign service career on behalf of his home country. Having worked overseas under a tax-free salary, he assumed his pension would also remain exempt from taxation, regardless of where he resided.

To his surprise, upon settling in the U.S., Alfred discovered that his pension income was subject to American taxes—even though he had never worked within the country. A tax preparer, recommended by his pastor, explained the relevant U.S. tax laws, including the requirement to file annual tax returns and report all foreign income and assets.

The idea of "giving money to Caesar"—or in this case, Uncle Sam—was unfamiliar and somewhat bewildering to Alfred. However, he came to understand that living in a developed society brings with it certain obligations, including paying taxes to maintain the services and infrastructures that had attracted him to the U.S. in the first place.

Alfred chose to comply fully with U.S. tax regulations and now enjoys a peaceful life, free from concerns about tax enforcement or legal complications.

Immigrants are often drawn to developed nations like the United States by the promise of security, functioning infrastructure, social services, and opportunity for self-development. Incidentally, what most immigrants don't immediately realize is that these benefits are not free. They come at a cost—one largely paid through taxes. Taxes are how governments fund public goods--roads, schools, healthcare, public safety, and infrastructure.

These benefits, which often attract immigrants in the first place, rely on broad and consistent financial contributions from all residents—native born and immigrants alike. In short, the services immigrants benefit from must be paid for, and taxes are the primary vehicle for doing so. Therefore, immigrant should go to any of the global-North countries with a *quid pro quo* mindset, that is, not only expecting to receive from the host countries but also be willing to give back to the host countries. This is a fair and mutually beneficial attitude. The most effective way to give back is paying taxes when due, using your talents to develop your community, and being law abiding.

FROM AVOIDANCE TO ACCOUNTABILITY

In the Global South with a high outflow of immigrants, especially parts of Africa, Asia, and Latin America, tax evasion is often widespread due to systemic dysfunction. Citizens, rich or poor, may pay taxes only under threat of punishment. But without strong tax systems, public sectors crumble, e.g., teachers go unpaid, hospitals lack supplies, and critical infrastructure decays.

This is perhaps the kind of situation that drove you and other skilled workers to flee to more functional countries thus, unintentionally worsening the crisis back home.

In the developed countries like the U.S., tax systems, while complex, are transparent and enforced. Failing to comply can result in fines, asset seizures, or imprisonment. The Internal Revenue Service (IRS) invests heavily in collecting owed taxes, demonstrating how seriously the government takes this obligation.

This is not merely about legality, it is about morality. Paying taxes is part of a social contract. It reflects a collective commitment to building and maintaining the kind of society immigrants seek - fair, functional, and full of opportunity.

SUCCESSFUL IMMIGRANTS UNDERSTAND THE TRADE-OFF

Many of the most successful immigrants fully embrace their civic responsibilities, including tax compliance. They "give to Caesar what belongs to Caesar," not begrudgingly, but as a reflection of their understanding of the social ecosystem they now belong to. They recognize that taxes support the very systems that enable their children to attend quality schools, their families to access healthcare, and their businesses to grow in a stable economy.

These immigrants are not only law-abiding, but they are also contributors. They build businesses, volunteer in communities, support local causes, and serve in public offices. They know that becoming part of a new country involves more than residency-- it requires investment, responsibility, and trust.

A CULTURAL SHIFT TOWARD CIVIC DUTY

To ensure long-term integration and contribution, immigrants from tax-evasive cultures must undergo a mental shift. They must learn to see taxes not as a burden, but as a civic duty and a form of gratitude, a concrete way to give back to the society that welcomed them.

Compare that to countries like Switzerland, where I lived for seven years. There, citizens sometimes call tax offices proactively, eager to know their tax obligations in advance. As one Swiss citizen told me, *"Our schools are well-funded, our streets are safe, and our services work—because we all pay our fair share of taxes."* This sense of shared responsibility should be the aspiration for any democratic society, and immigrants must be welcomed into that culture of trust and mutual obligation.

FOR POLICYMAKERS: BRIDGING THE GAP WITH EDUCATIONAND SUPPORT. THE CIVIC EDUCATION GAP

Thanks to the policymakers in the receiving countries for opening their borders for immigrants from other countries. However, they need to know that many immigrants arrive with little to no understanding of how taxation works in their new country. Some may come from places where filing taxes is unnecessary or ignored altogether. Others may fear interacting with tax authorities due to negative experiences back home. As a result, without proper education, many immigrants unintentionally fall into noncompliance—exposing themselves to audits, penalties, or worse.

Suggested solution

Governments and civic organizations in the receiving countries should develop and support culturally sensitive financial literacy programs aimed specifically at immigrant communities. These programs should:

- Explain tax obligations clearly and in multiple languages.
- Provide community-based assistance in filing taxes.
- Address common misconceptions about the role of taxes in democracy.
- Promote trust between immigrant communities and tax authorities.

By investing in culturally sensitive financial literacy programs, governments and civic organizations can bridge the gap between legal obligation and civic participation. Empowering immigrants with clear, accessible information will not only promote compliance but will also fosters a deeper sense of belonging and trust. When immigrants understand their role in the tax system, they are better equipped to contribute meaningfully to their new society—economically, socially, and democratically.

Civic participation begins with economic inclusion

If integration is the goal, then economic participation must be at the center. Paying taxes is one of the most fundamental forms of civic engagement. When immigrants understand their role as taxpayers, they are more likely to:

- Vote (when eligible)

- Serve on school boards or local councils
- Volunteering in community programs
- Open businesses and create jobs

Tax compliance, then, is more than a legal issue, it's an entry point into full democratic participation.

A NEW NARRATIVE: FROM LAW-ABIDING TO NATION-BUILDING SUCCESS STORIES: IMMIGRANTS WHO UNDERSTAND THE TRADE-OFF

Across the United States and other developed nations, many immigrants are successful not just by working hard, but by embracing their civic duties. They build businesses, send their children to good schools, support local causes, and contribute to national progress. They understand that paying taxes is a reflection of trust—a belief that their contributions matter. These immigrants don't just live in their new countries; they belong. Some of the immigrants I interviewed said they were not paying taxes in their countries of origin, but I was surprised to hear one saying, *"When I pay my taxes here in the US, I feel like I am investing in my community. It's not money lost, it's money planted."* That sounds like confidence that his money will be used for the advancement of the community or country.

CHANGING THE CULTURAL MINDSET AROUND TAXES

Changing how immigrants think about taxes means shifting cultural norms that have often been shaped by dysfunction. In some countries, taxes fund political elites, not public goods. In others, public services are so poor that people see no benefit in paying taxes.

CONCLUSION: A WORD OF WISDOM

Immigrants should not resent paying taxes in their new country of residence. They emigrated, often at great personal risk in search of a better life, and that better life comes with a price tag. Taxes fund the very systems that enabled their journey and support their success. In that sense, paying taxes is not a penalty; it is a privilege and a powerful expression of belonging.

To new immigrants: take pride in contributing to the society you now call home. Pay your taxes not just to avoid penalties, but to honor the values of fairness, reciprocity, and shared prosperity. Because in a thriving democracy, giving to Caesar what belongs to Caesar is the mark of a responsible citizen.

PRINCIPLE OF SUCCESS #24

SUCCESSFUL IMMIGRANTS ARE FAMILY CONSCIOUS

Real Life Story #21

Malik Addo was not born with a silver spoon in his mouth. Raised in a family of limited means, he learned early on that poverty was not a life sentence; it was a condition he believed could expire with perseverance and vision. Determined to break the cycle, he made a solemn vow: he would be the last in his family to be called illiterate or poor.

Fortune favored Malik's determination when he won a lottery to immigrate to Canada. While many advised him to move first and send for his family later, Malik stood firm. He had not applied for the lottery just for himself - he had done it with his wife and two children in mind. For him, success meant nothing if it came at the cost of being separated from those he loved. And so, they moved together.

Once in Canada, Malik acted swiftly and decisively. He enrolled his children in school, secured jobs for both him and his wife, and found affordable housing to give his family stability and a sense of belonging. Every decision he made was guided by one principle: family first. Being family-oriented is more than simply loving your family.

It is about shaping your life around them, putting their needs above your own, and making time to be present. Malik embodied this in every way.

Whenever I spoke with him, Malik's first thoughts were always about his family - how his children were coping with the cold Canadian winters and how his wife was adjusting to the new environment. Even the house he eventually purchased reflected his priorities: it was close to his children's school, had a school bus service, and was near both a hospital and an amusement park - ensuring safety, education, and joy were all within reach. Meeting these goals gave Malik a deep sense of peace and purpose. With his family safe, settled, and thriving, he could finally turn his attention to building a professional future, not just for himself, but for the generations to come.

Malik Addo's journey is a powerful reminder that success is not only about personal achievement, but also about the people you carry with you along the way. His life is a testament to the strength of resilience, the depth of sacrifice, and the enduring power of family.

Migration is rarely just about the individual. Whether fleeing conflict or seeking opportunity, most immigrants move with a dream that goes far beyond personal success: the dream of providing a better life for their families. At the heart of every meaningful migration story lies one common thread - family.

True success for many immigrants is not measured solely by degrees earned, money made, or positions attained.

Instead, it is reflected in the ability to support, nurture, and remain present for their loved ones. **Successful immigrants are deeply family conscious.** They understand that no matter how far they go or how high they rise, their greatest achievement is building and maintaining strong family bonds.

FAMILY: THE ROOT OF SUCCESS

Family is the foundation of identity. It is where values are first learned, character is shaped, and emotional resilience is formed. As important as family is, as Archbishop Desmond Tutu of South Africa once said, for better or worse, *"You don't choose your family. They are God's gift to you, as you are to them."* From birth, we are shaped by the people closest to us— parents, siblings, grandparents - who teach us what it means to live, love, and lead.

For immigrants, this connection is often what fuels their perseverance. Many works multiple jobs, sacrifice comfort, and endure loneliness just to see their children thrive and their extended families back home supported. They send remittances, stay in touch across time zones, and dream of reunion. This devotion is not just admirable, it is transformative.

THE DANGERS OF NEGLECTING FAMILY

Yet, the immigrant journey is also filled with risk - not just physical or financial, but relational. In the pursuit of upward mobility, many immigrants fall into the trap of overworking and under-prioritizing family life. The desire to "make it" in a new land can, ironically, lead to emotional and relational failure if family is left behind, either literally or figuratively.

I knew a friend who lived this painful reality.

He arrived in the U.S. with determination and drive. He rose quickly in his field, but his ambition kept him away from home. His wife became emotionally distant, and his children barely knew him. Though he achieved financial stability, he lost what mattered most: his family's affection and unity. Years later, he confessed that the wealth he worked so hard to build brought him little joy because he had no one left to truly share it with.

This story is not unique. In countless immigrant families, spouses drift apart, children grow up disconnected, and marriages end not from lack of love, but from lack of time, presence, and communication. **Being family conscious means recognizing that emotional presence is just as important as, if not more important than, financial provision.**

FAMILY AS A SOURCE OF STABILITY

HAPPY IMMIGRANT FAMILY TOGETHER

Many successful immigrants realize early that the family unit provides strength, direction, and resilience. Especially for African immigrants, the family vision extends beyond the nuclear household to include extended relatives. Bringing family together, or staying connected despite separation, offers emotional grounding and a sense of purpose that fuels perseverance.

When spouses are united and present in each other's lives, marriage is strengthened. Children grow up feeling secure and supported. Family-oriented immigrants tend to be more focused, balanced, and fulfilled, not just in their careers, but in life. They are not only building wealth; they are building legacy.

In contrast, those who neglect family ties often find success hollow. As Spanish philosopher Miguel de Unamuno noted, *"Man habitually sacrifices his life to his purse, but he sacrifices his purse to his vanity."* In chasing success, we risk losing the very relationships that give life its deepest meaning. A house full of things but empty of love is no home at all.

CHALLENGES FOR IMMIGRANT FAMILIES

Immigrant women, in particular, face unique challenges. Many African women arrive in the West with hope and ambition, only to discover the painful absence of the communal support they once knew. In their home countries, raising a child is a shared experience. In the West, it often becomes a solitary burden.

Without extended family or community support, immigrant mothers can feel isolated and overwhelmed. If their spouses are consumed by work, the emotional load becomes even heavier.

Family-conscious immigrants recognize this struggle and work intentionally to be present and supportive - emotionally, not just materially.

HOME AS A SANCTUARY

The home should be more than a place to eat and sleep; it should be a sanctuary, a source of comfort and connection. Before immigrants can fully integrate into their new communities, they must first strengthen the community within their homes. Spouses must become each other's first line of emotional support. When that connection breaks, the family becomes vulnerable to disintegration.

Escaping into work, social distractions, or even extramarital affairs may offer temporary relief from stress, but they ultimately leave lasting wounds. Being family conscious means resisting these escapes and investing in the people who matter most.

A CALL TO CONSCIOUSNESS

To immigrants building new lives in unfamiliar lands: **Build your family before you build your fortune**. Do not allow ambition to blind you to your partner's needs or your children's longing for connection. Do not let the office become your home. When the applause fades, when the promotions stop, it is your family that will remain, if you have nurtured them along the way.

Success is not just about what you achieve but who you bring along on the journey. A healthy family is a deeper wealth than any bank account can hold.

FINAL REFLECTION

Successful immigrants are not just hardworking - they are family conscious. They know that family is not an obstacle to success, but the reason for it. They make daily decisions with their loved ones in mind. They nurture relationships, preserve unity, and protect the priceless currency of love.

So, wherever you are on your journey, remember this: family is not just part of your story – it is the reason you are writing it. Nurture it, cherish it, and never lose sight of where your true wealth lies.

Principles of success #25

Successful immigrants invest in their health.

Real Life Story #22

I recently had the privilege of helping to organize a seminar on healthy living, specifically tailored for members of an immigrant community. I took extensive notes during the event, inspired by the passion and relevance of the discussions. The presenters highlighted several major health risks that are especially prevalent in immigrant populations: excessive alcohol consumption, chronic stress, cigarette smoking, promiscuity, and overeating.

The seminar sparked a meaningful exchange among participants, many of whom shared personal stories that echoed the concerns raised. One attendee shared his ongoing struggle with overeating, which had led to obesity. Despite understanding the consequences, he expressed how difficult it was to control his eating habits.

Another participant offered a powerful testimony about the pressures of working long hours to cover financial responsibilities such as car loans and mortgage payments. He shared that the resulting stress had pushed him into drinking, smoking, and, added "womanizing," with a smile.

His message to others was clear and heartfelt: good health is not something that can be bought. It requires mindfulness, discipline, and intentional self-care. He emphasized that maintaining one's health is not only essential for well-being but is also a foundational part of achieving long-term success.

This seminar served as an important reminder of the health challenges many immigrants face, and of the critical need for awareness, support, and lifestyle changes that promote physical and emotional well-being.

A healthy lifestyle is not just important, it is essential. That is why this chapter concludes with a critical takeaway: **your health is your greatest asset**. The old saying "health is wealth" rings truer than ever. Real success, whether professional, financial, or relational, depends on the strength and vitality of your body and mind. With good health, almost anything is possible. Without it, even the loftiest ambitions can collapse.

Money can buy doctor's time and medication, but not health itself. That is why we must prioritize wellness. Just as Egypt could not exist without the Nile River, our dreams cannot flourish without our well-being. Successful individuals - immigrants included - understand this and take daily steps to maintain both their physical and mental health. It is a conscious, consistent investment that yields lifelong dividends.

THE HIDDEN HEALTH CHALLENGES OF MIGRATION

Immigrants face unique health challenges. Starting life in a new country often brings stress, uncertainty, and overwhelming responsibility. The pressure to succeed and support loved ones, both locally and abroad, can push health to the bottom of the priority list. Many work long hours, skip meals, sacrifice sleep, and abandon regular exercise. Some fall into unhealthy habits they never practiced before - overeating, excessive drinking, smoking, or poor diet - often as a coping mechanism for stress and isolation.

Sadly, these behaviors can be passed on to children, leading to cycles of chronic illness, emotional instability, and substance abuse. **The dream of a better life can quickly become a source of harm if health is not consciously protected.** This is not a matter of blame, but a call to awareness. Immigrants bring with them deep cultural values and remarkable resilience. By preserving healthy traditions from home while embracing informed health choices in their new environment, they can build not only a better life, but a healthier one.

HEALTH IS THE FOUNDATION OF ALL SUCCESS

We live in a world driven by ambition, where the chase for more - more money, more power, more recognition - often drowns out the quiet voice of health. Across boardrooms, construction sites, classrooms, and kitchens, people push themselves to the edge in pursuit of their goals. Yet in doing so, they often ignore the very thing that makes all achievements possible: their health.

The COVID-19 pandemic was a global reminder that sickness does not discriminate. Rich or poor, powerful or powerless - no one is immune. Despite scientific advancements, new illnesses continue to emerge, and old ones resurface. Meanwhile, many still live as if health is guaranteed - until it is gone.

True health is not accidental. It demands intention, discipline, and education. The World Health Organization defines health as *"A state of complete physical, mental, emotional, and social well-being - not merely the absence of disease."* Successful immigrants recognize this and **treat health not as a luxury, but as a non-negotiable priority.**

YOUR HEALTH IS YOUR REAL INSURANCE

The pursuit of success is noble, but not at the expense of your body. You can recover from a failed business; you can rebuild lost wealth. But you cannot always recover from years of physical neglect. No amount of money is a substitute to a healthy heart, strong lungs, or peace of mind.

If billionaires with access to the best doctors still die from preventable conditions, it is proof that **wealth does not guarantee well-being**. A smart investor diversifies assets. A wise immigrant **invests first in health**, through nutrition, exercise, sleep, mental health care, and preventative medicine. These are not optional; they are success strategies.

And here is a sobering truth: if you die chasing money, your wealth does not follow you - not to heaven, not to hell. It stays behind, often taxed before your family even sees it. What matters most is what you did with your time, your energy, and your health, while alive.

Body intelligence: The immigrant's
silent partner

Successful immigrants do not take good health for granted. They develop body intelligence - the awareness of what their body is saying, how to respond, and when to act. Be mindful of the old saying: *"We can do nothing without the body; let us take care that it is in the best condition to serve us."* That insight still holds true today.

Your body sends daily signals - fatigue, tension, hunger, restlessness. Are you listening? High body intelligence begins with checking in: Am I rested? Am I energized? Am I in pain? Awareness helps prevent burnout and illness. And contrary to popular belief, managing your health does not require perfection, just consistency in small, sustainable habits.

The basics are clear: eat nutritious food, drink water, sleep well, limit alcohol, exercise regularly, and manage stress. These are not just wellness tips, they are **performance enhancers**. Physical well-being fuels clarity, confidence, resilience, and high achievement. A healthy immigrant is a productive one.

Faith, wisdom, and personal responsibility

It is important to trust doctors, but it is equally important to trust yourself - and, for many, to trust in God. Your physician is a partner, not a savior. Do not outsource your health entirely. **You are your first line of defense**. Prayer without action is incomplete. Faith must be matched with responsibility: eat wisely, move your body, rest, think clearly, and love deeply.

Even more, **your health choices ripple outward**. A healthy parent raises healthy children. A strong body supports a peaceful mind. And a sound mind builds a meaningful life. As immigrants, we must reject the myth that hard work alone guarantees success. Without good health, "hard work" becomes "hardship."

Final insight:
Good health is the immigrant's first victory

Immigrants do not uproot their lives to suffer or die early. They come to thrive. But thriving begins with taking care of the vessel that carries you: your body. Health is not just one aspect of success - it is the starting point.

In a culture that glorifies hustle, it is easy to overlook rest. In a society driven by consumerism, it is easy to forget simplicity. But if you want to enjoy your success - and live long enough to see your children and grandchildren flourish - you must invest in your health.

So, to every immigrant building a new life: build your health first. It is the one investment that guarantees the strength, stamina, and serenity to enjoy everything else you have worked for.

CONCLUSION TO SECTION III

The journey of an immigrant is never easy - but it can be incredibly rewarding. In this section of the book, we have explored twenty-five key principles that define the mindset, habits, and values of highly successful immigrants. These principles are not just strategies for survival; they are blueprints for thriving.

Whether it is staying rooted in family, investing in health, embracing education, or building resilience in the face of adversity, each principle reflects a deeper truth: success is not just about what you achieve, but who you become in the process.

As you continue your own journey, remember that success is not a destination, it is a daily commitment. Hold on to your values, stay focused on your purpose, and never forget why you started. Because when immigrants succeed, they do not just change their own lives - they uplift families, enrich communities, and inspire nations.

Always keep in mind the three "g's." Keep 'g'rowing, keep 'g'iving, and keep 'g'oing. Your story matters, and it is just beginning.

EPILOGUE

Think Like an Immigrant is more than just another book about immigration—it's a heartfelt guide, written by an immigrant, for immigrants. Whether you have just arrived in a new country, have lived abroad for decades, or are still preparing for your journey, my purpose in writing this book is simple: to share hard-won truths, offer practical insight, and help you not just survive, but thrive in a world that may often see you as different. The first step to a successful journey is believing in yourself. The world will not believe in you until you believe in yourself.

Every meaningful achievement, or let me say, every step forward, starts with self-belief. Maybe you chose to emigrate because you felt called to something greater, something different. That decision required courage. You left behind the familiar, and stepped into uncertainty.

On your journey, you have encountered countless barriers - cultural, financial, physical, and emotional. Some people similarly situated gave up halfway. Others never reached their goals. But you are still here. You kept going. As Pastor Olumide Ogunjuyigbe of Jesus House, DC, once said, "We were created on purpose, for a purpose." That purpose didn't vanish when you left your homeland. In fact, for many of us, the very act of emigrating, regardless of the reason, was a step toward fulfilling that purpose. Bravo.

Now you find yourself in a land that is not your ancestral. You may feel like a stranger. You may even be treated like one. And while that can hurt, try not to take it personally. People often fear what they do not understand. As the saying goes, *"No matter how hard the bird tries, it cannot fly in the ocean."* It is a reminder that no matter your talent or ambition, you may still be seen as "other;" an immigrant, with limited rights and uncertain status. But hear this clearly: your dreams are still valid. You deserve the right to hope for a better future. Just understand that not all hopes will come true. And not everyone will care about your struggle. In fact, most will only care about what you can offer them. That is why it is so important to know who you are. Know your strengths. Know your weaknesses. Know what drove you to leave your homeland and why you chose this particular country. Only you can define your journey.

Every decision you have made, whether it seemed right or wrong, was the best decision you could make at that time. And here is another truth: a good decision can turn bad, and a bad one can lead to something unexpectedly good. Everything depends on how circumstances evolve.

Immigration laws change all the time. No country, rich or poor, is immune. Your new country of residence will not rewrite its laws to make you feel more welcome. Its leaders are focused on their own citizens, their own needs. Do not expect special treatment.

Do not get too comfortable. And no matter what color your passport is - blue, red, green, or brown - it does not erase your immigrant identity. You may have new papers, but they do not always come with full acceptance.

Still, if you are better off now than you were in your country of origin, that is all that matters. That is progress. That is worth holding onto. Don't forget to celebrate achievements, small or large. So, embrace your journey. Embrace your story. Embrace your immigrant status - not as a burden, but as a badge of resilience. You left for a reason. And you are here for a purpose.

We live in a world where people are rarely satisfied with what they have. Many immigrants leave their home countries in search of things they already possess, including happiness, stability, or community. But they also want more: more money, more comfort, more status, more everything. They chase bigger houses, luxury cars, designer clothes, multiple relationships, and fame. These desires, while understandable, often overshadow the very reasons they left their countries of origin.

The truth is, many of the things immigrants seek, though perhaps not in the quantity or form they imagine, are within reach through hard work and time. And while they may not have it all yet, it is worth remembering that "little joys aren't that little." If you think like an immigrant - grateful for progress, conscious of how far you have come, you will recognize that your current life, even with its challenges, is often better than the one you left behind.

As discussed in Principle of Success #1, happiness begins with understanding life backward but living it forward. That means acknowledging your past while actively shaping the future you want to live - because that future is where you will spend the rest of your life.

Often, people fail to reach their goals because of a negative mindset. Self-doubt, fear of failure, lack of belief, and a tendency to give up too soon are common obstacles. A pessimistic attitude undermines the motivation and persistence needed to succeed. Still, these challenges should not discourage you; they should motivate you to push harder.

Upon arriving in a new country, many immigrants become consumed by the pursuit of wealth and material success. In this relentless chase, it is easy to forget the original goal: a better life for oneself and one's family. That better life includes not just wealth, but safety, freedom from persecution, access to quality education and healthcare, job opportunities, and the freedom to pursue your dreams. However, always remember that freedom is not free. In most countries, while you are free to pursue your goals, you are also under the watchful eye of the law. Authorities have a duty to maintain order and security. If you step out of line, you will be held accountable. As an immigrant, it is crucial to respect and follow the laws of your new home.

This book is titled *Think Like an Immigrant* because it offers practical insights on how and why you should embrace this mindset. Your new country is your adopted home. Its laws, values, and cultural norms are different from those of your homeland. To succeed, you must adapt. This does not mean abandoning your heritage; rather, it means learning to live in harmony with the culture around you. Assimilating does not mean losing yourself. It means expanding who you are - learning the language, tasting the food, building relationships. Without shared experiences, deep friendships can be hard to form. But when you open yourself up to your new environment, you gain more than a new home; you gain the chance to thrive.

You made a courageous decision to leave your country of birth, likely driven by circumstances beyond your control - political instability, economic hardship, or the pursuit of a better life. With grace and generosity, your new country opened its doors and granted you the opportunity to start afresh. This is now your country by choice, not by chance. You may have chosen this nation for its stability, its values, or the opportunities it offers. Whatever your reasons, you are now part of a society built on the efforts, struggles, and sacrifices of those who came before you. You are reaping the harvest they sowed. And now, the responsibility to contribute - to give back - becomes part of your journey.

As author Joan Marques wisely said, *"It's easier to take than to give. It's nobler to give than to take. The thrill of taking lasts a day. The thrill of giving lasts a lifetime."*[21] Giving back is more than a noble act; it is a moral obligation. In the words of Albert Einstein, *"It is every man's obligation to put back into the world at least the equivalent of what he takes out of it."*[22] Whether you are wealthy or modest in means, you will never run out of something valuable to give. If you cannot give money, give your time. If you lack time, offer your skills. If you are still finding your way, give your compassion, your prayers, your effort - these, too, have the power to build a stronger, more inclusive society. Every act of giving contributes to the safety, prosperity, and future of your new home - for you, your children, and generations to come.

But giving back is only part of the equation. Staying relevant, adaptable, and intentional is essential. You must:

---

21 "Joan Marques Quotes," Quotefancy, accessed May 22, 2025, https://quotefancy.com/quote/2022892/Joan-Marques-It-s-easier-to-take-than-to-give-It-s-nobler-to-give-than-to-take-The-thrill.

22 "Albert Einstein Quotes," Goodreads, accessed May 22, 2025, https://www.goodreads.com/quotes/423709-it-is-every-man-s-obligation-to-put-back-into-the.

- Keep up to date with immigration laws and legal requirements.
- Re-examine your skillset regularly. The world changes, and so must you. Learn new things. Sharpen your tools.
- Review your habits; abandon the ones that hinder your growth and adopt those that support your progress.
- Choose your community carefully. The people around you shape your future. Surround yourself with those who inspire, support, and challenge you to grow, not those who pull you backward.

In this new land, you are not just a guest. You are a builder, a contributor, a citizen in spirit and action. Let your presence be a blessing. Let your life reflect the values of gratitude, service, and purpose. Strive not only to live well here, but to contribute to make this country better than you found it.

REFERENCES

Adepoju, A. "Patterns of Migration in West Africa" in T. Manuh (ed), At Home in the World: International Migration and Development in Contemporary Ghana and West Africa. (Accra: Sub-Saharan Publishers, 2005), p.32.

AIC – American Immigration Council (2021). "Immigrants in the United States—Facts Sheet." Retrieved from: https://www. americanimmigrationcouncil.org/research/immigrants-in-the-united-states.

Alcorn. "Silicon Valley Home to One of Largest Foreign-Born Populations in the US." Retrieved from: https://www.alcorn. law/immigration.

American Immigration Council (AIC), Special Report (September 9, 2024). "New American Fortune 500 in 2024. The Largest American Companies and Their Immigrant Roots." Retrieved from: https://www.americanimmigrationcouncil.org/research/ new-american-fortune-500-2024#:~:.

Anderson, Monica & Phillip Connor (2018). "Sub-Saharan African Immigrants in the U.S. Are Often More Educated Than Those in Top European Destinations...also more highly educated than U.S. native-born population." PEW Research Center Report. Retrieved from: https://www.pewresearch. org/global/2018/04/24/sub-saharan-african-immigrants-in-the-u-s-are-often-more-educated-than-those-in-top-european-destinations.

Anderson, Stuart (2023). "Immigrant Maria Telleria: From Mexico To MIT And Entrepreneur." Forbes. Retrieved from: https:// www.forbes.com/sites/stuartanderson/2023/09/19/immigrant-maria-telleria-from-mexico-to-mit-and-entrepreneur/

Anderson, Stuart (2016). "Immigrants and billion dollars startups." National Foundation for American Policy (NFAP) brief. Retrieved from http://nfap.com/wp content/uploads/2016/03/ Immigrants-and-Billion-Dollar-Startups.NFAP-Policy-Brief. March-2016.pdf.

Anderson, Stuart (2020). "A Review of Trump Immigration Policy." Forbes. Retrieved from: https://www.forbes.com/sites/ stuartanderson/2020/08/26/fact-check-and-review-of-trump-immigration-policy/#5ddc8da656c0.

Anderson, Stuart. ACLU in Samma v. U.S. Department of Defense (2020). Retrieved from: https://www.aclu.org/cases/samma-v-us-department-defense-lawsuit-challenging-policy-denying-us-military-service-members

Appel, Allan (2015). Roosevelt: Kick Out "Hyphenated Americans." In New Haven Independent. Retrieved from: https://www.newhavenindependent.org/index.php/archives/entry/war_declall_sounded_to_kick_out_hyp.

Arnold, Peters and Liefbroer Aart C. (1997). "Beyond Marital Status: Partner History and Well-Being in Old Age." Journal of Marriage and the Family 59(3):687–99. [Google Scholar].

Aubry, Amandine, Michał Burzyński, & Frédéric Docquier (2016). "The welfare impact of global migration in OECD countries." In Journal of International Economics, July 2016. Retrieved from: https://www.sciencedirect.com/science/article/abs/pii/S002219961630040X.

Azose JJ, Raftery AE (2019) Estimation of emigration, return migration, and transit between all pairs of countries. PNAS 116(1):116–122. Retrieved from: https://appliednetsci.springeropen.com/articles/10.1007/s41109-020-00322-x.

Batalova, Jeanne, Michael Fix and James D. Bachmeier (2016). "Untapped Talent: The Costs of Brain Waste among Highly Skilled Immigrants in the United States." Retrieved from:

https://www.migrationpolicy.org/research/untapped-talent-costs-brain-waste-among-highly-skilled-immigrants-united-states. See also: New American Economy (2016). "Billions of Dollars in Tax Receipts Forgone Annually as Nearly 2 Million Highly Skilled Immigrants in U.S. Are Stuck in Low-Skilled Jobs or Unemployed." Retrieved from: https://www. newamericaneconomy.org/press-release/billions-of-dollars-in-tax-receipts-forgone-.

Batalova, Jeanne, Michael Fix and Sarah Pierce (2020) "Brain Waste among U.S. Immigrants with Health Degrees: A Multi-State Profile." Retrieved from:

https://www.migrationpolicy.org/research/brain-waste-immigrants-health-degrees-multi-state-profile.

Boak, Josh (2022). Associated Press. "US Unveils Changes to Attract Foreign Science, Tech Students." Retrieved from: https://www. usnews.com/news/world/articles/2022-01-21/biden-admin-unveils-changes-to-attract-foreign-stem-students.

Booker, Brakkton (2020). "Trump Administration Diverts $3.8 Billion In Pentagon Funding To Border Wall." Retrieved from: https://www.npr.org/2020/02/13/805796618/trump-administration-diverts-3-8-billion-in-pentagon-funding-to-border-wall.

Borjas, George J (2016). "The Case for Extreme Immigrant Vetting. It's a practice as American as apple pie—and for good reason." Retrieved from: https://scholar.harvard.edu/files/gborjas/files/

pol081706.pdf.

Boubtane, Ekrame (2022). "France Reckons with Immigration Amid Reality of Rising Far Right." Migration Policy Institute. Retrieved from: https://www.migrationpolicy.org/article/france-immigration-rising-far-right.

Bowen, Alison, and Alexia Elejalde-Ruiz (2017). "Skilled immigrants often struggle to put degrees, credentials to use in U.S." Retrieved from: https://www.chicagotribune.com/business/ct-merit-immigration-brain-waste-20170326-story.html.

Brown, Emma (2015) Former Stanford dean explains why helicopter parenting is ruining a generation of children. Retrieved from: https://www.washingtonpost.com/news/education/wp/2015/10/16/former-stanford-dean-explains-why-helicopter-parenting-is-ruining-a-generation-of-children.

Britannica. "Know-Nothing Party." Retrieved from: https://www.britannica.com/topic/Know-Nothing-party.

Brown, Emma (2015) Former Stanford dean explains why helicopter parenting is ruining a generation of children. Retrieved from: https://www.washingtonpost.com/news/education/wp/2015/10/16/former-stanford-dean-explains-why-helicopter-parenting-is-ruining-a-generation-of-children.

Bryan, Van (2014). " Five Reasons Why Socrates Was A Terrible Husband." Retrieved from:

https://classicalwisdom.com/people/philosophers/five-reasons-socrates-terrible-husband.

Budiman, Abby (2020). "Key findings about U.S. immigrants." Pew Research Center. Retrieved from: https://www.pewresearch.org/fact-tank/2020/08/20/key-findings-about-u-s-immigrants.

Cardenas, Cat (2022). "A Reformed "Model Immigrant" shares what it costs to become an American." In TexasMonthly. Retrieved from: https://www.texasmonthly.com/arts-entertainment/julissa-arce-book-rejecting-assimilation/

Chaloff, Jonathan, and George Lemaitre (2009), "Managing Highly-Skilled Labour Migration: A Comparative Analysis of Migration Policies and Challenges in OECD Countries."

Camus, Renaud (2011), Le Grand Remplacement (Great Replacement). Reinharc, 2011.

Chamberlin, Jamie (2013). 'Tiger parenting' doesn't create child prodigies, finds new research." Retrieved from: https://www.apa.org/monitor/2013/09/tiger-parenting.

Chen, James (2020). Investopedia. Retrieved from: https://www.investopedia.com/contributors/101529.

Child Protective Services (CPS) promotes the safety and well-being of children through intervention in reported child abuse cases. The goal of CPS is to keep children in their homes when it is deemed safe, and to provide them with a safe environment when they are determined to be at risk.

Chishti, Muzaffar, Sarah Pierce, and Jessica Bolter (2017). "The Obama Record on Deportations: Deporter in Chief or Not? In Migration Policy Institute report. Retrieved from: https://www.migrationpolicy.org/article/obama-record-deportations-deporter-chief-or-not.

Clemens, Michael A. and Gunilla Pettersson (2008). "New data on African health professionals abroad." Quoted from Johnson James Speech to Annual Representative Meeting of BMA. http://www.bma.org.uk/ap.nsf/Content/ARM05ChCo, June 27, 2005. Retrieved from: https://www.ncbi.nlm.nih.gov/pmc/articles/PMC2254438.

Connolly, Daniel (2023). "Homelessness, Success, Self-Doubt: A Brazilian Atty's Story." Retrieved from: https://irp.cdn-website.com/aec2e4c5/files/uploaded/CALIFORNIA%20PULSE%20-%20Homelessness-

Cooks-Campbell, Allaya (2022). "The importance of knowing yourself: your key to fulfillment." Retrieved from: https://www.betterup.com/blog/the-importance-of-knowing-yourself.

Corrigan, Jack (2022). The Hill. "The advantages of foreign STEM students staying in the US." Retrieved from: https://thehill.com/opinion/immigration/3522679-the-advantages-of-foreign-stem-students-becoming-us-citizens.

Croucher S (2009) Migrants of privilege: the political transnationalism of Americans in Mexico. Identities Glob Stud 16(4):463–491. Retrieved from: https://appliednetsci.springeropen.com/

articles/10.1007/s41109-020-00322-x.

Docquiera, FrÈdÈric and Hillel Rapoport (2011). "Globalization, brain drain and development." Retrieved from: https://core.ac.uk/download/pdf/6339066.pdf.

Dodani, Sunita & Ronald E. LaPorte (2005). "Brain drain from developing countries: how can brain drain be converted into wisdom gain?" In Journal of Social Medicine, Vol. 98 (11). Retrieved from: https://www.ncbi.nlm.nih.gov/pmc/articles/PMC1275994.

Duvivier, Robbert, J., Vanessa C. Burch & John R. Boulet (2017). "A comparison of physician emigration from Africa to the United States of America between 2005 and 2015." Retrieved from: https://human-resources-health.biomedcentral.com/articles/10.1186/s12960-017-0217-0.

Echeverria-Estrada, Carlos and Jeanne Batalova (2019). "Sub-Saharan African Immigrants in the United States." Retrieved from: https://www.migrationpolicy.org/article/sub-saharan-african-immigrants-united-states-2018?gclid.

Edwards, Frank, Hedwig Lee & Michael Esposito (2019). "Risk of being killed by police use of force in the United States by age, race-ethnicity, and sex." Retrieved from: https://pubmed.ncbi.nlm.nih.gov/31383756.

Eisenbruch M. (1991). "From post-traumatic stress disorder to cultural bereavement: diagnosis of Southeast Asian refugees."

In Soc Sci Med. 1991; 33:673–680. Retrieved from:

https://www.ncbi.nlm.nih.gov/pmc/articles/PMC1414713/#:.

Elfers, Richard (2014). Chishti, Muzaffar, Sarah Pierce, and Jessica Bolter (2017). "The Obama Record on Deportations: Deporter in Chief or Not? In Migration Policy Institute report. Retrieved from: https://www.migrationpolicy.org/article/obama-record-deportations-deporter-chief-or-not. In The Courier-Herald. Retrieved from: https://www.courierherald.com/opinion/republicans-can-learn-from-federalists-rich-elfers.

Eurich, Tasha (2018) "What Self-Awareness Really Is (and How to Cultivate It)." Retrieved from: https://hbr.org/2018/01/what-self-awareness-really-is-and-how-to-cultivate-it.

Fonte, John. "To Possess the National Consciousness of an American (Louis Brandeis, July 4, 1915." Center for immigration studies. Retrieved from: https://cis.org/Possess-National-Consciousness-American-Louis-Brandeis-July-4-1915.

Gamillo, Elizabeth (2024). "Meet Katya Echazarreta, the first Mexican-born woman to travel to space." In Astronomy magazine. Retrieved from: https://www.astronomy.com/space-exploration/meet-katya-echazarreta-the-first-mexican-born-woman-to-travel-to-space/

Gelatt, Julia (2024). "Explainer: Immigrants and the U.S. Economy." MPI. Retrieved https://www.migrationpolicy.org/sites/default/files/publications/mpi-immigrants-us-economy-explainer-2024_final.pdf.

Gilbert D.T. (2006). Stumbling on Happiness. Random House; New York: 2006.

Gove, Walter R., Hughes Michael and Briggs Style Carolyn. 1983. "Does Marriage Have Positive Effects on the Psychological Well-Being of the Individual? "Journal of Health and Social Behavior 24(2):122–31.

Gray, Alex (2018). World Economic Forum. "These countries are the most attractive for foreign workers." Retrieved from: https://www.weforum.org/agenda/2018/09/worlds-most-attractive-countries-for-foreign-workers.

Gray, Paul (1991). "Whose America? A growing emphasis on the U.S.'s "multicultural" heritage exalts racial and ethnic pride at the expense of social cohesion." In TIME International, July 8, 1991.

Gubernskaya, Z., & Debry, J. (2017). "US Immigration Policy and the case for family unity. Journal on Migration and Human Security, 5(2) 417-430. doi:10.14240/jmhs.v5i2.91; See also Heim, C., & Nemeroff, C. B. (2001). "The role of childhood trauma in the neurobiology of mood and anxiety disorders: Preclinical and clinical studies." Biological Psychiatry, 49(12), 1023-1039. doi:10.1016/S0006-3223(01)01157-X.

Hagopian, Amy; Matthew J. Thompson, Meredith Fordyce, Karin E. Johnson, & L. Gary Hart (2004). "The migration of physicians from sub-Saharan Africa to the United States of America: measures of the African brain drain." Retrieved from: https://www.ncbi.nlm.nih.gov/pmc/articles/PMC544595.

Hansen, Claire (2020). "Trump Administration significantly increased the visa processing fees by 80%." Retrieved from: https://www.usnews.com/news/national-news/articles/2020-07-31/trump-administration-nearly-doubles-cost-to-apply-to-become-a-us-citizen.

Hathaway, Ian (2017). "Almost half of Fortune 500 companies in 2017 were founded or co-founded by an immigrant or the child of an immigrant." Retrieved from: https://www.brookings.edu/blog/the-avenue/2017/12/04/almost-half-of-fortune-500-companies-were-founded-by-american-immigrants-or-their-children.

Hayes M (2014) "We gained a lot over what we would have had": the geographic arbitrage of North American lifestyle migrants to Cuenca, Ecuador. J Ethn Migr Stud 40(12):1953–1971. Retrieved from: https://appliednetsci.springeropen.com/articles/10.1007/s41109-020-00322-x.

HerAgender (2023). "Why It Is Important To Learn From Inspiring People." Retrieved from: https://heragenda.com/p/reasons-to-learn-from-those-who-inspire-you/#:~:text=.

Hesson, Ted. "Explainer: Why is the new U.S. policy for international students causing backlash from colleges?" Reuters. Retrieved from: https://www.reuters.com/article/us-usa-immigration-student-explainer/explainer-why-is-the-new-u-s-policy-for-international-students-causing-backlash-from-colleges-idUSKBN2492V8.

Hoang Lan Anh, and Yeoh Brenda SA. 2011. "Breadwinning wives and "left-behind" husbands: Men and masculinities in the Vietnamese transnational family." Gender & Society 25(6): 717–739. [Google Scholar].

Ighobo, Kingsley (2017). "Diagnosing Africa's medical brain drain." In African Renewal. Retrieved from: https://www.un.org/africarenewal/magazine/december-2016-march-2017/diagnosing-africa%E2%80%99s-medical-brain-drain

IOM. International Organization for Migration (2022). "World Migration Report." Retrieved from: https://worldmigrationreport.iom.int/wmr-2022-interactive.

IOM (2023) "Migration and Migrants: A Global Overview. International remittances." Retrieved from: https://worldmigrationreport.iom.int/what-we-do/world-migration-report-2024-chapter-2/international-remittances.

IOM – UN Migration (2023). "Deadliest Quarter for Migrants in the Central Mediterranean Since 2017." Retrieved from: https://www.iom.int/news/deadliest-quarter-migrants-central-mediterranean-2017.

IOM (2024). "World Migration Report." Retrieved from: https://worldmigrationreport.iom.int/msite/wmr-2024-interactive.

Jaffe, Greg & Souad Mekhennet (2019) "Omar Ilhan's American story: It's complicated." Retrieved from: https://www. washingtonpost.com/politics/2019/07/06/ilhan-omar-is-unlike-anyone-who-has%20served-congress-this-is-her-complicated-american-story.

Jalali, Ujwal (2024). "Tried and failed, yet 'Donkey route' preferred to reach US, greener pastures." Retrieved from: https://www. newindianexpress.com/cities/delhi/2024/Oct/31/tried-and-failed-yet-donkey-route-preferred-to-reach-us-greener-pastures.

James, William (1890): Habit. New York: Henry Holt and Company. Retrieved from: https://www.ncbi.nlm.nih.gov/pmc/articles/ PMC6701929.

Kakissis, Joanna (2019). NPR, "In Trump, Hungary's Viktor Orbán Has A Rare Ally In The Oval Office." Retrieved from: https:// www.npr.org/2019/05/13/722620996/in-trump-hungarys-viktor-orban-has-a-rare-ally-in-the-oval-office.

Kleinfeld, Rachel & John Dickas (2020). "Resisting the call of nativism: What the US political parties can learn from other democracies." Carnegie Endowment for International Peace. Retrieved from: https://carnegieendowment.org/2020/03/05/ resisting-call-of-nativism-what-u.s.-political-parties-can-learn-from-other-democracies-pub-81204.

Klitzke, Erin (2001). "The Unblended. The Problems of Assimilation in 19th Century America." Retrieved from: https://www2.gvsu. edu/klitzkee/efforts/schoolwork/theunblended.htm#:.

Krogstad, Jens Manuel and Jynnah Radford (2016). "Education levels of US immigrants are on the rise." PEW Research Center report. Retrieved from: https://www.pewresearch.org/fact-tank/2018/09/14/education-levels-of-u-s-immigrants-are-on-the-rise/, See also Lorenzi, Jane & Jeanne Batalova (2022), op.cit.

Livingston, Amy (2021). "How to deal with sudden wealth syndrome and manage newfound riches." Retrieved from: https://www.moneycrashers.com/deal-manage-sudden-wealth-syndrome.

Liu Hui and Umberson Debra J. (2008). "The Times They Are a Changin': Marital Status and Health Differentials from 1972 to 2003." Journal of Health and Social Behavior 49(3):239–53.

Lorenzi, Jane & Jeanne Batalova (2022). "Sub-Saharan African Immigrants in the United States." Migration Policy Institute (MPI). Retrieved from: https://www.migrationpolicy.org/article/sub-saharan-african-immigrants-united-states-2019.

Loudenback, Tanza (2016). "International students are now 'subsidizing' public American universities to the tune of $9 billion a year. Retrieved from:

https://www.businessinsider.com/foreign-students-pay-up-to-three-times-as-much-for tuition-at-us-public-colleges-2016-9.

McPhillips, Deidre (2020)— "Deaths From Police Harm Disproportionately Affect People of Color." Retrieved from: https://www.usnews.com/news/articles/2020-06-03/data-show-deaths-from-police-violence-disproportionately-affect-people-of-color.

Macaulay, Cecilia (2022). "African brain drain: "90% of my friends want to leave." African Youth Survey. Retrieved from: https://www.bbc.com/news/world-africa-61795026.

Madhavan, Sangeetha, Nicholas W. Townsend, and Anita I. Garey (2010). "Absent Breadwinners": Father–Child Connections and Paternal Support in Rural South Africa." In Journal of South African Studies. Retrieved from: https://www.unicef.org/media/83581/file/Children-Left-Behind.pdf.

Malkin, Michelle (2015). "Immigration and the Values of Our Founding Fathers." In National Review. Retrieved from: https://www.nationalreview.com/2015/12/immigration-founding-fathers-view-michelle-malkin.

Marklein, Mary Beth (2016). "Credentials fraud now a global threat for universities." Retrieved from https://www.universityworldnews.com/post.php?story=20160603175611493.

Monroe, Myles (2008). The Fatherhood Principles. Whitaker House

National Foundation for American Policy, 2019. "Immigrants and Nobel Prizes: 1901—2019." Retrieved from: https://nfap.com/wp-content/uploads/2019/10/Immigrants-and-Nobel-Prizes.NFAP-Policy-Brief.October-2019.pdf.

Neal, Joan F (2020). "Being black and immigrant in America." Center for Migration Studies. Retrieved from: https://cmsny.org/

being-black-and-immigrant-in-america/.

NFAP Policy Brief (October 2017). "Immigrants and Nobel Prizes: 1901—2017." Retrieved from: http://nfap.com/wp-content/ uploads/2017/10/Immigrants-and-Nobel-Prizes-1901-to-2017. NFAP-Policy-Brief.October-20171.pdf.

Nicholson, Amy (2021). "Operation Varsity Blues' Review: Failing the Ethics Test." Retrieved from: https://www.nytimes. com/2021/03/17/movies/operation-varsity-blues-review.html.

Nedlund, Evelina (2019) CNN Business. "The US economy is losing billions of dollars because foreign students aren't enrolling." Retrieved from: https://www.cnn.com/2019/11/19/business/ international-students-decline/index.html.

Network. "The History of Immigration Policies in the U.S." Retrieved from: https://networklobby.org/historyimmigration.

New American Economy (2016). "Billions of Dollars in Tax Receipts Forgone Annually as Nearly 2 Million Highly Skilled Immigrants in U.S. Are Stuck in Low-Skilled Jobs or Unemployed." Retrieved from: https://www.newamericaneconomy.org/press-release/billions-of-dollars-in-tax-receipts-forgone-.

New American Economy (2020). "New American Fortune 500 in 2020: Top American Companies and Their Immigrant Roots." Retrieved from: https://data.newamericaneconomy.org/en/ fortune500-2020.

New American Economy (2021). "Immigrants and the U.S.

Educational System." Retrieved from: https://research. newamericaneconomy.org/report/immigrants-america-educational-system.

New American Economy (2022). "Entrepreneurship." Retrieved from: https://www.newamericaneconomy.org/issues/ entrepreneurship/page/60/#:~.

Organization for Economic Co-operation and Development OECD, 2008a.

Olsen-Medina, Kira and Jeanne Batalova (2020). "College-Educated Immigrants in the United States." Migration Policy Institute. Retrieved from: https://www.migrationpolicy.org/article/ college-educated-immigrants-united-states.

O'Malley, Katherine 920240. "Guest column: Stopping 'brain waste' for foreign-born workers in US." Retrieved from: https:// www.telegram.com/story/opinion/columns/guest/2024/05/12/ guest-column-stopping-brain-waste-for-foreign-born-workers-in-us/73614987007.

Owens, Mackubin Thomas (2026). "Hamilton's actual view on immigration." Retrieved from: https://www.iwp.edu/ articles/2016/12/21/hamiltons-actual-view-on-immigration.

Passel, Jeffrey S., Wendy Wang, and Paul Taylor (2010). "Marrying Out: One-in-Seven New U.S. Marriages Is Interracial or Interethnic." PEW Research Report. Retrieved from: https:// www.pewresearch.org/wp-content/uploads/sites/3/2010/10/755-

marrying-out.pdf.

Pew Research Center (2019). "Remittance flows worldwide in 2017" Retrieved from: https://www.pewresearch.org/global/interactives/remittance-flows-by-country.

Pew Research Center (2023). "Gender pay gap in U.S. hasn't changed much in two decades." Retrieved from: https://www.pewresearch.org/short-reads/2023/03/01/gender-pay-gap-facts/#:~.

Portes Alejandro and Zhou Min. 1993. "The New Second Generation: Segmented Assimilation and Its Variants." Annals of the American Academy of Political and Social Science 530:74–96. Retrieved from: https://www.ncbi.nlm.nih.gov/pmc/articles/PMC10706603.

Rachel, St. John (2018). "The Raging Controversy at the Border Began With This Incident 100 Years Ago." In Smithsonian Magazine. Retrieved from: https://www.smithsonianmag.com/history/raging-controversy-border-began-100-years-ago-180969343.

Ramsey Solutions (2024). "Three Keys to Leaving a Lasting Legacy." Retrieved from: https://www.ramseysolutions.com/retirement/will-your-retirement-leave-a-legacy.

Rapoport, Hillel, Sulin Sardoschau, and Arthur Silve (2021). "Migration and Cultural Change." CATO Institute. Retrieved from: https://www.cato.org/research-briefs-economic-policy/

migration-cultural-change.

Ratha, Dilip, Sonia Plaza & Eung Ju Kim (2024). "In 2024, remittance flows to low- and middle-income countries are expected to reach $685 billion, larger than FDI and ODA combined." Retrieved from: https://blogs.worldbank.org/en/peoplemove/in-2024--remittance-flows-to-low--and-middle-income-countries-ar#:~:text.

Redden, Elizabeth (2018). "International students enrollments decline again." Retrieved from: https://www.insidehighered.com/news/2018/11/13/new-international-student-enrollments-continue-decline-us-universities.

Reuters (2023). "Over 400 migrants died crossing Mediterranean early in 2023." Report by IOM-UN agency. Retrieved from: https://www.reuters.com/world/europe/over-400-migrants-died-crossing-mediterranean-early-2023-un-agency-2023-04-.

Ruiz Soto, Ariel, Jeanne Batalova and Michael Fix (2016). "The Costs of Brain Waste among Highly Skilled Immigrants in Select States." Retrieved from: https://www.migrationpolicy.org/research/costs-brain-waste-among-highly-skilled-immigrants-select-states.

Sandner, Philipp (2023) "Do Chinese firms employ convicts from China in Africa?" In DW News. Retrieved from: https://www.dw.com/en/do-chinese-firms-employ-convicts-from-china-in-africa/a-67802241.

Schlesinger Jr, Arthur (1991). "The Cult of Ethnicity, Good and Bad." Retrieved in: https://content.time.com/time/subscriber/article/0,33009,973355,00.html.

Schnitker, Sarah A. & Robert A. Emmons (2007). "Patience as a virtue: Religious and psychological perspectives." Retrieved from: https://www.semanticscholar.org/paper/Patience-as-a-virtue%3A-Religious-and-psychological-Schnitker.

Schofield, Norman (1984). "Economic integration in Africa: a venture in self-reliance." In Crisis in economic Relations between North and South." Gower Publishing Company.

She, Qianru & Terry Wotherspoon (2013). "International student mobility and highly skilled migration: a comparative study of Canada, the United States, and the United Kingdom." Retrieved from: https://www.ncbi.nlm.nih.gov/pmc/articles/PMC3648681.

Sherman, Arloc, Danilo Trisi, Chad Stone, Shelby Gonzales and Sharon Parrott (2019). "Immigrants contribute greatly to U.S. economy, despite administration's "public charge" rule rationale." Center on Budget and Policy Priorities. Retrieved from: https://www.cbpp.org/research/poverty-and-inequality/immigrants-contribute-greatly-to-us-economy-despite-administrations.

Sonmez, Felicia & Mike DeBonis (2019). "Trump tells four liberal congresswomen to 'go back' to their countries, prompting Pelosi to defend them." Retrieved from: https://www.washingtonpost.com/politics/trump-says-four-liberal-congresswomen-should-go-back-to-the-crime-infested-places-from-which-they-came/2019/07/14/b8bf140e-a638-11e9-a3a6-ab670962db05_story.html.

Stangel, Luke (2017). "Study: More than a third of Silicon Valley's population is foreign-born." In Silicon Valley Business Journal. Retrieved from: https://www.bizjournals.com/sanjose/news/2017/02/28/immigration-silicon-valley-impact.html. See also, Public Policy Institute of California (PPIC). "Silicon Valley's Skilled Immigrants Becoming Agents of Global Economic Change, Survey Finds." Retrieved from: https://www.ppic.org/press-release/silicon-valleys-skilled-immigrants-becoming-agents-of-global-economic-change-survey-finds.

Stokes, Bruce (2017). "What It Takes to Truly Be 'One of Us." Pew Research Center. Retrieved from: https://www.pewresearch.org/global/2017/02/01/what-it-takes-to-truly-be-one-of-us.

Stoller-Conrad, Jessica (2015). "Why high earnings don't protect you from bankruptcy." Retrieved from: https://www.weforum.org/agenda/2015/04/why-high-earnings-dont-protect-you-from-bankruptcy.

Toffler, Alvin (1984). Future Shock. United Nations (2019). "The number of international migrants reaches 272 million, continuing an upward trend in all world regions, says UN." Retrieved from: https://www.un.org/uk/desa/number-international-migrants-reaches-272-million-continuing-upward-trend-all#:~:text.

The Federalist Papers, 1961.

The New American Fortune 500 (2011) "Partnership for a New American Economy." Retrieved from: https://www. newamericaneconomy.org/sites/all/themes/pnae/img/new-american-fortune-500-june-2011.pdf.

The USA Reporter (2024). "From Athlete to Advocate: The Journey of Sekou Clarke." Retrieved from:

https://theusareporter.com/from-athlete-to-advocate-the-journey-of-sekou-clarke/

The World Bank (2021). "Defying Predictions, Remittance Flows Remain Strong During COVID-19 Crises." Press Release. Retrieved from: https://www.worldbank.org/en/news/press-release/2021/05/12/defying-predictions-remittance-flows-remain-strong-during-covid-19-crisis.

The World Conference on Human Rights. Vienna Declaration and Programme of Action. Retrieved from: https://www.ohchr.org/en/professionalinterest/pages/vienna.aspx.

Thomas, June (2002). "Les Bleus et Les Noirs." International Papers. Retrieved from: https://slate.com/news-and-politics/2002/04/le-pen-vs-les-bleus.html.

Tong, Yuying, Feinian Chen & Binbin Shu (2019). "Spousal Migration and Married Adults' Psychological Distress in Rural China: The Roles of Intimacy, Autonomy and Responsibility." Retrieved from: https://www.ncbi.nlm.nih.gov/pmc/articles/PMC7319256.

TSB News (2020). "Number of Nigerian doctors in United Kingdom rises to 7,875." Retrieved from: https://tsbnews.com/2020/07/number-of-nigerian-doctors-in-united-kingdom-rises-to-7875-woodberry.

Udom, Udoh Elijah (2014). What Makes Students Tick: Unlocking the Passion for Learning. Balboa Press.

Uecker, Jeremy E. (2012). "Marriage and mental health among young adults." Retrieved from: https://www.ncbi.nlm.nih.gov/pmc/articles/PMC3390929.

Umberson Debra. 1987. "Family Status and Health Behaviors: Social Control as a Dimension of Social Integration." Journal of Health and Social Behavior 28(3):306–19.

UN/IOM (2018). International Migration (Global Issue). Retrieved from: https://www.un.org/en/global-issues/migration.

United Nations (2019). Dept. of Economic and Social Affairs. "The number of international migrants reaches 272 million, continuing an upward trend in all world regions, says UN." Retrieved from: https://www.un.org/sw/desa/number-international-migrants-reaches-272-million-continuing-upward-trend-.

UN-DESA, 2023. "International migrants are important agents of change." Retrieved from: https://www.un.org/en/desa/international-migrants-are-important-agents-change.

UN News (2021). "Families came first' for remittances in year of pandemic, says Guterres." Retrieved from: https://news.

un.org/en/story/2021/06/1094102.

UN News (2022) "South Africa 'on the precipice of explosive xenophobic violence.' Global perspective Human stories." Retrieved from: https://news.un.org/en/news/topic/human-rights?

UNHCR (2023). "Ukraine Emergency." Retrieved from: https://www.unrefugees.org/emergencies/ukraine.

United Nations (2022). "Intolerable tide" of people displaced by climate change: UN expert." Retrieved from: https://www.ohchr.org/en/press-releases/2022/06/intolerable-tide-people-displaced-climate-change-un-expert.

US Dept of Agriculture (2024). "Ag and Food Sectors and the Economy." Retrieved from: https://www.ers.usda.gov/data-products/ag-and-food-statistics-charting-the-essentials/ag-and-food-sectors-and-the-economy/#:~:text=.

US Dept of Justice (2022). "Federal Jury Finds Three Men Guilty of Hate Crimes in Connection with the Pursuit and Killing of Ahmaud Arbery." Retrieved from: https://www.justice.gov/opa/pr/federal-jury-finds-three-men-guilty-hate-crimes-connection-pursuit-and-killing-ahmaud-arbery.

United States General Accounting Office (2004). "Diploma Mills: Federal Employees Have Obtained Degrees from Diploma Mills and Other Unaccredited Schools, Some at Government Expense." Testimony Before the Committee on Governmental

Affairs, U.S. Senate by Robert J. Cramer, Managing Director, Office of Special Investigations. Retrieved from: https://www. gao.gov/new.items/d04771t.pdf.

Voegele, Juergen (2021). Vice President of Sustainable Development, World Bank. "Climate change could force 216 million people to migrate within their own countries by 2050." Retrieved from: https://www.worldbank.org/en/news/press-release/2021/09/13/ climate-change.

UVU - University Valley of Utah (2024). "Self-Actualization vs Self-Awareness." Retrieved from: https://www.coursesidekick. com/psychology/3065749#:.

Wagner, John (2018). "Trump: Immigration is 'changing the culture' of Europe and its leaders 'better watch themselves." Retrieved from:

https://www.washingtonpost.com/politics/trump-immigration-is-changing-the-culture-of-europe-and-its-leaders-better-watch-themselves/2018/07/13/afb5d9a6-868b-11e8-8f6c-46cb43e3f306_story.html.

Walker, Shaun (2018). "Hungarian leader says Europe is now 'under invasion' by migrants." Retrieved from: https://www. theguardian.com/world/2018/mar/15/hungarian-leader-says-europe-is-now-under-invasion-by-migrants.

Wamugu, Leah (2022) "Remittances to Sub-Saharan Africa Grows 14% to $49 billion in 2021." Retrieved from: https://

kenyanwallstreet.com/remittances-to-africa-grows-14-to-49-b-2021/#:~:text=.

Waters Mary C. (1999). Black Identities: West Indian Immigrant Dreams and American Realities. New York, NY: Russel Sage Foundation. Retrieved from: https://www.ncbi.nlm.nih.gov/pmc/articles/PMC10706603.

Waters Mary C., Tran Van C., Kasinitz Philip and Mollenkopf John H... (2010). "Segmented Assimilation Revisited: Types of Acculturations and Socioeconomic Mobility in Young Adulthood." Ethnic and Racial Studies 33(7):1168–1193. Retrieved from: https://www.ncbi.nlm.nih.gov/pmc/articles/PMC10706603.

Weiss, Avrum (2021). Hidden in Plain Sight: How Men's Fears of Women Shape Their Intimate Relationships. Lasting Impact Press.

Weiss, Avrum (2022). "Why Men Are Intimidated by Their Intimate Partners." In Psychology Today. Retrieved from: https://www.psychologytoday.com/us/blog/from-fear-to-intimacy/202209/why-men-are-intimidated-by-their-intimate-partners.

Wharton, Penn: Budget Model (2016). "The effect of immigration on the United States economy." Retrieved from: https://budgetmodel.wharton.upenn.edu/issues/2016/1/27/the-effects-of-immigration-on-the-united-states-economy.

White House (2017). "Executive Order: Border Security and

Immigration Enforcement Improvements." Retrieved from: https://www.whitehouse.gov/presidential-actions/executive-order-border-security-immigration-enforcement-improvements.

World Bank (2021). "Remittance Flows Register Robust 7.3 Percent Growth in 2021." Retrieved from: https://www.worldbank.org/en/news/press-release/2021/11/17/remittance-flows-register-robust-7-3-percent-growth-in-2021.

World Bank (2021). "Climate Change Could Force 216 million people to migrate within their own countries by 2050." Retrieved from: https://www.worldbank.org/en/news/press-release/2021/09/13/climate-change-could-force-216-million-people-to-migrate-within-their-own-countries-by-2050.

World Bank (2023). "Remittance Flows Continue to Grow in 2023 Albeit at Slower Pace." Retrieved from: https://www.worldbank.org/en/news/press-release/2023/12/18/remittance-flows-grow-2023-slower-pace-migration-development-brief.

World Economic Forum (2017). "Stop telling immigrants to assimilate and start helping them participate." https://www.weforum.org/agenda/2017/01/stop-telling-immigrants-to-assimilate-and-start-helping-them-participate.

World Social Report, (2020). "International migration: A force for equality, under the right conditions." Retrieved from: https://www.un.org/development/desa/dspd/wp-content/uploads/sites/22/2020/02/World-Social-Report-2020-Chapter-5.pdf.

Yameogo, Nadege Desiree (2019). "Non-economic impacts of migration - winners and losers." Retrieved from: https://blogs. worldbank.org/peoplemove/non-economic-impacts-migration-winners-and-losers.

Walker, Shaun (2018). "Hungarian leader says Europe is now 'under invasion' by migrants." Retrieved from: https://www. theguardian.com/world/2018/mar/15/hungarian-leader-says-europe-is-now-under-invasion-by-migrants.

Yi Jinyao, Zhong Bin and Yao Shuqiao. 2014. "Health-Related Quality of Life and Influencing Factors among Rural Left-Behind Wives in Liuyang, China." BMC Women's Health 14(1):67–72.

Zagorsky, Jay L. (2012). "Do People Save or Spend Their Inheritances? Understanding What Happens to Inherited Wealth." In Journal of Family and Economic Issues, Vol. 34(1). Retrieved from: https:// www.researchgate.net/publication/257579648_Do_People_ Save_or_Spend_Their_Inheritances_Understanding_What_ Happens_to_Inherited_Wealth#:.

INDEX

O

Opportunity – 9–16, 35–44, 154–156, 200–202
Optimism – 8–14

P

Philip Effiong – 3–5

R

Racism – 18, 51–58, 113–120, 230, 292, 297
Remittances – 22–30
Resilience – 10–17, 93–100, 204–211, 328–333
Respect – 10–14, 175–178, 208–210
Return – 10–13, 165–168, 170–172

S

Shadow citizens – 10–19
Social inclusion – 9–21, 185–193, 233
Success – 10–18, 309–347, 355–377
Survival – 8–14, 43–49, 62–67

T

Thomas Jefferson – 27

U

Unity – 9–15, 23–32

V

Vivek Ramaswamy – 27
Volunteering – 11–14, 238–242

W

Work ethic – 10–13, 219–222, 278–282

ABOUT THE AUTHOR

The author has lived and worked in many countries, both developing and developed, during his career as a diplomat with the United Nations. His lifelong interest in the immigrant experience is informed by extensive personal and professional exposure to life in foreign countries. In addition to his diplomatic career, he is an educator who has taught law and public policy to undergraduate and graduate students at major universities in the United States. He holds a PhD in Government from the University of Texas at Austin, a Juris Doctor (JD) from the University of Iowa, and a Master of Law (LLM) from the University of Leicester in the United Kingdom. He is the author of four books and peer reviewed articles.

.

www.ingramcontent.com/pod-product-compliance
Lightning Source LLC
Chambersburg PA
CBHW072337090426

42741CB00012B/2814